INSIDE Art

CULTURE • HISTORY • EXPRESSION

BOOK TWO

Rebecca Brooks, Ph.D.
Professor of Art Education
The University of Texas at Austin

W.S. Benson and Company, Inc., Austin, Texas

ACKNOWLEDGEMENT

We wish to thank the following people who
were helpful in the completion of this book:

ANN FEARS CRAWFORD, Ph.D.
Consulting Editor

Stephanie Amster   Don Haughey   John Smithers
Hans Beacham   Frank Puente Harris   Marilyn Stewart, Ph.D.
Bob Burden   Louise Hudgins   Lisa Lundgren Watson
Elaine Burden   Sue Mayer   Iris Williams
Laurie Condrasky   Emma Lea Mayton   Fred Woody
Katherine Reid

Book design by: Jean O. Bollinger
Art Research: Contemporary Art Services, Ltd., New York
ISBN: 0-87443-102-6   Printed in United States of America.
W.S. Benson & Company, Inc., P.O. Box 1866, Austin, Texas 78767.

To my nephew Chris Vinklarek whose 8th grade wisdom kept me in focus.

TABLE OF CONTENTS

TABLE OF CONTENTS

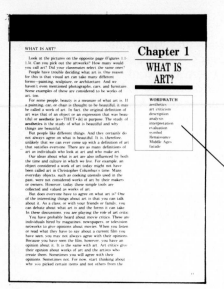

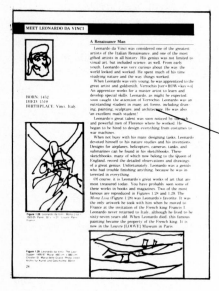

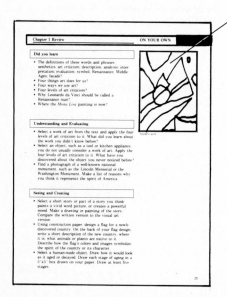

How to Use *Inside Art*

This book has been arranged so that you can use it easily. It is divided into 5 units and 20 chapters.

Units cover big blocks of related information, such as the art elements and design principles. Each unit is made up of chapters.

Chapter Organization

Each chapter begins with WORDWATCH. This is a list of important vocabulary words to watch out for as you read. These words will be shown in bold type and defined for you. They can also be found in the Glossary at the end of the book. Most have a pronunciation guide next to them in parenthesis.

Many visuals are included throughout each chapter. These are photographs of natural and humanmade environments and artworks created by professional and student artists. You will also find drawings and diagrams to help you see something special, or practice something new.

At the end of each chapter you will find two sections called MEET THE ARTIST and ON YOUR OWN.

MEET THE ARTIST presents more information about an artist featured in the chapter. The page will show additional samples of the artist's works, and ask you questions about these works. Many of these questions have no right or wrong answers. They are intended to sharpen your art evaluation skills and keep you thinking about art.

ON YOUR OWN gives you a chance to review and use some of the information you have read about in each chapter.

Several different kinds of activities let you explore art-making and art-thinking.

Symbols

As you read *Inside Art,* you will come across the following symbols next to a part of the text.

This is a safety warning. When you see this symbol, it means that the art material, tool, or process you are reading about, needs to be used with caution. Even materials that can stain your clothes, will have this symbol next to them. When you see the symbol, read the text carefully. You will be instructed how to use the material or tool properly and safely.

When you see this symbol, you should be ready for some thinking! It indicates a question in the text that needs an answer. You can answer these questions in your own mind, since they are asked to make you think about art. Most of the questions have no right or wrong answers! Its your opinion that counts. And remember, everyone has an opinion.

In Book One of *Inside Art* you learned how important visual art has always been to human beings and how important it is still today. Whether it is used to communicate personal feelings and emotions or to enclose a living space, rally people to a national cause or inspire religious devotion, art matters to people. Communication through art is as essential to the human spirit as eating and sleeping are to the human body.

Art is a big subject. What you learned in Book One of *Inside Art* was just a beginning. In Book Two you will have a chance to explore the fascinating world of visual art in more detail. You will meet not only more artists, but also other individuals who helped shape both the art and history of their times.

Visual art has a rich and exciting history. It is a history that spans more than 25,000 years and hundreds of cultures. The art you see today is in many ways influenced by the creative tradition of centuries and the heritage of countless civilizations. Understanding something of this history will reveal new ways to look at art and to communicate through art.

Part One
FOCUSING ON ART

Unit I
ART ROLES

Some people believe that if you don't create art as an artist, you can't take part in the experience of art. This is a mistake. Everyone can be involved in visual art. When you walk up to a painting or sculpture in a museum and look at it, you are experiencing art. When you make the decision to buy something beautiful and well-designed over something ugly and poorly designed, you are taking part in art. Unlike many other subjects you will study, art has a place for everyone. Being an artist is just one of the many roles to play in the world of art. Each role has its own purposes, activities, and responsibilities. In the following chapters, you will discover more about these roles and how each is essential to the existence of visual art.

Pieter Brueghel. *The Artist and The Connoisseur.* 1565. Pen and ink, 25 cm. x 21.6 cm. Graphische Sammlung Albertina, Vienna.

Chapter 1

VIEWERS AND PATRONS

The role of the **viewer** or the spectator in art is a very important one. You may not have considered "viewing" art as a part of the art experience at all. After all, you just walk up to a work of art and look at it. That doesn't appear to take any special talent or training, since everybody does it. Well, not everyone views art the same way. Some viewers see more than others—but more about that later. What is important to understand is that art, as we know it, could not exist without the viewer.

For it is you—the viewer or audience—that gives art purpose and life. Without someone to look at visual art there is little reason for it.

Of course, some people believe that artists would create art whether there was anyone to see it or not. This is probably true. But, art would have little meaning without the communication and sharing between artist and viewer. Both are needed to keep visual art alive. The greatness of a work of art, or whether it **is** a work of art, is measured by its effect on and value to different people throughout the years. Such works are said to be **universal** in communicating their artistic messages. In other words, they are meaningful and inspirational to people, regardless of time period and culture. This universal message cannot exist without an audience.

BECOMING A SKILLED VIEWER

But what is so hard about walking up to a painting, sculpture, or building and looking at it? Isn't that all that an art viewer does? Yes, but being a skillful viewer takes both knowledge and practice. Skillful viewers look carefully at works of art. If at first they don't like what they see, they don't just walk away. They are patient with art. They continue to look, searching the image for meaning.

What does it mean to look carefully? To be patient with art? First, it means keeping an open mind. It means not making judgments until you have learned more about what you are seeing. It is fine to dislike an artwork, even one in a museum, as long as you know *why* you dislike it. The test is whether you can explain your dislikes to someone else and can support your opinion.

"But, some art looks like a two-year-old painted it." "Why should I bother to look at it?" Well, if you know the artist isn't a two-year-old, aren't you curious as to why he or she paints like one? With further investigation, you might discover a reason—and some interesting information about both the artist and the work. Knowing this

---

WORDWATCH
viewer
universal
subject
form
content
patron
Medici
pietà
abstract

Figure 1.1. Michelangelo Buonarroti. *Pietà.* 1498-99. Marble, 174 cm. h., 195 cm. x 69 cm. b. St. Peters Cathedral, Rome. Photo credit: Archiv fur Kunst und Geschichte, Berlin.

information may not change your opinion of the work, but you will be able to make a more knowledgeable judgment.

"There are so many different kinds of art. How can I ever learn to understand them all?" A good place to start is with the three parts that all works of art have in common—**subject, form,** and **content.**

Look for a moment at the work shown in Figure 1.1. This is a famous sculpture by Michelangelo Buonarroti [michel • ANG • ee • low bu • on • ah • ROT • tee] or as the artist is best known—Michelangelo. Many consider Michelangelo one of the greatest artists who ever lived. This sculpture of Christ and his mother Mary, is called a **pietà** [pea • a • TAH]. A **pietà** is a scene in painting or sculpture of Mary mourning the dead Christ. This sculpture is presently located in St. Peter's Cathedral in Rome. It is seen daily by thousands of people from all over the world. These thousands of viewers see a figure of a woman holding the dead body of a man across her lap. This is the **subject** of the sculpture. Those viewers, who like you, know it is a pietà, also know who the woman and man are meant to represent. This additional piece of information, though small, adds greatly to the understanding and appreciation of the work.

Although both a painter and an architect, Michelangelo loved sculpture the most. He carved this work from marble, his favorite medium, and gave it a high polish. The figures are very realistic and shown in great detail. All this information tells us about the **form** of the work.

The final, and most important, part of the work of art is **content**. This is the meaning of the work. The content is what the artist is trying to say to the viewer through the subject and form. The personal feelings and emotions artists put into their works are part of the content of art. Like the reader of a mystery novel, a careful viewer will not stop with a quick look at the evidence of subject and form. He or she will want to search deeper for clues to the artist's message and purpose. Only then can he or she truly appreciate the work and draw pleasure from it.

Figure 1.2 is a work of art that has a far different subject than Michelangelo's pietà. In fact, you may wonder if it has a subject at all! As you learned in Book One, this painting is **abstract** or **non-representational.** This simply means that the subject of the painting is not a recognizable object. Does this mean that all abstract art lacks subjects? Of course not. All artworks have subject, form, and content. In abstract or non-representational art, the subject is the way the art elements have been arranged or composed using the principles of design. In a work like that pictured in Figure 1.2, the *main* subjects are color and shape, although other elements are used. By looking at the work, can you tell why these elements should be the main subjects? If the subjects are color and shape, what is the form?

Look for a moment at how the artist has applied the paint to the canvas. Can you see brushstrokes, drips? This is part of the form of this work. In other words, the artist decided to apply paint in this way, just as Michelangelo decided to carve and polish marble to express his thoughts about the death of Christ.

But what is the content of the painting in Figure 1.2? Is there any way to know for sure? Probably not, unless we ask the artist, and artists rarely tell us their exact feelings when they create art. As you learn more about art and artists, and see more abstract works of art, you will grow in your ability to form opinions about works like this one by Robert Gottlieb. You should never be afraid to voice your opinion. So long as you have taken time to really look at a work and try to understand it,

Figure 1.2. Adolph Gottlieb. *Cadmium Red Over Black.* 1959. Oil on canvas, 108″ x 90″. Archer M. Huntington Art Gallery, The University of Texas at Austin, Lent by Mari and James Michener.

Figure 1.3. Verrocchio. *Lorenzo De Medici.* (1449-92), Il Magnifico. Painted terra cotta, 25⅞ " x 23¼ " x 12⅞ ". National Gallery of Art, Washington, D.C., Samuel H. Kress Collection.

your opinion is valuable. What do you think the content ? or meaning of *Cadmium Red Over Black* is?

PATRONS

Along with Leonardo Da Vinci, whom you met in Book One, Michelangelo lived and worked during the Italian Renaissance. During this time, there were many rich and powerful families in Italy. One of the most powerful was the **Medici** [MED • ah • chee]. Led by Lorenzo the Magnificent (Figure 1.3), as he was called, this amazing family distinguished themselves in politics and as **patrons** of art.

A **patron** [PAY • tron] is an individual who hires an artist to create a work of art. Since the patron pays for the work, he or she may even have a say in the choice of subject matter or media. Many artists throughout history have been supported by patrons. Both Michelangelo and Leonardo worked for the Medici family.

Patrons like the Medicis made up a very special viewing audience for art. Their wealth, power, and education allowed them to hire artists to create art just for themselves. As true art lovers, they also built large art collections. Fortunately for us, many of these collections are now part of public museums around the world. Viewers everywhere can enjoy the works of the greatest artists in history. Art that once was reserved only for the eyes of the very rich is now available to all. In a later chapter you will read more about the importance of museums in preserving our art heritage.

There are not many individuals or families today like the Medicis. Although wealthy art lovers still support art through contributions to museums and commissions to artists, the days of the great patrons are over. Some feel this is a good thing. They believe that artists shouldn't be influenced by anyone.

Giant of the Renaissance

Like the great Leonardo, many consider Michelangelo to be one of the greatest artistic geniuses of all time. Did he inherit his talent from his family? Apparently not. His father was a very ordinary individual with no artistic talent and little sympathy for art talent in others. One of five brothers, Michelangelo was the only one to show any special ability. In fact, in later years this "ordinary" family was to prove a great burden to him. His father and brothers were lazy, greedy, and demanded assistance from Michelangelo their entire lives. Being a generous and faithful son and brother, he provided as best he could.

Though Michelangelo's family was less than supportive of his genuis, there were others who saw his greatness. The first was Lorenzo the Magnificent or Lorenzo de Medici. One of the greatest art patrons who ever lived, Lorenzo soon recognized the young Michelangelo as having artistic ability without equal.

After an early apprenticeship with a well-known local artist, Michelangelo was invited to become a student in Lorenzo's school for sculptors. Even the wise Lorenzo could hardly have foreseen the great works of art that would eventually be created by the quiet, frowning, seventeen-year-old boy.

Lorenzo treated Michelangelo as a son, including him in many family activities. At the home of Lorenzo the Magnificent, Michelangelo was introduced to many wealthy and powerful individuals. His fame grew, reaching finally to Rome and the Pope himself. Pope Julius II became Michelangelo's second great patron and the torment of his life.

Though he created many great works for Pope Julius, including his painting masterpiece—the ceiling of the Sistine Chapel—Michelangelo was very unhappy working for this difficult and demanding individual. Stories of their arguments are legendary and make fascinating reading. Michelangelo's stubbornness and rude manner seemed always to anger the Pope, who expected honor and respect from everyone. At one famous confrontation, the enraged pontiff struck Michelangelo over the back with a walking cane! It is difficult to believe that this fiery relationship produced some of the greatest art the world has ever known.

Figure 1.4. *Bronze Portrait of Michelangelo.* c. 1564. Bust by Daniele da Volterra (or Giovanni da Bologna after Volterra). Bronze, 60 cm. Collection Casa Buonarroti, Florence. Photo credit: Archiv fur Kunst und Geschichte, Berlin.

BORN: 1475
DIED: 1564
BIRTHPLACE: Florence, Italy

Figure 1.5. Michelangelo Buonarroti. *Moses.* 1513-15, reworked 1542. Marble, 235 cm. h. St. Pietro in Vincoli. Photo credit: Archiv fur Kunst und Geschichte, Berlin.

Student work.

Student work.

- The definitions of these words and phrases: viewer; universal; subject; form; content; abstract; patron; Medici; pietà?
- Why the role of viewer is an important one for art?
- Some ways to become a more skilled viewer?
- The role a patron plays in art?
- The three parts that all artworks have in common?
- Two patrons of Michelangelo's?

Understanding and Evaluating

- Find, either in this book or another art book, three artworks you think have a **universal** message. For each, decide what the message is and write a short paragraph about it.
- Look again at the Gottlieb painting (Figure 1.2). What other art elements do you think are used in this work? If necessary review the art elements in Book One, Unit 2 or in Part Two of this book.
- Is the Gottlieb painting symmetrical or asymmetrical in balance? What about the pietà (Figure 1.1)? How do you know?

Seeing and Creating

- Select some simple objects to draw, such as fruits or vegetables. On a large sheet of white drawing paper [18"x24" or 22"x28"] mark off 4 three-inch squares. In the first square, draw your object to emphasize **subject**. In the second square, emphasize **form**. In the third and final square, emphasize **content**. In this square you will want to show the viewer something new or unexpected about the object. Remember **content** is the artist's message, and **form** is the way the message is delivered. Use either crayon or chalk pastels for your drawing.
- Select one of the above drawings to use as an idea for a tempera or acrylic painting. Does the idea or expressive content change when you paint rather than draw? How? Which do you prefer?

There have been many books written and movies made about the lives of artists. The reason is that the public has always had a fascination with artists and the sometimes unconventional lives they lead. In movies the artist is usually shown with a beard, in shabby clothes, and barely making enough money to keep food on the table. His temperament or personality is wild and unruly, given to outbursts of rage or uncontrolled joy. This Hollywood image of artists has had an influence on the way the public thinks about them. How true is it? Not very.

Yes, there have been artists who fit the movie image. Artists such as Van Gogh and Salvador Dali were definitely emotional and flamboyant characters. And it is also true that most artists struggle for recognition and reward, sometimes until the end of their lives. But, many other artists lead lives that are not much different from bankers, store clerks, or teachers.

The public's idea of how an artist looks and behaves is also the result of a very old theory—artists are born, not made. Many people believe that the artistic genius of a Michelangelo or Leonardo cannot be taught or learned, no matter how hard one studies or practices. There is probably some truth to this. Just as in areas, such as science and math, some individuals seem to be born with special abilities for these subjects. This doesn't mean that instruction and practice don't play a part. They do. A large part. Both Leonardo and Michelangelo studied and worked hard to learn and improve their skills.

HOW TO MAKE AN ARTIST

Think for a moment of artistic ability as a long line with the great artists at one end. Everyone else falls somewhere along the line. Yes, everyone is on the line! For, there is some art ability in everybody. So, how do you work your way to the end to be with the great artists? We have already discussed the importance of study and practice, but, most great artists also share another characteristic—they *must* make art.

This need to create in an art medium can be so overpowering in some that they drive themselves and everyone else crazy. Vincent Van Gogh, for example, had difficulty holding on to friends and jobs because of his passion for art. Most of the ordinary people he met could not understand his devotion to creating paintings. For them, art was enjoyable and pleasant, not a matter of life or death.

Chapter 2
ARTISTS

WORDWATCH
Parthenon
cartoon
mural
fresco

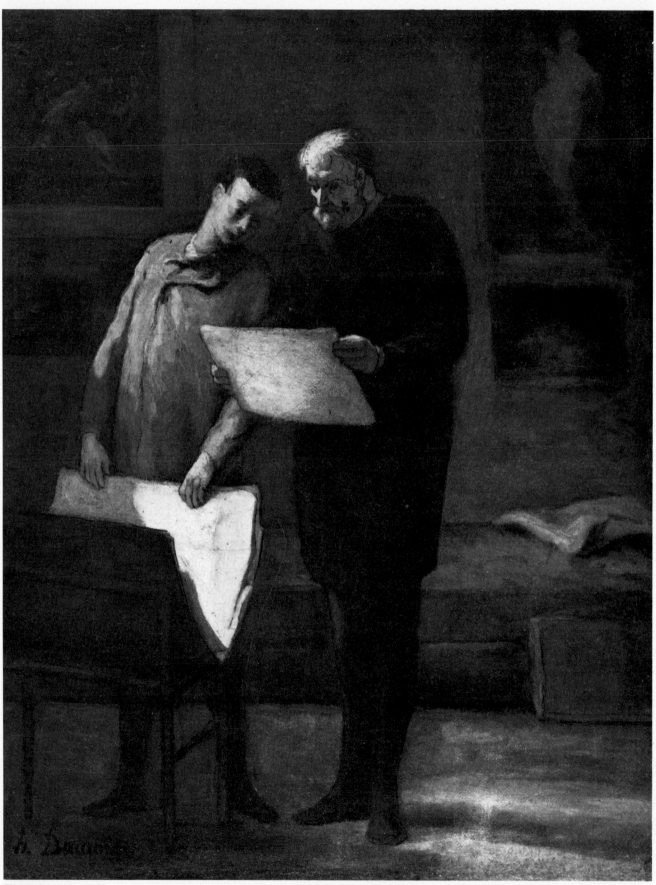

Figure 2.1. Honoré Daumier. *Advice to a Young Artist.* After 1860. Oil on canvas, 16⅛″ x 12⅞″. National Gallery of Art, Washington, D.C. Gift of Duncan Phillips.

Even another great artist, Paul Gauguin [go • GAN] could not completely understand Van Gogh's obsession. Gauguin tried to befriend Van Gogh, but soon realized the hopelessness of it. His portrait of Van Gogh (Figure 2.2) shows that he recognized his friend's passion for painting. The distortion of the artist and the sunflowers he painted shows this. Look at Van Gogh's face in the painting. His concentration seems complete. Why do you think Gauguin used so many diagonal lines and shapes in the painting?

Michelangelo was not called *terribilita* [terry • bee • LEE • tah] or the "little terror" for nothing! He too was a man obsessed with his art. When he thought that his artistic expression was threatened, even by the Pope, he stubbornly stood his ground. This cost him years of suffering, not to mention a sound whack on the back from the pontiff's cane!

Although great artists, through their works, bring inspiration and pleasure to the rest of the world, it may be a good thing that most of us don't share their terrible obsessions.

What else does it take to make an artist, besides talent, hard work, and a great desire to create art? Well, the ability to see is important.

Figure 2.2. Paul Gauguin. *Portrait of Vincent Van Gogh.* 1888. Oil on canvas, Vincent van Gogh Foundation/National Museum Vincent van Gogh, Amsterdam.

ARTISTS SEE IN SPECIAL WAYS

Artists see the world in a special way. They see the same things as the rest of us, but they see them as *ways* to express thoughts, ideas, feelings. Art is about expression. Artists find ways to use the objects and scenes of life to express feelings and ideas.

For example, Figure 2.3 by American artist William Harnett is titled *My Gems.* This wonderful painting is greatly admired by most people for its photographic realism. The stil life objects are painted with amazing precision and detail. Harnett was one of the masters of realistic painting. It is true that a viewer can marvel at the realism of the objects and then walk away. Surely, Harnett's painting skill is enough to insure his place among the master artists.

But, is there more here than first meets the eye? If art is the expression of thoughts and feelings, what else can we make of this work? What is the content? The meaning? Is it only a beautifully painted still life of ordinary objects?

Figure 2.3. William Harnett. *My Gems.* 1888. Wood, 18″ x 14″. National Gallery of Art, Washington, D.C. Gift of the Avalon Foundation.

Figure 2.4. William Turner. *Rain, Steam and Speed.* 1844. Oil on canvas, 90.8 cm. x 121.9 cm. Reproduced by courtesy of the Trustees, The National Gallery, London.

No matter how realistically the subject is presented, great art will express meanings beyond the subject matter of the work. From a world of objects, Harnett selected certain ones to paint. He saw in them something that he could use to express an idea. The title of the painting may give us a clue as to why these particular items were selected. How does Harnett *see* these objects? How is he able to express his ideas through his painting?

Figure 2.4 *Rain, Steam, and Speed*, by English artist, William Turner, though more abstract in subject, may be easier to understand in content. Turner has taken the objects of a scene—rain, trains, bridges, and steam—and transformed them into a unique personal expression. He sees in the driving rain and the billowing steam from the locomotive's smokestack a way to say something about how rain and steam blank out details. How an ordinary scene can be changed into a place of beauty and mystery. If we could see the actual scene Turner painted, we would probably not find any of the magic and beauty the painting expresses. Black steel locomotives, smoke-blackened bridges, and the wet, depressing weather would probably be what we saw. Unless, of course, we saw them with the eyes of an artist!

ARTISTIC INFLUENCES

There are few artists, no matter how original and creative, who are not influenced by art of the past, the time and culture in which they live, and the art of others. Some even find inspiration in the art of cultures far different from their own. Being influenced by art from other times and cultures is not a bad thing. Unless, of course, the artist brings nothing new or personal to the work. Few artists can claim not to be influenced by something or someone.

Even the great Michelangelo carefully studied and borrowed ideas and techniques from the works of ancient Greek sculptors. In fact, that was one of the reasons he so enjoyed being a part of the Medici household. Lorenzo de Medici was an avid collector of ancient Greek and Roman sculptures. As ancient treasures were unearthed from the soil of Italy, rich collectors like Lorenzo could take their pick. These works provided inspiration for many of the Renaissance artists.

Figure 2.5. Parthenon East Pediment. Aphrodite and two other Godesses. 438-432 BC. Courtesy the Trustees of the British Museum.

Look again at Michelangelo's *Pietà* (Figure 1.1) and compare the way the cloth of Mary's robe is carved with that shown in Figure 2.5. Figure 2.5 is a group of figures from the **Parthenon** [PAR•tha•non]. The Parthenon was an ancient Greek temple, built high above the city of Athens. It is famous not only for its architecture, but for its carved decoration. Although it is not known whether Michelangelo saw this particular Greek sculpture, he was able to study others like it. Figure 2.6 shows a figure from a Roman wall painting. How like the statue of *Moses* (Figure 1.5) it appears!

Artists are influenced by their fellow artists as well. One of the most influential works of art, during the Renaissance and for more than a century later, was created by Leonardo Da Vinci. No, it is not the Mona Lisa!

Figure 2.7, known as *The Battle of Anghiari* [an•gee•R•ee] shows a drawing by artist Peter Paul Rubens. He made the drawing from the original **cartoon** drawing by Leonardo. A cartoon, in this case, isn't a funny drawing.

Cartoons were large sketches made by artists in preparation for painting **murals**. **Murals** are wall-size paintings. During the Renaissance, most were painted in a technique called **fresco**. When painting in **fresco**, the artist applies paint directly onto a wet plaster wall. When the plaster dries, the color becomes part of the wall. Obviously, careful planning and sketching beforehand are necessary. This is where the **cartoon** came in.

Figure 2.6. *Pompeii Wall Painting.* Roman ca. 70 B.C. Collection National Archaeological Museum, Naples.

Figure 2.7. Peter Paul Rubens. *The Battle of Anghiari.* c. 1605. Collection of The Louvre, Paris. Photo: ©R.M.N.

Figure 2.8. Pablo Picasso. *Bust of a Woman.* 1962. Metal cut-out, folded and painted 27½". Private collection.

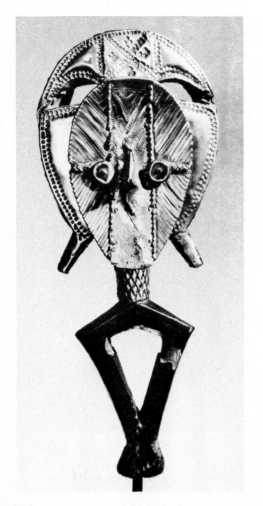

The original mural for which this cartoon was made was never completed. In typical "Leonardo fashion," he left the work unfinished, except for the magnificent cartoon. The fame of this drawing spread throughout Europe. Artists came from many countries to see this wonderful drawing. Most made drawings from it. The most famous being the one by Rubens (Figure 2.7). The power and movement of the fighting figures influenced the work of artists for years to come. How unfortunate that the world was deprived of the completed fresco from the hand of Leonardo, himself.

Closer to modern times, the art of Pablo Picasso (Figure 2.8) has had an enormous effect on other artists. In fact, many consider Picasso the "father" of modern art. Interestingly, Picasso was, himself, influenced by the primitive, but highly expressive, work of Africa (Figure 2.9). Picasso liked the idea that African artists felt free to simplify details of the human figure and to show more than one point of view at a time! It is interesting that this one idea would become identified with the art of Picasso and with modern art itself.

Another work by Picasso is an excellent example of how world events influence the work of artists. Figure 2.10, titled *Guernica* [GARE•nee•kah], was painted to protest the senseless destruction of an entire Spanish city during the Spanish Civil War. The twisted, dramatic figures express both the pain and despair of war.

Even though the images are abstracted, with few realistic details, the content or message is clear and unforgettable. The painting has no color. It is painted entirely in black, white, and shades of gray. This only increases the stark terror of the scene. Picasso could not stop the terrible event that inspired his work, but he left a powerful memorial to the dead of Guernica and a grim reminder of the human cost of war.

Figure 2.9. Gabon. *African Sculpture.* Metalwork sculpture, Kota XIX-XX. 42.4 cm. h. The Metropolitan Museum of Art. The Michael C. Rockefeller Memorial Collection, Bequest of Nelson A. Rockefeller, 1979.

Figure 2.10. Pablo Picasso. *Guernica.* 1937. Oil on canvas, 350 cm. x 782 cm. Courtesy the Prado Museum, Madrid, Spain.

Some artists have been so influenced by the political movements of their countries that their artworks are as much a political statement as a work of art. The work of the great Mexican muralists of the 1920s and 1930s are examples of this political influence.

José Clemente Orozco [hoe • SAY o • ROWS • co] used his art to protest the treatment of the poor people of Mexico during a time of political upheaval. Figure 2.11 gives an idea of the power of his images. As a muralist, Orozco could use the wide, interior spaces of buildings to express his beliefs. Though inspired by the struggle of common people for freedom and security, Orozco's murals have a more universal appeal. Their vibrant colors and dynamic figures speak clearly of the power of images to express great ideas and to touch human emotions.

Figure 2.11. Jose Clemente Orozco. *The People and their False Leaders.* 1937. Jose Clemente Orozco Studio Museum.

Portrait by Aline Fruhauf
India ink, 4 3/16″ x 4 3/16″
National Portrait Gallery, Smithsonian
Institution; Gift of Erwin Vollmer.

BORN: 1883
DIED: 1949
BIRTHPLACE: Jalisco, Mexico

The Voice of the People

José Clemente Orozco learned at an early age how unfair life could be. As a young man, he lost the sight of one of his eyes and the use of his left hand. This did not stop him from continuing to pursue a career in art, although he soon decided that formal art instruction was not for him.

After receiving instruction in drawing at the School of Fine Arts in Mexico City, he dropped out. He taught himself how to paint.

Like some other artists, Orozco began as a cartoonist, working for various journals and magazines. He traveled to the United States in 1917 and finally to Europe in 1934.

He had long been an admirer of Michelangelo and other Renaissance masters. At last he was able to admire their work first hand. The frescos were of particular interest to him.

When he returned to Mexico, he was prepared to begin his greatest works. Figure 2.12, *Man in Flames,* is considered one of his finest frescos. Painted on the dome of the Hospicio Cabañas in Guadalajara, Mexico, the exaggerated perspective and vivid flames surrounding the figure create a memorable, if disturbing image.

During this time Orozco also painted a number of other great works dealing with the history of Mexico and its people before the Spanish conquest.

He became an international celebrity, receiving awards and praise from many countries. His dramatic murals, which depicted with such passion, the richness of Mexican culture and the splendour of its history, are preserved today, as is his studio. A statue of Orozco was erected after his death in 1949.

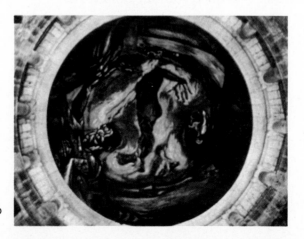

Figure 2.12. Jose Clemente Orozco. *Man in Flames.* 1938-39. Jose Clemente Orozco Studio Museum.

Did you learn

- The definitions of these words and phrases: Parthenon; cartoon; mural; fresco?
- What makes the way artists *see* the world different from the way most people see it?
- Why Harnett's *My Gems* is more than a realistically painted still life?
- At least three ways artists can be influenced?
- What Michelangelo studied in the Medici household?
- The name and artist of one of the most influential works of the Renaissance?
- An important influence on the work of Picasso?

Student work.

Understanding and Evaluation

- Read a biography of an artist discussed in this chapter. Write a short report on the biography (three to five pages). What events or personality characteristics of the artist do you believe influenced his artworks? Add your thoughts on this in a paragraph at the end of your report. Could you defend your opinion in a class debate?
- Using Harnett's painting (Figure 2.3) as a model, briefly describe the subject, form, and content. Compare it with Turner's work (Figure 2.4). In which work do you think form plays the most important part. Why? Review Chapter 1 on subject, form, and content, if necessary.

Seeing and Creating

- Create a tempera or acrylic painting of a sport or activity you enjoy playing or watching. Try to express the excitement and pleasure you feel by using intense colors and strong contrasts.
- Select a color scheme to express the way you feel about a place you have seen. Create a tempera or acrylic painting of the scene. Try to add even more feeling and deeper mood by using strong brushstrokes or by using other paint applicators, such as those made of cardboard or sponges.

Chapter 3
CRITICS AND HISTORIANS

WORDWATCH
consumers
interpretation
description
analysis
evaluation
credit line
art critic
art historian

Figure 3.1. Honoré Daumier. *The Connoisseurs.* c. 1858. Watercolor, charcoal and pencil, 10¼″ x 7⅝″. The Cleveland Museum of Art, Dudley P. Allen Fund.

ART CRITICISM

If artists are the producers or makers of art and viewers are the users or **consumers** of art, then what roles do art critics and historians play? It might be helpful to compare both roles to that of a teacher.

When students must learn and use certain knowledge and skills, teachers show students the best way to use the information and develop their skills. Teachers also help students **interpret** or understand what they are learning. This is very similar to the role of the art critic and the art historian.

An **interpretation** is a form of explanation. **Art critics** offer interpretations of artwork to the public. The public may not agree with a critic's interpretation, but they almost always learn from it. Remember, to criticize art doesn't mean you necessarily dislike it. Art criticism is a system for understanding and evaluating works of art and artists.

ANALYZING AND EVALUATING

In Chapter 1 you read about the three parts of every work of art—subject, form, and content. By examining works or art through these three categories, you increase your understanding of the work and your appreciation and pleasure in it. The art critic is also interested in subject, form and content but has a system or procedure for examining works of art. You were introduced to this system briefly in Book One of *Inside Art.* There are four stages or levels of criticism—**description, analysis, interpretation,** and **evaluation.** Let's review each level.

Level One—Description

Information gathered at this level deals with what is in the work of art, who made it, what is it made of, and other such "facts." The activity of description is very similar to finding the subject of a work of art. Take, for example, Figure 3.2. A description of this work would include what you see in the painting—flowers, a bowl of fruit, a window, and a table. It also includes who painted it—Marc Chagall [shah•GALL]. Look at the **credit line** beneath the work. All the information printed there is part of the description. What medium is used in this painting? Where is the painting located? Who donated the work? When you answer these questions, you have provided a description of the artwork.

Level Two—Analysis

At the analysis level, you are looking for information about how the artist has put the work together. In other words, you are discovering how the art elements and design principles are used. If you need to review the art elements and design principles, look at Unit II in Book One. You can also refresh your memory by checking Part Two of this book.

At the analysis level, you are also looking closely at the techniques the artist used to apply paint, to carve stone, or to weave fabric. As you can see, this level is similar to finding out about the form of a work of art.

Figure 3.3 shows a painting of a famous event in American history. This painting, *Washington Crossing The Delaware,* is by Emanuel Leutz [e•MAN•u•el LOYTSE]. When we analyze this work, we want to pay attention to how the artist used a wide range of color values. By placing dark values next to light values, the artist has increased contrast in the painting. This adds drama to the whole scene. Have you noticed the use of line direction? How many diagonal lines or edges can you find? Is there any part of the painting that is vertical? What other elements has the artist used? What about texture? Color? What kind of space has been used? What kind of compositional balance is used—symmetrical or asymmetrical?

Level Three—Interpretation

At this level, the role of critic becomes very important. Like a detective, the art critic, after careful description and analysis of the evidence, will make an interpretation of the evidence. This level deals with the content of a work of art.

Through interpretation, the art critic gives an opinion about the meaning or content of a work of art. Through interpretation, the art critic explains what he or she thinks a work means. For this explanation to be more than a "guess," the critic must have carefully completed the previous levels.

Figure 3.2. Marc Chagall. *Dream Village.* 1929. Oil on canvas, 39½″ x 29⅛″. Bequest of Marion Koogler McNay, Marion Koogler McNay Art Museum. San Antonio, Texas.

Figure 3.3. Luetze. *Washington Crossing the Delaware.* 1851. Oil on canvas, 149″ x 255″. The Metropolitan Museum of Art. Gift of John Stewart Kennedy, 1897.

In interpretation there is never one final answer. The accuracy of a critic's interpretation depends not only on the care and thought that has gone into the previous levels, but also the experience and background of the critic's life and education. You should never be afraid to offer a different opinion on the meaning of a work of art. As long as you have taken time to look carefully and thoughtfully, you too can assume the role of art critic. Try your hand at interpreting the work shown in Figure 3.3. Study it carefully. There is much to see and think about.

Level Four—Evaluation

When you **evaluate** something, you make a judgment or decision about it. After completing the other three levels, the art critic is in a position to decide whether a work of art is successful or not. Interestingly, this is usually the level at which most people *begin*, when looking at art. They may make statements like: "I like it," or "I don't understand why a work like this is allowed in a museum." These opinions are fine. However, they are more valid if voiced *after* the individual has taken the time to go through the first three levels of art criticism or investigation.

You might have noticed that following the levels of art criticism takes time. It slows the viewer down. This is good. To understand art takes time and patience. All art that is created in a serious, thoughtful way deserves equally serious, thoughtful viewers and critics.

ART HISTORIANS

The role of art historian is similar in many ways to that of art critic. Art historians study and research the lives and works of artists to help us understand more about how and why art is created.

They, however, have a different purpose for their investigations. Their main concern is not to evaluate the quality of a work of art, but to place it in time. They make a judgment about its place and standing in art history. They are concerned with how a work of art fits into the culture and time in which it was created. They want to know how the artist was influenced by time, culture, and the works of other artists.

By discovering new information about artists and the times in which they lived, art historians can add to our understanding and appreciation of art. A good example is the work shown in Figure 3.4. This famous painting and the artist who created it provide a treasure trove of material for art historians. Their study and research into

the historical period of this painting have increased our knowledge of both the artist and his work. This adds greatly to our enjoyment and appreciation of the work. But even for the casual viewer this painting is full of interest and mystery.

Titled *The Ambassadors,* it was painted in 1533 by Hans Holbein [HOLE • bine]. The history of the artist and the time and place in which he worked is as fascinating as the painting itself.

A German by birth, Holbein quickly established a reputation as an artist of great skill. As word of his abilities spread throughout Europe, he found himself a position as official royal painter to the court of King Henry VIII of England. Our image of the obese and dangerous monarch (he had a habit of beheading wives to get rid of them) comes mainly from the portraits Holbein painted of him (Figure 3.5).

What a time and place King Henry's court must have been in which to live and work! One wonders if Holbein was ever nervous about painting so unpredictable a person as King Henry. What if the king didn't like his portrait? Would the royal painter lose his head? Apparently, from what historians have discovered, King Henry was well pleased with his talented court artist.

The Ambassadors (Figure 3.4) was painted one year after Holbein moved to London. The two figures in the painting are real people. The one on the left was the

Figure 3.5. Holbein. *Portrait of King Henry VIII.* 1542. Courtesy Castle Howard, England.

French ambassador to the court of Henry VIII. The gentleman on the right was a French bishop. Both are painted full size. This was one of the first paintings to depict full-length portraits. And the detail! The richness of their clothes and the articles scattered so casually on the table demonstrate Holbein's great ability to paint with photographic realism. We can be assured that had cameras existed in 16th-century England, they could not have shown us a more accurate picture.

The more one looks at this work, the more one discovers. For example, the age of the ambassador (figure on the left) is carved into the hilt of his dagger. He's 29. The age of the bishop is 25. It is written on his book. Even the time of day, 10:30 a.m. and the date, April 11, are shown on the dials and instruments scattered about.

Paintings as interesting and full of details as this Holbein offer rich material for art historians or for anyone who loves to unravel mysteries. In a way, art historians work with mysteries all the time. Each work of art presents its own puzzles to solve. Knowing about the artist's life and the historical period in which he or she worked can help solve the puzzle and answer some of the questions. However, it is you, the viewer, who must finally decide and judge whether a work has a message and meaning for you.

Art historians also provide a time frame for art. This timeframe is called art history. By placing artists and artworks in their correct time periods, comparisons can be made and interesting relationships discovered. In the following chapters, you will read about some of the major time periods in art history. As you read, you will recognize many artworks. You will also see similarities between works from very different time periods and from very different cultures. These connections are important for understanding how one style of art influences another. You will also be able to see connections between art and major world events. This will give you a better perspective of how art and world history connect.

One thing you need not worry about is finding art history dull. It is one of the most fascinating subjects you can study.

A True and Royal Witness

Like many of the other artists you have read about, Hans Holbein was born into a family devoted to art. His father, known as Hans Holbein the Elder, was a well-known painter of religious works. He too painted portraits, although never of the scale and quality as those of his talented son.

By age seventeen or eighteen, Hans Holbein had attracted the attention of some very important people. He was much sought after as a portrait artist. His incredible ability to draw and paint the likenesses of faces and the textures of materials brought him commissions from the wealthy and powerful.

After all, this was an age of magnificent clothes. Velvets, satins, silks, and furs were part of the everyday dress of the rich. They loved to wear great gold chains and jewels to show their status in society. Of course, it would be essential for a successful portrait artist to be able to paint these items with absolute realism. Holbein was a master at realistic painting.

Most of Holbein's great works came from the time he was court painter to England's Henry VIII. He painted and drew many members of the royal family, as well as the ladies and lords of the court. His portraits are time machines, sweeping away the hundreds of years separating us from these individuals.

We come face to face with the great King Henry himself, without fear for our heads! And what about the frail, sickly young Prince Edward (Figure 3.6)? At the time this portrait was painted he was six years old. Four years later, at age ten he would be king of England. But his reign was cut short by his death at sixteen.

Holbein also painted portraits of two of King Henry's more unfortunate wives—Anne Boleyn [bow•LYN] and Catherine Howard. Both were beheaded. Figure 3.7 is Holbein's portrait of Queen Catherine Howard.

Holbein was an accurate and truthful witness to a fascinating time in history. He has left us a treasure of memorable portraits from a time and place long past.

Hans Holbein the younger. *Self Portrait.* The Uffizi Gallery. Photo courtesy Scala/Art Resource.

BORN: 1497/8
DIED: 1543
BIRTHPLACE:
Augsburg, Germany

Figure 3.6. Holbein. *Edward VI* (1537-1553), King of England when Duke of Cornwall. Tempera and oil on wood, 12¾ d. The Metropolitan Museum of Art. The Jules Bache Collection, 1949.

Figure 3.7. Holbein. *Lady of Cromwell Family.* ca. 1535-40. Oil on wood panel, 28⅜″ x 19½″. The Toledo Museum of Art, Toledo, Ohio. Gift of Edward Drummond Libbey.

Student work.

Did you learn

- The definitions of these words and phrases: consumers; interpretation; description; analysis; evaluation; credit line; art critic; art historian.
- The four levels of criticism?
- Information that would be included in the description of a work of art?
- One of the purposes of studying the history of art?
- At least three art history facts that add to our understanding of *The Ambassadors*?

Understanding and Evaluating

- Use the four levels of art criticism to evaluate the painting, *Washington Crossing the Delaware*. Write your evaluation down. Compare it with the evaluations of other students in the class.
- In your American history book or another book about the American Revolution, read the account of Washington's crossing of the Delaware River. After reading, look once again at the Luetze painting. Make a list of other connections you find between the event and the painted version.

Seeing and Creating

- Research a historical building in your community. Create a tempera, acrylic, or watercolor painting of the structure. Use color, value, and emphasis to increase visual drama.
- Try your hand at creating a miniature. On a piece of scratchboard, mark off a circle three inches in diameter. Make a self-portrait drawing. Scratchboard can be made by coating a piece of white posterboard with white crayon.
  Mix a few drops of liquid soap into India ink and apply with a brush over the white crayon. The liquid soap keeps the ink from beading up over the crayon. Ink should be applied as smoothly as possible, but not too thick. When dry, a drawing can be made by scratching through the ink with a straightened paper clip. Mistakes can easily be corrected by covering with more ink. [CAUTION: India ink will stain clothes. Use carefully. Cover clothes with an old shirt or smock if possible.]

Like any other subject you study, visual art has a history. Its history is closely tied to the main periods and events of human history. While a more detailed study of art history would fill a book much larger than the one you are holding, this unit will give you an introduction to the main time periods and some of the artworks typical of each period. You will also learn about **style** in art.

Style is a characteristic way an artist or group of artists have of expressing themselves in an art medium. Artworks from the same historical time period share similarities or characteristics of style. You will learn to recognize these styles when you see them in museums or in art books.

"But doesn't the study of history mean learning a lot of dates?"

Don't worry. The timeline shown on the following page will help. Remembering individual dates of artworks is not as important as remembering the general time period from which they come. The timeline will help you with this. There are also maps for each period. With these, you will be able to locate the civilizations discussed and the main art centers and monuments.

One other thing to remember about the timeline is that it represents the main periods of **Western art**. We are not talking about cowboys and Indians here! A history of Western art is about art whose roots are in the culture and heritage of Europe. There are many other Non-Western cultures with rich and wonderful artworks and histories—Asia, Africa, Mexico, South America, and the art of Native Americans, to name just a few.

We will also look at art from some of these Non-Western cultures. We could create a visual art time-line for each of these cultures, if we had another ten volumes! The Western or European art tradition has been influenced by many of these cultures. When you see art-works from these Non-Western Cultures, try to place them on the timeline. This will help you see how cultures have touched and blended throughout recorded history.

WHY STUDY ART HISTORY?

"Why do I have to study art history? I just want to draw and paint in art class."

As you found in the previous chapter, knowing something of the history of the time in which an artist worked can add to your understanding and enjoyment of art. It will also help the development of your own art skills and creative ideas. Seeing the expressive possibilities of

Unit II
INTRODUCING ART HISTORY

others can help you make decisions about your own work; what materials to use; how to work with different subject matter.

Another reason to study art history is that art changes. Art history gives you a framework in which to place artists and their works. It is then easier to see how artists of later periods changed and built upon the work of artists before them. Remember, no artist works without the influence of both time and culture.

A final reason to study art history is simply because it is fun! The history of art is one of the most eventful and "colorful" you can study. Art history is filled not only with artistic geniuses, but also with a whole population of odd and fascinating personalities. Pirates and popes, swordsmen and slaves, magicians and monarchs are all part of the glorious history of art. The importance of art to humankind has always placed its creation and collection at the swirling center of world events. Art history, dull? Hardly. Art history is an adventure!

B.C.	A.D.	1700
18,000 — Cave Art of Lascaux (18,000) — *Prehistoric*	**A.D.** — Colosseum (72-80); Eruption of Vesuvius (79); Pantheon (118-125)	*Roccoco* — Watteau (1684-1721); Declaration of Independence (1776); American Revolution (1775-83); French Revolution (1789-99)
Sumer (3000-2500)	**500** *Medieval* — Hagia Sophia (532-537); Mayan Civilization (100B.C.-900A.D.); Tang Dynasty—Ceramics (618-906)	**1800** — David (1748-1825); Goya (1746-1828); Texas Independence (1836); Constable (1776-1837); Turner (1775-1851); Delacroix (1799-1863); American Civil War (1861-65); Van Gogh (1853-1890); Seurat (1859-1891)
3000 — Stonehenge (2800); Great Pyramids of Egypt (2600-2460)	**1000** *Renaissance* — Norman Invasion (1066); Mesa Verde (1100); Song Dynasty—Painting (960-1279); Giotto (1266-1337); Van Eyck (1395-1441); Ghiberti (1378-1455); Donatello (1386-1466); Columbus discovers America (1492); Leonardo da Vinci (1452-1519)	**1900** *Modern* — Cezanne (1839-1906); Rodin (1840-1917); World War I (1914-1918); Founding of Bauhaus (1919); Renoir (1841-1919); Cassatt (1845-1926); Monet (1840-1926); Mondrian (1892-1944); World War II (1939-1945); Matisse (1869-1954); Pollock (1912-1956); Wright (1867-1959); Mies van der Rohe (1886-1969); Picasso (1881-1973); Vietnam War (1954-1975); Calder (1898-1976); Ernst (1894-1976); Dali (1904-1989); Christo (1935-)
Ancient — King Tut (1450)	**1500** — Raphael (1483-1520); Dürer (1471-1528); Michelangelo (1475-1564); Bruegel (1525-1569)	**2000**
1000 — Founding of Rome (753)	**1600** *Baroque* — Caravaggio (1565-1609); Pilgrims land at Plymouth Rock (1620); Rubens (1577-1640); Velasquez (1599-1660); Rembrandt (1606-1669)	
500 — Parthenon (447-432) — B.C.	**A.D.**	

Chapter 4
ANCIENT BEGINNINGS

Prehistoric means before history, or more accurately, before written records of history were kept. The art of this period, beginning about 25,000 years ago, is sometimes referred to as **Stone Age** art. The term **Stone Age** is used because tools found at these ancient sites were made of stone.

The image most of us have of prehistoric times was probably created by the movies. We imagine huge, lumbering, dim-witted dinosaurs chasing hairy, skin-clad, dim-witted cave people across a vast, empty landscape covered with erupting volcanos. Sound familiar? The truth is quite different.

First, dinosaurs, fortunately for everyone, had long disappeared from the earth before prehistoric humans threw their first rock. Mammoths (something like a hairy elephant), deer, bison, and wild horses were the primary objects of worship and hunting for the cave dwellers of the Stone Age.

Were prehistoric people as slow-witted as the movies and comics portray them? Hardly. Archeologists have discovered that they were highly intelligent, though primitive. They made stone tools with the sharpness and precision of surgical instruments. They buried their dead with compassion and dignity. And though they did not have a written language, they did create wonderful art.

Prehistoric Art

The most famous prehistoric or Stone Age artworks are the cave paintings from two sites or locations: Lascaux [lass•COE] in France (Figure 4.1), and Altamira [al•tah•MEE•rah] in northern Spain (Figure 4.2). The cave of Lascaux was discovered by two small boys searching for a missing puppy!

Each cave contains giant paintings of a variety of animals galloping across the landscape of the cave walls. The images, drawn with great skill, are hidden deep within the caves, far from the light of day and prying eyes.

Archeologists now believe that these paintings had a religious meaning to Stone Age hunters. They may have been created to cast a kind of spell over the animals targeted for the hunt. Maybe the hunter/artist believed that the animals captured in the imagination and in a painting on the walls of a cave, would be easy game for a real hunt. The power of art has a long history.

> **WORDWATCH**
> prehistoric
> Stone Age
> paleolithic
> neolithic
> megalith
> cuneiform
> ziggurats
> relief
> pharoah
> mummification
> hieroglyphics

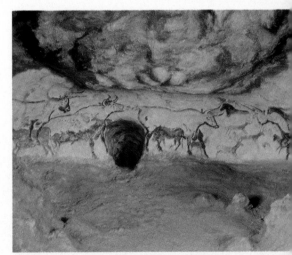

Figure 4.1. Lascaux Cave, France. *Hall of Bulls.* Photo credit: Archiv fur Kunst und Geschichte, Berlin.

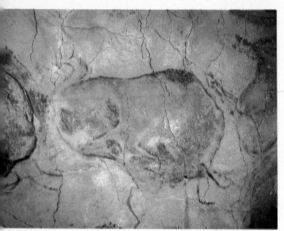

Figure 4.2. Altimira, Spain. *Bison.* c. 21,000-13,000 B.C. Photo credit: Archiv fur Kunst und Geschichte, Berlin.

Figure 4.3. Stone Age Sculpture. *Bison.* La Madeleine, St. Germain. Photo credit: Reunion des Musees Nationaus, France.

Figure 4.4. *Stonehenge,* England. Photo credit: Lee Botlin Picture Library, New York.

Most prehistoric art is in the form of cave paintings. However, there have been pieces of sculptures found also. Figure 4.3 shows a famous example. This beautiful carving of reindeer antler is believed to be a weapon. Historians think that it was used as a club or throwing stick. What is remarkable about it is the clever way the artist has made the image of a bison follow the shape of an antler. Since there was no part of the antler that looked like a head, the artist shows the bison turning its head across the back. He looks as if he is flicking a fly away with his tongue! Like the animals of the cave paintings, the bison is drawn with amazing skill and understanding of animal anatomy.

The animals in prehistoric paintings are usually drawn with simple, but strong outlines. Some colors and textures are included, as seen in Figures 4.1 and 4.2. No effort was made to use value or shading to give an appearance of roundness or volume. The animal figures overlap. This may have been an attempt to show space. It might also have been an effort to reuse wall space! When color is used, it has a very limited range. This is because color pigments were all made from natural materials. There is black, brown, red, and ocher [O•kur], a kind of yellowish-brown.

The Place of the Hanging Stones

Cave art is part of the "old" Stone or **paleolithic** [pay•leo•LITH•ic] Age. **Paleo** means old. You may have seen words in your science textbook with "paleo" as part of them. **Lithic** means stone. Put the two parts together and you have "old stone." There is also a historical period known as the "new" Stone Age. The word for this is **neolithic** [nee•o•LITH•ic]. **Neo** means new; **lithic** means stone.

During the neolithic period, the first architecture or free-standing structures were built. One of the most famous and mysterious is Stonehenge (Figure 4.4) in England. Stonehenge means "hanging stones" in Old English. Standing alone on a windy, empty plain, this circle of great stone arches has fascinated people for thousands of years. It is believed that the first circle, no more than a pit and earth mound, was built around 2,800 B.C. The **megaliths** or large stones seen standing today were probably erected around 2,000 B.C.

Because no one really knows what Stonehenge was used for, it has been the focus of many interesting myths, legends, and theories over the centuries. People once believed it had been built by Merlin, the magician and advisor to King Arthur. It did seem that it would have taken magic to place huge stones weighing tons on top of other enormous stones. How could primitive stone tools and human strength alone accomplish such a feat? To this day, no one knows for sure. But, there it stands, as mysterious and remote as ever.

Was Stonehenge once the site of strange rites where human sacrifice was practiced or an astronomical observatory? Both these theories have been suggested. The latest theory is that Stonehenge is a giant computer! We will probably never know for sure. But in a way, that is what is so wonderful about this remarkable structure. Stonehenge makes people dream and imagine. In this, at least, its magic is as powerful as ever. What do you think Stonehenge was used for?

Figure 4.5. Middle East map. The area between the Tigris and Euphrates rivers was known in ancient times as Mesopotamia.

CHILDREN OF THE RIVERS—MESOPOTAMIA AND EGYPT

It is no accident that the two greatest civilizations of the ancient world were built along the banks of rivers. The rivers not only provided water for drinking, but water for irrigating crops and transporting people and goods. The Tigris [TIE•gris] and Euphrates [u•FRAY•tees] rivers gave life to the civilization known as Mesopotamian [mes•uh•puh•TA•mi•un]. Mesopotamia is a Greek word which means "between the rivers." And this is exactly where Mesopotamia was located, between the Tigris and Euphrates rivers (Figure 4.5). This area is now known as Iraq.

This valley was an ideal place to build a great civilization. Although the desert stretched for hundreds of miles, the land between the rivers was fertile. It allowed many different crops to grow. The people could not only feed themselves, but could also establish trade with other cultures. The region became the home of many different people. The first group called themselves Sumerians [soo•MAR•ee•uns]. The area where these people lived in small city-states, was called Sumer.

Sumer

We owe much to these clever and inventive people. For example, they invented writing. Using a wedge-shaped tool, they pressed triangles into damp clay tablets. Each group of triangles made up a letter or phrase in

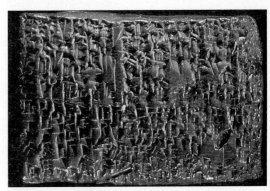

Figure 4.6. *Cuniform tablets.* Photo credit: Lee Boltin Picture Library, New York.

Sumerian. This type of writing is called **cuneiform** [QUE • nee • form] (Figure 4.6).

Of course, as soon as someone learns to write, someone else decides that records and accounts must be kept. This is what happened in Sumer. Archeologists have uncovered thousands of clay tablets covered with cuneiform writing. Most, when translated, turned out to be tax accounts and lists of merchandise bought and traded. Nevertheless, the Sumerians can claim to be the first "historic" civilization. Do you remember what word describes those societies or cultures that existed *before* writing was invented?

If you had to choose the most important invention or discovery in the history of humankind what would you choose? Fire? Electricity? What about the wheel? How would we manage without wheels? Well, we also owe the invention of the wheel to the Sumerians.

The Sumerians were "first" in other areas, as well. They created the first representative government and the first public schools. Can you imagine attending school in ancient Sumer with a stack of wet, clay tablets instead of notebook paper!

The written records of Sumer tell us much of the everyday lives and activities of these amazing people. But it is the art that gives us the best picture of this remarkable civilization.

The Art of Mesopotamia

As the first great culture to occupy Mesopotamia, the Sumerians were accomplished in architecture, sculpture, and the creation of decorative objects. Unfortunately, because they constructed their buildings, called **ziggurats** [ZIG • goo • rots], of clay bricks, not stone, these human-made mountains have all but disappeared. (Figure 4.7). What we do have are some impressive sculptures and wonderful jewelry and art objects. Figure 4.8 shows one of the most famous.

Found in a royal tomb, this sculpture of a goat is decorated with gold, silver, and colored stones. He is rearing on his hind legs to nibble the tender flowers and leaves from the golden bush. There were two of these sculptures found in the tomb. Historians believe that both were used as the supports or legs of a table. Study the goat carefully. Do you think the Sumerian artist who made it understood the anatomy of the animal? How would you compare this animal portrait with those from the Stone Age?

Figure 4.9 shows a sculpture that is typical of the Sumerian style. This portrait, thought to be one of the rulers of Sumer, known as Gudea [goo • DEE • ah], has few details of features or clothing. The head seems large

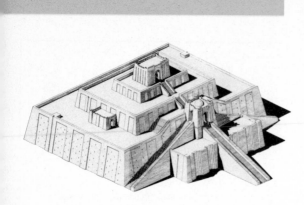

Figure 4.7. *Sumerian Ziggurat of Ur-Nammu Restored.* Reproduced by courtesy of the Trustees of the British Museum.

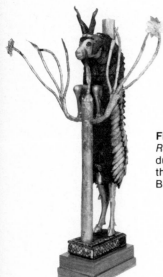

Figure 4.8. Sumerian. *Ram in Thicket.* Reproduced by courtesy of the Trustees of the British Museum.

Figure 4.9. *Sumerian. Gudea.* Collection The Louvre, Paris. Photo © R.N.M.

for the body; the eyes large and staring. The hands are quietly folded, as if in prayer. Unlike architecture, Sumerian sculpture is made from hard stone. That is why today we can stare into the face of a king who ruled over 5,000 years ago.

Unfortunately for the clever Sumerians, the richness of their valley and the advances of their civilization attracted invaders. The Assyrians [as•SEER•ee•uns] conquered the people of Mesopotamia about 900 B.C. Though warlike, the Assyrians were also great artists. Two examples of their art are shown in Figures 4.10 and 4.11. Figure 4.10 is a **relief** sculpture. A **relief** is a shallow carving, similar to a drawing in stone. The Assyrians produced some of the greatest relief sculptures ever made.

Unlike the Sumerian artists, the Assyrians liked to show as much detail as possible. Just look how much you can tell about the clothing of the winged figure. The elaborate robe is trimmed with heavy fringe. The figure's wings and beard are carefully arranged so that the smallest details can be shown. Notice the position of the figure. The top part of the body is turned to face you, while the arms, legs, and face are shown in profile. This is a position you will notice in the art of ancient Egypt, as well.

The Assyrian artists were famous for their relief sculptures. Figure 4.11 is another example of their art. A winged figure holds a small animal in his arms. Can you tell what kind of animal this might be? The Assyrian artists were very skilled in carving animals realistically. Compare this animal with those in the Stone Age cave and with the playful Sumarian goat.

Eternal Egypt

Without the Nile river there would likely have been no Egyptian civilization. The great river which cuts its way across the continent of Africa (Figure 4.12) made the Nile valley one of the richest on earth. Like the Sumerians, the Egyptians were able to grow many different crops for eating and trading. The width and length of the river provided a perfect "highway" for trade and transportation. The Egyptians soon took advantage of this watery "highway" and the fertile valley it protected. Along its banks they built one of the great civilizations of the world. They built it to last.

Figure 4.10. Assyrian. *Winged Genius.* Late 9th century B.C. From the Nimrud Palace of Ashurnasirpal II, 93″ x 77¼″. Los Angeles County Museum of Art: Los Angeles County Funds donated by Anna Bing Arnold.

Figure 4.11. Assyrian. *Nimrud: Plaque of Protective Spirit with Cuniform Description.* c. 865-850 B.C. 4′10″. Photo credit: Lee Boltin. Picture Library, New York.

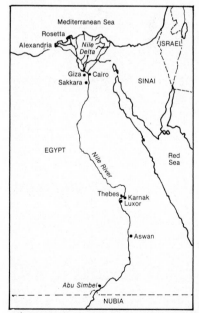

Figure 4.12. This map shows the Nile valley. The most famous pyramids of Egypt are located at the base of the Delta at Giza. Modern day Cairo is about a thirty minute drive from the pyramids.

Figure 4.13. *Overview of Pyramids of Egypt.* Photo by Erich Lessing. Archiv fur Kunst und Geschichte, Berlin.

Figure 4.14. *Sphinz at Giza.* Photo credit: Rosenthal Art Slides.

Architecture

There are few more famous monuments in the world than the pyramids of Egypt (Figure 4.13). This pyramid is located at Giza [gee•zah] at the foot of the Nile delta. Find Giza and the delta on the map in Figure 4.12. The pyramids in Mexico may be higher (you will read about them in a later chapter), but those of Egypt are older and more famous. Rising from desert-like, mysterious mountains, they have mystified human beings for centuries. How were they built and why?

The answer to the first part of the question is still in doubt. How human beings were able to build a structure that could cover ten football fields and contained over two-million blocks of stone is still something of a mystery. Some people think that the blocks were dragged up mud ramps until the last block was in place. We may never know exactly how this architectural feat was accomplished. However, we do know something of *why* they were built.

Ancient Egyptian society was dependent on the rule of the king or **pharoah** [fay•row]. People believed that the pharoah was also a god. Pyramids were built to be the tombs of the pharoahs of Egypt.

Figure 4.14 shows the huge stone sculpture known as the Sphinx [SFEENX]. This massive sculpture is positioned in front of the largest of the pyramids at Giza. The head is a portrait of the Pharoah Khafre [KAH•fray]; the body is that of a lion. The Sphinx has become as famous a symbol of Egypt as the pyramids. Why do you think the sculptor showed the pharoah with the body of a lion?

The people of ancient Egypt believed in an afterlife. In this afterlife, the pharoah would take his place with the other gods. This could only be assured if the remains or body of the pharoah were protected and preserved for eternity. Placing it under tons of stone seemed a perfect way to insure an afterlife for the pharoah.

But the most perfect plans do not always work. Though the architects of the pharoah's tomb and pyramid used many clever devices to hide the king's mummy and the treasures he needed in the afterlife, thieves always found a way into the royal burial chamber. The only pharoah's tomb to be found with most of the treasures still in place was that of Tutankhamon [two•tank•amon] or King "Tut," as he is best known. Figure 4.22 shows one of the most famous treasures found in his tomb—the solid gold mummy mask.

Because of their interest in preserving things for as long as possible, the Egyptians devised ways to preserve the human body after death. This process was called

mummification [mummy•fy•KAY•shun]. The climate of Egypt is very hot and dry. This helped preserve people and objects for thousands of years. When King Tut's tomb was found in 1922 by archeologist Howard Carter, the flowers that had been placed on the mummy, perhaps by the grieving young widow, still retained some of their color!

The pyramids at Giza, impressive as they are, are not the oldest in Egypt. That particular honor goes to the Step pyramid at Saqqara [sah•KAH•ra] (Figure 4.15). It is easy to see where this pyramid gets its name. Constructed in a series of stages or steps, this was the first large stone structure ever built on earth. It was built to hold the remains of a pharoah named Zoser [ZOE•sir].

There is something else very special about this monument. We know the name of the architect who designed it—Imhotep [em•HOE•tep]. His is the only architect's name that has come down to us from ancient times. He must have been a remarkable individual. Unfortunately, other than his name, we know little about him. However, his pyramid design became, with some changes (can you see what they are?), the model for all the others that followed. The Step pyramid was built around 2,600 B.C. What a special date this seems to be! Can you remember the other works you have read about in this chapter that were made around that time?

Imhotep's reputation became so great in Egypt that like the pharoah, he was made a god. This is surely an honor no other artist in history can claim! Legend has it that his tomb was as splendid as the Pharoah's, but to this day, it has never been found. Wouldn't you like to try to find it?

Egyptian architecture was not limited to pyramids. Many magnificent temples and palaces dot the desert along the Nile. Figures 4.16 through 4.18 give you an idea of the size and variety of ancient Egyptian architecture. Notice the columns in Figure 4.16. These represent a type of plant called a lotus. These plants were found all along the banks of the Nile, along with palms and papyrus [pah•PIE•russ]. Many structures and decorations in Egyptian architecture use these plants as subjects. Can you find them in any other decorative motifs?

Sculpture

Egyptian artists also created many wonderful sculptures. Figure 4.19 is a sculpture portrait of the Pharoah Khafre. One of the pyramids at Giza belongs to this great king. Compare this portrait with that of Gudea (Figure 4.9). How are they similar? How are they different?

Figure 4.15. *Step Pyramid.* Saggara, Egypt. Photo credit: Rosenthal Art Slides.

Figure 4.16. *Kom Ombo.* Upper Egypt. 332-320 B.C.

Figure 4.17. *Colossal Statues of Ramesses II.*

Figure 4.18. *Temple of Khonsu.* Karnak.

41

Figure 4.19. Seated *Portrait of Chefren (Khafre) with falcon,* from his Death Temple at Giza. Diorite. 4th dynasty. Photo: Foto Marburg/Art Resource, New York.

Egyptian sculpture always shows the figure facing forward in a stiff, posed position. The faces are idealized portraits, but are probably closer to a true likeness than the Sumerian portraits. You will see in the next chapter how the Romans really changed this tradition. They sculpted true likenesses—warts and all!

The subjects of Egyptian portraits are shown with great dignity as is this portrait of Khafre. Can you see the wings of the hawk on either side of his head? The hawk represents one of the most famous Egyptian gods called Horus. His power protects the king and gives him strength and wisdom.

The headdress the pharoah is wearing represents the mane of a lion. Do you remember the Sphinx? Look again at Figure 4.14. This headdress is one of the ways you can tell that a sculpture is Egyptian and that the subject is the Pharoah.

Look at Figure 4.20. This sculpture portrait of Queen Nefertiti [nef•fur•TEE•tee] is considered one of the finest portraits ever created. This beautiful woman was King Tut's aunt. Her name is well suited to her face. Nefertiti means "the beautiful one is come." Do you think the sculptor idealized this portrait? Compared to other ancient portraits you have seen, doesn't she seem strangely modern? Would you be surprised to see her face on the cover of a fashion magazine?

Figure 4.20. *Nefertiti.* 1360 B.C. Photo credit: Archiv fur Kunst und Geschichte, Berlin.

Painting

What surprises most visitors when they visit the monuments of ancient Egypt today is how well buildings and sculptures are preserved. Even more amazing is the amount of painting that can still be seen on the walls of tombs and temples. The Egyptians enjoyed color and beautifully decorated walls. They covered almost every inch of wall surface with paintings. Even the walls of tombs, covered over by tons of stone or earth, were covered with magnificent, painted scenes of the activities that the dead had enjoyed in life. Figure 4.21 shows just such a scene. Here a rich young man is hunting geese and ducks. Do you recognize the lotus and papyrus plants near the edge? The strange symbols are **hieroglyphics** [hy•row•GLIF•iks]. This was the Egyptian style of writing.

Egyptian paintings of figures are similar to the Assyrian reliefs, such as that in Figure 4.10. The upper part of the body faces forward, while the head, arms, and legs are shown in profile. Though the painting has many details, there is no illusion that the figures or objects are three-dimensional, or rounded. No value or shading has been used at all. These techniques would come much later with Greek and Roman painting.

Figure 4.21. Egyptian Wall Painting. *Fowling Scene.* Reproduced by courtesy of the Trustees of the British Museum.

Figure 4.22. *Gold Mask of Tutankahamun.* Gold and Lapiis Lazuli. Photo credit: Lee Boltin Picture Library, New York.

Figure 4.23. Egyptian. *Vessel in Shape of a Fish.* Reproduced by courtesy of the Trustees of the British Museum.

For the Glory of The Pharoah

Though their individual names are unknown to us, the artists and craftspeople of ancient Egypt were as skilled and creative as any working today. In the working of materials like ivory, glass, inlaid wood, precious stones and metals, the Egyptians had few equals. Using the simplest of tools, craftspeople were able to create masterpieces like the famous solid gold mask of Tutankhamon (Figure 4.22). This remarkable object is not only a wonderful portrait, it is also one of the finest examples of gold crafting ever made. The young pharoah (he died at nineteen) looks dignified and peaceful.

Although the portrait is probably idealized, we still have a feeling that this is how the Pharoah looked in life. Notice the elaborate headdress inlaid with semi-precious stones, as are the eyes. This mask covered the face of King Tut's mummy. Both mummy and mask were then placed inside a case made of over a ton of solid gold! From works like this, it is easy to see why the riches and crafts of the Egyptians were legendary.

Though of less value than the gold mask, the fish bottle shown in Figure 4.23 shows another side to the people and crafts of Egypt. This charming bottle in the shape of a fish was used to hold perfumes or cosmetics. It is made of glass.

It is unknown when the making of glass was first used. It is known that the craftspeople of Egypt soon established themselves as masters of the process. In Figure 4.23 many different colors of glass have been combined to represent the color and scales of a fish. The mouth, which probably once held a stopper, was designed to be a pouring spout.

The Egyptians were very interested in their appearance. They enjoyed looking their best, just as we do today. Both men and women used a variety of cosmetics and perfumes. To hold these items, craftspeople created hundreds of small containers. To amuse their wealthy owners, many were cleverly shaped like animals or people. To the rich Egyptians, this lovely and precious item may have been no more important than a plastic bottle is to us. Fortunately for us, many of these wonderful glass containers have survived without a chip for over five thousand years.

Student work.

Did you learn

- The definitions of these words and phrases: prehistoric; Stone Age; Paleolithic; Neolithic; megalith; cuneiform; ziggurats; relief; pharoah; mummification; hieroglyphics?
- At least three important contributions of the Sumerians to modern civilization?
- Three characteristics of the Egyptian style of figure painting?

Understanding and Evaluating

- Write a short story about Stonehenge (3-5 pages).
- Compare the portrait of Gudea (Figure 4.9) with that of Khafre (Figure 4.19). Make a list of ways they are similar and ways they are different.
- In a paragraph or two, write an imaginary speech for each king to speak to his people on a great occasion.

Seeing and Creating

- Under the direction of your teacher prepare some plaster slabs about 8″x10″ and one inch thick.
- © [CAUTION: if you are allergic to plaster dust, be sure to wear a protective mask. Never pour plaster down a sink. Wipe all containers and hands into a wastebasket.] On a sheet of paper create a design using animal or plant forms. Transfer the design to the smooth side of the plaster slab. Using simple carving tools such as paper clips and old kitchen knives, carve the design as a low relief into the plaster. Look again at the Assyrian relief shown in Figure 4.11. Notice how an illusion of space is shown by carving objects at different levels. Be sure to include detail in your relief.
- Make an imaginary drawing of a pyramid or other Egyptian architecture. Add sculptures and other structures to decorate the surrounding landscape, as well as any other details you imagine. You might even want to show an interior view of the pyramid and where you think the pharoah's tomb would be hidden. Finish your drawing in India ink and pen. Watercolor wash can then be added for color.

Chapter 5

GLORY AND GRANDEUR— THE ART OF GREECE AND ROME

GREECE—BIRTHPLACE OF WESTERN CIVILIZATION

There is something very familiar about the art of ancient Greece. Not only does it appear right and beautiful to our eyes, but it seems to almost be a part of American history. The reason for this is not so surprising. From the architecture of government buildings to the design of democratic structures, the founding fathers of the United States borrowed many ideas and images from ancient Greece.

In fact, many consider Greece the true birthplace of **Western Civilization**. Civilization includes all people who share a common heritage of ideas, customs, and culture. Most of the art we will examine in this text has its origins in the artistic traditions of ancient Greece.

But what made this ancient civilization so special, so different from others? Why were men like Thomas Jefferson so influenced by the spirit and art of people dead for thousands of years? At its most powerful time, ancient Greece was never a match for the cultures of Egypt and Rome. Living in a collection of small city-states, the people of Greece were as likely to be at war with each other as with the rest of the world.

Was it size? Hardly. Ancient Greece was about the size of the state of Arizona. (Figure 5.1) So, what gave this civilization such influence? The answer is people. The greatest difference between Greece and other ancient civilizations was that in Greece the individual was important. Most of the people of Mesopotamia and Egypt were completely overshadowed by the will and might of absolute rulers. If they were artists, their fame was known only through the works they produced for the king or pharoah. But in Greece, things were different.

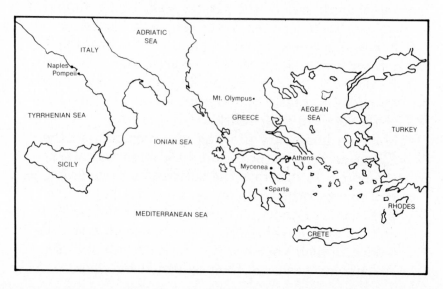

Figure 5.1. Map of ancient Greece.

The Greeks considered themselves citizens with certain basic rights. They took pride in themselves and their individual accomplishments. Every task, every work of art was completed with care and attention. Art, as the visual expression of individual feelings and ideas, was especially valued. And it is art that was the true glory of Greece.

Greek Architecture and Sculpture

Figure 5.2 is a photograph of what many consider the most beautiful and perfect building ever constructed. It is called the Parthenon [PAR•tha•non]. Although today it is a mere echo of its former magnificence, for centuries it was the model and standard against which all other buildings were measured. Doesn't it look familiar? Compare it to our nation's Capitol building shown in Figure 5.3. There are many similarities. What other buildings have you seen that look similar? Even Thomas Jefferson's home, Monticello (Figure 5.4), borrowed many design ideas from Greek architecture.

Figure 5.2. View of *Parthenon.*

The Parthenon was built during a period known as the "the Golden Age." The art of this period is also referred to as **classical** Greek art. **Classical** really means two things: First, it means art that was made during the 4th and 5th centuries B.C. If something is made during the 4th century B.C., its date will be 300-399. For example, the Parthenon was built in the 5th century B.C. Its dates are 448-432 B.C. It is considered an example of classical Greek architecture. Second, art that is classical in design, follows certain artistic principles.

For example, the Greeks believed that some physical proportions were perfect or ideal. A column had to be just the right size and shape to fit the design of a building. All parts of the architectural design or composition had to work together in harmony to create balance and unity. The ancient Greeks believed, if all these elements worked together, classical beauty would be achieved. The Parthenon is a wonderful example of classical design and beauty.

Figure 5.3. *United States Capitol,* Washington D.C. Photo credit: Rosenthal Art Slides.

Who built this wonder? Two names have come down to us. Ictinus [IK•tee•nus] and Callicrates [cal•i•KRAY•tis], architects and engineers. Why was the Parthenon built? It was a temple to the goddess Athena [ah•THEE•na]. Athena was the patron goddess of the ancient city-state of Athens. Modern-day Athens is the capital of Greece. The Parthenon was built on a high plateau overlooking Athens called the Acropolis [ah•CROP•o•liss]. (Figure 5.5)

Because of the importance of Athena to the city of Athens, every possible care and attention was lavished on the Parthenon. Although destroyed many centuries ago, a

Figure 5.4. Thomas Jefferson's *Monticello.* Photo credit: ©1991 James Tkatch.

Figure 5.5. *Acropolis.* 5th century B.C. View from southwest. Photo credit: Rosenthal Art Slides.

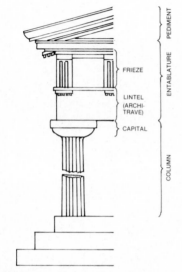

Figure 5.6. The main parts of a Doric column and post and lintel construction.

Figure 5.7. The Ionic capital is shaped somewhat like the coiled horns of a goat. It is more elaborate than the Doric, but simpler than the Corinthian.

Figure 5.8. The Corinthian capital looks like a plant. This is no accident, since its design is based on the shape of the leaves of the acanthus plant that grows in Greece.

roof once covered the interior of the building. This was important, since one of the rooms contained one of the seven wonders of the ancient world—a gigantic statue of the goddess herself.

Unfortunately, this remarkable sculpture has long since disappeared. We know it only from poor copies made by Roman artists and the written descriptions of visitors. But what a sight it must have been. Just imagine, a statue of a goddess thirty-five-feet tall! No simple marble or granite for the patron goddess of Athens. This sculpture was covered in pieces of ivory to represent the glowing skin of the beautiful Athena. Her clothes were made of sheets of solid gold. Over a ton of gold was used. How she must have shone in the flickering light of the torches!

Did her eyes seem to follow awe-struck visitors? They were made of precious stones, as were the glittering eyes of the huge snake that lay coiled at her side. We know the name of the sculptor who created this masterpiece and designed the other sculptures on the Parthenon. His name was Phidias [FID•dee•us].

As magnificent as the sculpture of Athena must have been, it was not the only wonder of the Parthenon. Thanks to Phidias and the architects of the Parthenon (do you remember their names?), the building and its decorations were so perfectly made and matched that it is difficult to talk about one without discussing the other.

Look at Figure 5.2 again. The first part of the Parthenon that catches your attention are the columns. They are of a special design called **Doric** [DOOR•ric]. You can identify Doric-style columns in two ways: 1) they have no base and stand directly on the floor of the building; 2) their tops or **capitals** are very simple, like small cushions. Figure 5.6 shows you the main parts of the Doric column. The Greeks used two other types of columns as well, **Ionic** [i•ON•ik] (Figure 5.7) and **Corinthian** [core• IN•the•ahn] (Figure 5.8). What differences can you see between the three types of capitals?

If you look above the columns, you will see a long flat surface. This is called the **entablature** [in•TAB•let•chur] (Figure 5.6). The entablature is divided into two parts: the **architrave** [ARC•i•trave] and the **frieze** [FREEZE]. The architrave is the part just above the capitals of the columns. The frieze is above the architrave. Locate all these parts in Figure 5.6.

Look above the architrave of the Parthenon (Figure 5.2). What do you see? Not much is left of the final part of the temple called the **pediment** [PED•i•mint]. The pediment (find this part on Figure 5.6) was a triangular-shaped section below the roof. The Greeks used this part of their buildings as a space for sculpture and decoration.

Figure 5.10. *Birth of Athena* (detail). Reconstruction of Parthenon east pediment. Courtesy of the Trustees, British Museum.

The pediment sculptures of the Parthenon, designed by Phidias, were some of the greatest ever created. Unfortunately, only fragments now remain, scattered throughout the museums of the world. The British Museum in London, England, has some of the most well-preserved pieces.

Figure 5.9 shows one of the magnificent horse's heads that was part of a corner section. Figure 5.10 shows how the completed sculptures looked when they were part of the east pediment. Can you find the horse's head from Figure 5.9 in this photograph? What do you think the horses are part of? Look at the other corner of the pediment. There are three other horses. The seated figure in the center of the pediment represents Zeus, the greatest of the Greek gods. Standing beside him is the figure of the goddess Athena.

There were two pediments on the Parthenon, one at the west end and one at the east end. Why do you think the Greeks placed their temple facing east?

The sculptures of both pediments are carved in the round. That is, they are three-dimensional. Sculptures that were carved on the frieze are reliefs. This frieze of figures ran around the entire temple (Figure 5.11). The frieze sculptures represented figures of the citizens of Athens, as well as figures from Greek **mythology.** This was a collection of stories about the gods and goddesses. These stories provided the main subject matter of Greek art.

Although sculpture and architecture were the favorite art forms of the ancient Greeks, painting also played an important part. Most Greek painting that has come down to us is found on vases and other ceramic containers.

You might be surprised to discover that the Greeks also painted their elegant temples! Long since washed away by sun, wind, rain, and time, strong, intense colors once covered the sculptures of the Parthenon! Today, it is hard to imagine these wonderful structures, with their creamy white columns, in full color!

More to modern tastes are Greek vase paintings, like that pictured in Figure 5.12. This type of painting is

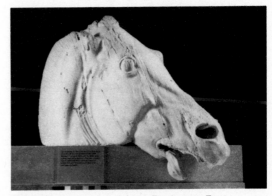

Figure 5.9. Horse head from Parthenon East Pediment. c. 430 BC. Marble. Reproduced by courtesy of the Trustees of the British Museum.

Figure 5.11. Poseidon and Apollo Frieze Relief from Parthenon east cella frieze. c. 440 BC. Marble, 37"h. Reproduced by courtesy of the Trustees of the British Museum.

Figure 5.12. *Attic Black Figure Hydria, Five Women at Well.* ca. 510 B.C. Ceramic, 20½″ h. Courtesy of the Museum of Fine Arts Boston. William Francis Warden Fund.

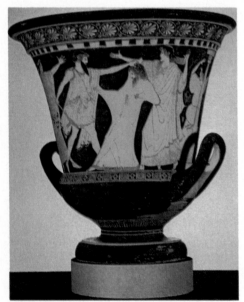

Figure 5.13. *Red Figured Vase.* Reproduced by courtesy of the Trustees of the British Museum, London.

called a **black-figured** design. The background is light in color, while the figures are black. Details on the figures also appear light in color. The Greeks also reversed this painting technique. They created **red-figured** designs (Figure 5.13).

The subject matter for most Greek vase paintings was taken from mythology. However, human heroes and heroines from Greek history are also used. What part of a Greek temple do the vase decorations remind you of? Why? In which style—black-figured or red-figured—do you think the negative space (space around the figures) shows up best? Why?

ROME—AN EMPIRE IS BORN

Borrowing ideas from the Greeks began early. The first important culture in Italy, the Etruscan [e•TRUS•cun] culture, borrowed many ideas from the clever Greeks. But, it was the people of Rome that completely absorbed the images and art of Greece. In fact, if Roman artists had not been so impressed with Greek painting and sculpture, we might not have known the Greek works at all. The Roman artists made copies of everything Greek, from jewelry to wall paintings.

But the Romans did not become the masters of the known world without having some original ideas of their own!

Legend has it that Rome was founded on April 21, 753 B.C. by two boys, Romulus and Remus, who had been raised by a wolf. At least the date seems fairly accurate. Situated on the seven hills along the Tiber river (Figure 5.14), the city of Rome would become in time the center of Western Civilization and power. The great cultures of Greece and Egypt would eventually fall to the might of the Roman army and be added to an expanding empire. This empire, one of the greatest the world has ever known, was managed by an emperor and a group of elders or senate. At one time it must have seemed as though no army could stand against the power of imperial Rome.

Part of the Romans' success had to do with the fact that they were great organizers. They knew how to organize and manage armies and the people they conquered. They also knew how to make use of the knowledge and skills of the people they conquered. Greek art was not only copied by Roman artists, but Greek artists were brought to Rome to teach their skills. This passion for organization and order was reflected in the

Figure 5.14. The Roman empire spread far beyond its original area in Italy. At its height it reached from North Africa to the British Isles.

Figure 5.15. Exterior view of the *Colosseum*. Photo credit: Archiv fur Kunst und Geschichte, Berlin.

government of Rome, as well as in its body of laws.

Although Rome borrowed most of its art images and decoration from Greece, there were areas in which the Romans made improvements and discoveries. These advances can be seen mainly in Roman architecture. For architecture was the gift of Rome to Western Civilization.

Figure 5.15 shows one of the most famous ancient Roman buildings—the Colosseum [Col•uh•SEE•um]. From its shape, you can probably guess its use. Our modern stadiums have changed very little in design from this ancient one.

While our stadiums are designed to hold hundreds of spectators for sporting events, the Flavian Amphitheater [FLAY•vee•un AM•fy•thee•a•ter], the real name of this structure, served a far darker purpose. Among other things, it was the site of gladiatorial [glad•ee•ah•TOR•ee•all] contests. **Gladiators** were slaves highly trained in fighting with a variety of weapons.

Look again at Figure 5.15. The Colosseum represents the genius of the Roman architects. As in modern stadiums, easy access was made to each level of seats within the stadium. This permitted enormous crowds of spectators to move freely and rapidly throughout the structure.

Figure 5.16. Interior view of the *Colosseum*. Photo credit: Archiv fur Kunst und Geschichte, Berlin.

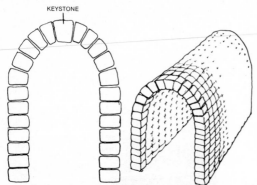

KEYSTONE

Figure 5.17. Roman architects used the greater strength of the arch to span larger spaces, both inside and out. If extended, the arch can easily become a tunnel or barrel vault.

Figure 5.18. Pont du Gard, Nimes, France. Photo credit: Rosenthal Art Slides.

Figure 5.19. Appollodorus of Damascus. *Forum of Trajan.* c. 113 A.D. Photo credit: Rosenthal Art Slides.

Figure 5.20. Giovanni Paolo Pannini. *Interior of the Pantheon.* 1740 Oil on canvas, 50½" x 39". National Gallery of Art, Washington. Samuel H. Kress Collection.

Probably the first thing you notice about the outside of the Colosseum are the many arches. This is one of the great Roman contributions to architectural design. Figure 5.17 shows you how the Roman arch was constructed. The Greeks used arches, but they were usually small and hidden. An arch, however, lets you build bigger, and cover a greater area, with less material and weight. Figures 5.18, 5.19 and 5.20 give an idea of the different kinds of buildings that the Romans constructed using the arch.

Roman-style architecture spread around the empire, from Egypt to England. Many of these works, though in ruin, are still impressive today.

Portraits

Though most Roman sculpture looks almost identical to Greek sculpture, there are some differences, especially in the portrait.

Figures 5.21 through 5.23 show examples of the Roman art of portraiture. Notice how real these individuals seem. If you met them on the street, dressed in modern clothes, you would take them for bankers, construction workers, or teachers. We know these are true likenesses. They show all the flaws of the face and character of the subject.

Compare them to the portraits of people of Mesopotamia and Egypt. The Roman portraits not only let us see the true features of the person, but they also allow us a glimpse into his or her personality. Although some of these individuals ruled the Roman empire, it is clear from these stone portraits, they were just people like everyone else. They could be cruel or kind, serious or silly. These wonderful images are the closest thing we have to photographs of the Romans. They help us feel closer to these people of the distant past.

Figure 5.21. *Lucio Cecilio Giocondo,* banker of Pompeii. Museo Nazionale, Rome. Photo: Alinari/Art Resource, New York.

Figure 5.23. Roman. *Portrait of a Lady.* Marble bust. Capitolino Museum, Rome. Photo credit: Archiv fur Kunst und Geschichte, Berlin.

Figure 5.22. Roman. *Pompeius.* Collection: Copenhagen Ny Carlsberg Glyptothek. Photo credit: Archiv fur Kunst und Geschichte, Berlin.

Figure 5.24. Street in Pompeii. The raised stones in the middle allowed shoppers to step over wet or muddy streets without ruining their shoes.

A Roman Time Capsule

Before we leave the subject of Roman art, we must pay a visit to a remarkable town—Pompeii [pom • PAY] (Figure 5.24). What makes this town so special is that because of its destruction, we know more about the daily lives of the Romans than any other ancient people. The death of Pompeii and its nearby neighbor city, Herculaneum [her • cule • LANE • ee • um], happened suddenly on a hot August morning in 79 A.D.

The citizens of both cities rose early to enjoy the cool sea breeze before the heat of the day closed in. Situated along the beautiful Bay of Naples (Figure 5.14), both cities enjoyed a glorious climate. In fact, this area of Italy had become a favorite resort and vacation spot for wealthy Roman citizens. Magnificent summer houses dotted the hillsides overlooking the blue Mediterranean. Life was wonderful.

Servants in the houses of the wealthy had begun preparing lunch—baked chicken, olives, and cheese were on the menu for this day. The kitchen of the bakery shop on the corner was filled with the delicious smells of baking bread and fruit tarts. Dogs lay sleeping in the shade, waiting for their masters to return for lunch, and for the promise of table scraps. It was just another normal day, until Mount Vesuvius [ves•SU•vee•us] awoke.

To the Romans who had built this charming and prosperous resort, the looming presence of the mountain known as Vesuvius was an added benefit to the town. The soil on the mountain was very rich. The Pompeians discovered that they could grow a variety of crops, including grapes for wine. They nestled their town at the very foot of the mountain. But what they didn't know was that in the heart of Vesuvius slept a fiery giant. Vesuvius wasn't just a mountain, it was one of the most active volcanos on earth!

The destruction began with violent earthquakes. But the mountain itself soon erupted. Enormous columns of rock, ash, and smoke exploded high into the air. Daylight turned into twilight. Panic filled the streets. People grabbed what possessions they could carry and ran for their lives. Fortunately, there were boats in the harbor. Even Roman naval vessels were sent to rescue the terrified citizens of Pompeii.

For many years, archeologists believed most people had escaped. But, a few years ago construction workers, digging along the old sea wall of the town, found the remains of hundreds of bodies. Many were still clutching the few valuables they had saved. They were soon trapped and poisoned by the deadly gases that poured from the volcano. What was a tragedy for the ancient citizens of Pompeii has become a historical treasure for modern archeologists and historians.

There was no hot lava to destroy Pompeii and Herculaneum. Vesuvius makes no lava. It erupted with rock, dust, and ash, much like Mount St. Helens in the United States did in 1980. However, the eruption of Vesuvius was ten times greater! The deadly gases poisoned many people before they could make it to safety, and then the ash, rock, and dust rained down for days. It buried Pompeii to a depth of seventeen feet!

Both Pompeii and Herculaneum were rediscovered in the 18th century. At present, both ancient towns can be visited. The ruins of Pompeii are almost entirely uncovered now. Herculaneum has been much harder to uncover. The stone-hard mud has to be removed with jack-hammers, not shovels! There is also another problem. Since all memory of this Roman town was lost,

Figure 5.25. Three scenes from Pompeii.

Figure 5.26. Roman. *Wall painting in Pompeii.* Fresco on lime plaster, 8′ h. Metropolitan Museum of Art, Rogers Fund, 1903.

a new city was built over its grave. To dig out the ancient city today, means destroying the homes and businesses of modern Italian citizens. This is a problem that may prevent us from ever seeing all the treasures that Herculaneum holds. But, we do have Pompeii (Figure 5.25).

You might have been wondering how we know what was being served for lunch on the day of the eruption, or how we know the bakeshop was cooking bread and tarts. The answer is that everything was found just as it was left. People left the food and dishes on the tables or in the ovens. Loaves of bread, 1,900 years old, were found still in their baking pans. Needless to say, the bread was quite stale! The tons of ash that buried and preserved loaves of bread, also preserved works of art.

The Art of Pompeii

Because of their wealth the Pompeians were able to hire the best architects and artists in the empire. They filled their villas (fine houses) with beautiful objects, and covered the walls of their houses with elegant paintings. Because of the eruption of Vesuvius, many of these works were preserved, as if sealed in a vault. We even have the witty and rude sayings of the local delinquents who wrote on the public buildings!

Figure 5.26 is a fine example of a wall painting or mural from Pompeii. It shows the street view of a fine townhouse. Notice the use of plants and sculpture to decorate the area around the house. We still landscape our houses today in much the same fashion.

The artist who painted this scene not only wanted to show how beautiful the architecture of Pompeii was, but also to create the illusion of looking out a real window. This technique has been given a French name **trompe l'oeil** [tromp•LOY]. The Romans loved this effect and used it throughout their buildings. For historians, it is almost like having photographs of Pompeii. From these paintings, we can even tell what kinds of fruit trees were planted in the gardens. These paintings were the Pompeians' "windows" to their surroundings. They are our "windows" into their lives.

Study Figure 5.26 more carefully. How has the artist created the illusion of space? Has linear perspective been used? Can you find any arches? Columns? Look at the two columns on either side of the doorway in the painting. Can you tell what style capitals they have?

MEET THE JEWELRY MAKERS OF ROME

Wearable Art

One of the many interesting facts we have discovered about the people of ancient Rome is their love for beautiful household articles and jewelry. Wealthy Romans liked to live well and to be well-dressed. From the looks of many items of jewelry found at Pompeii and Herculaneum, the Romans must have spent enormous sums of money on items for beauty and adornment. Figure 5.27 gives you an idea of the elegance and richness of Roman jewelry.

As with other art forms, the design and construction of Roman jewelry was greatly influenced by Greek jewelry design. All kinds of working with gold were used in the prosperous jewelry workshops of Rome. Many of the techniques for making jewelry, such as making molds of wax in which to pour liquid gold for casting or engraving, or the carving of precious stones were probably learned from Greek artisans. Though modern stone cutting with facets was not used (like those in a modern diamond ring), precious stones were polished and carved. Even portraits were cut or engraved into the stones.

As the Roman empire grew, so did its wealth and its resources for gold and precious stones. Customers could request any piece or shape of jewelry they wanted from earrings to bracelets. Bracelets shaped like snakes were very popular. Gold rings set with engraved stones were a special symbol of wealth and status, just as they are today.

Though both women and men wore jewelry, it was the women who wore the most. Figure 5.28 shows a wealthy Roman woman wearing many different pieces of jewelry. One wonders if this was her everyday jewelry, or was she dressed for some special occasion.

The love of jewelry and gold might have caused the death of some of the citizens of ill-fated Pompeii. Many of the skeletons recently found at Pompeii still wore gold bracelets and gold rings on their arms and hands. Skeletal hands still clutched small bags of other pieces of jewelry. One wonders if the owner would have made it to safety, if he or she had not stopped to collect these objects. A sad reminder that all the wealth and gold in the world is not worth the most precious of possessions—life.

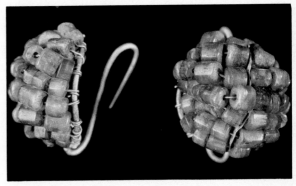

Figure 5.27. above. *Bracelet in the form of a Serpent.* National Museum Naples. Photo courtesy Scala/Art Resource. below. *Roman Earrings from Pompeii.* Photo courtesy Scala/Art Resource.

Figure 5.28. Palmyra. *Funerary Statue of Aqmat.* Late 2nd Century A.D. Limestone. Reproduced by courtesy of the Trustees of the British Museum.

57

Student work.

Did you learn

- The definitions of these words and phrases: Western Civilization; classical; capital; Doric; Ionic; Corinthian; entablature; architrave; frieze; pediment; mythology; black-figured; red-figured; gladiators; trompe l'oeil?
- What it was about the ancient Greeks that made their civilization so different than ones that had gone before?
- Why the Parthenon was built? The names of the architects who designed it?
- Three types of capitals used on Greek columns?
- Where the Greeks got most of the subjects for their art?
- A Roman contribution to architecture?
- Why Pompeii and Herculaneum are important to us today?

Understanding and Evaluating

- Look through your American history book for illustrations and photographs of famous American buildings and monuments. What parts of these buildings seem borrowed from Greek architecture? Make a list of all the similarities you can find. Can you identify the design of any column capitals?
- In the school library look up information on the discovery and history of Pompeii and Herculaneum. Write a short essay on any part that you find interesting. Quite a bit is known about the lives of the people who lived there. You might want to also write a short fiction story about the events in the lives of particular people on that fateful morning.

Seeing and Creating

- On a long sheet of paper (several small sheets can be glued together), design a sculpture frieze for a building to be dedicated to the natural environment. Begin your drawing in pencil. Later outline with India ink. Shading on figures can be added with watercolor wash. Select a section of your frieze for the design of a relief on a clay plaque.
- Using animal forms and characteristics, design several pieces of jewelry. Make models of your designs using construction paper, poster board, tempera paint, and other decorative materials.

The years between the 5th century A.D. (the years 400-499) and the 15th century are called the **Middle Ages.** It is easy to remember this period if you think of these years as being in the "middle" between the end of the Roman empire and the beginning of the Renaissance [ren • NAY • saunce]. The Renaissance was a time of great discoveries and explorations. It was also a time of great art.

The span of time covered by the Middle Ages is large—almost 1,000 years. Much took place during this time, not only in Europe, but in other parts of the world. However, some consider this time, in comparison with the glory of Greece and Rome, a time of darkness for civilization and for art. The Middle Ages are also known as the Dark Ages. Discoveries and advances made in science and in the arts by the Greeks and Romans were, for the most part, rejected or ignored. The focus of art and learning was no longer on the individual person, but on God. The Christian religion became the center of civilization in Europe.

THE HOLY ROMAN EMPIRE

After a thousand years, the power of Rome was challenged and destroyed. Like jackals attacking a lion weakened by age and battle, invaders from the "barbarian North" attacked the failing Roman empire. By the 4th century A.D. the might of Rome was broken. But from this destruction arose the new Holy Roman Empire. The word "holy" had been added to signify the importance of Christianity. The empire's center was no longer Rome, but Constantinople [con • stan • tah • NO • pull], now known as Istanbul, Turkey. Its leader was considered both emperor and head of the Christian church. His name was Constantine [CON • stan • teen]. He proclaimed Christianity as the official religion of the Holy Roman Empire. The art of this time is known as **Byzantine** [BIZ • un • teen].

Chapter 6
A TIME OF FAITH—ART OF THE MIDDLE AGES

WORDWATCH
Middle Ages
Byzantine
Hagia Sophia
mosaics
manuscript
illumination
interlace
Celtic
Gothic
flying buttress
facade
calligraphy
glazier

Figure 6.1. *Reims Cathedral.* The soaring arches of the Gothic cathedral represent the importance of religion to the artists of the Middle Ages.

BYZANTINE ART

The rule of Constantine the Great was followed by that of Emperor Justinian [jus•TIN•ee•un] (Figure 6.2). True patrons of art, Justinian and his wife the Empress Theodora [thee•o•DOOR•ah] (Figure 6.3), built churches and buildings on a grand scale. The greatest achievement of Justinian's reign is the great Church of Saint Sophia, or as it is known, **Hagia Sophia** [HAG•yah so•FEE•ah], which means Holy Wisdom. Figure 6.4 shows how this magnificent church looks today. The four towers at the corners are called minarets [MEN•nah•rets]. They were added in the 15th century when the church was changed into a mosque [mahsk] or Moslem church. It is now a museum, where thousands of visitors fill its enormous spaces every day.

Notice the huge dome and the arches. Does it remind you of the Roman Pantheon (Figure 5.20)? It is easy to see the influence of Roman architecture in this church. Figure 6.5 is a view of the interior. Compare it to the interior of the Pantheon. What similarities do you see?

The dome of Hagia Sophia rises 185 feet above the floor and has a diameter of 107 feet.

This great dome made a lasting impression on everyone who saw it. One observer thought it looked as if it were hung from heaven by a golden chain, rather than resting on the sides of the building. Its surface was covered with

Figure 6.2. *Emperor Justinian.* Mosaic before 547 A.D. Ravenna, San Vitale, Presbyterium, North wall of the Apse. Photo credit: Archiv fur Kunst und Geschichte, Berlin.

Figure 6.3. *Empress Theodora.* Mosaic before 547 A.D. Ravenna, San Vitale, Presbyterium, North wall of the Apse. Photo credit: Archiv fur Kunst und Geschichte, Berlin.

Figure 6.4. Exterior view of *Hagia Sophia.*

Figure 6.5. Gaspare Fossati. *Hagia Sophia-Interior View.* 1852. Photo credit: Archiv fur Kunst und Geschichte, Berlin.

magnificent **mosaics** [mo•SAY•iks]. **Mosaics** are pictures created by attaching small pieces of colored rock or glass to a surface. Figure 6.6 shows one of the mosaics of Christ from Hagia Sophia. It had been painted over with whitewash when the church was converted into a mosque. Some of the whitewash can still be seen.

Although Byzantine architecture has many of the characteristics of Roman architecture, including domes and arches, there is one major difference. The sculptures of the human figure that once filled the spaces of Roman buildings are nowhere to be found. The beauty of the human form is no longer of any concern or interest to artists. It is as if the creative eye of the artist had turned inward, away from life and toward the spirit. This attitude continues throughout the Middle Ages. And, although the human figure would reappear in sculptures on the great cathedrals and in beautiful illustrations in books and manuscripts, it would not regain its place as the supreme subject of art until the Renaissance.

THE AMAZING PAGES OF THE MIDDLE AGES

During the Middle Ages one art form that was quite unique and completely amazing developed. This was

Figure 6.6. *Mosaic of Christ.* Deesis Hagia Sophia, Istanbul. Photo credit: Scala/Art Resource.

manuscript [MAN•u•script] illumination [e•lum•i•
NAY•shun]. **Manuscripts** are simply collections of
writings on pages which are often bound together as a
book. **Illumination** is another word for illustration or the
drawing and painting of pictures to decorate and illustrate the text of a book.

Figure 6.7 shows an example of a page from a book
known as *The Book of Kells.* This is a title page, so a
letter is used as the main design. Just look at the
elaborate turning and twisting of this design! It is
difficult to believe that it was drawn and painted by
hand. Figure 6.8 is a page from a manuscript known as
the *Lindisfarne Gospels.* This particular page is called a
"carpet" page. Why do you think it is called this? What
does its design remind you of? If you look closely, you
will see how the lines of the design intertwine, looping
over and under each other. This is called **interlace.** There
are even animals and plants to be found among the
swirling patterns.

Most of these illuminated masterpieces were created in
Ireland, Scotland, and England. They were made by
monks. These were men who devoted themselves to the
Christian religion and lived shut away from everyday life.
The style of this art is known as **Celtic** [KEL•tik]. The
Celts were the people who lived in ancient Britain during
the time of the Greeks and Romans.

Figure 6.7. *Book of Kells.* Trinity College,
Dublin. Photo credit: Archiv fur Kunst und
Geschichte, Berlin.

STAR OF THE MIDDLE AGES— GOTHIC ARCHITECTURE

Look for a moment at Figure 6.1. This shows the
interior of one of the great cathedrals of the Middle Ages
known as Reims [reems]. Its style of architecture is
known as **Gothic** [GOTH•ik]. **Gothic** architecture, as you
can see, is very different from Byzantine architecture and
the architecture of Greece and Rome.

The first thing you may notice is how high the ceiling
is above the floor. It is almost impossible to keep your
eyes down. You want to look upward, toward the
delicate, pointed arches that soar above your head. This
is one of the ways you can tell you are looking at a
Gothic cathedral. The arches, walls, and columns are very
tall and delicate. Although made of stone, they seem
hardly able to support the roof. There are no heavy,
rounded Roman arches here. Walls are pierced by enormous stained-glass windows. The design of these windows
tells stories from the Bible. They were meant to teach, as
much as delight the eye with their beauty.

Figure 6.8. Page from the *Lindisfarne
Gospels.* Permission of the British Library.

Figure 6.9. Flying Buttress, Chartres Cathedral. Photo: Bildarchiv Foto Marburg/Art Resource, New York.

Figure 6.10. Chartres, Cathedral, West Facade.

The architects of the great Gothic cathedrals of Europe wanted the people who came to pray to feel a sense of awe and religious emotion. They wanted people to turn their eyes upward toward heaven and God. But, in order to build these very tall, delicate structures, the Gothic architects had to think carefully about the weight of things.

Never had buildings reached such heights and spanned such spaces without using thick walls, huge thick columns, and rounded arches. Gothic architects instead, wanted to treat stone like lace. They carved it, pierced it, and shaped it until it seemed as airy as the space it enclosed. But thin, delicate columns and lace-like walls and windows won't support a roof.

Figure 6.9 shows an architectural design invented by the Gothic architects to solve this problem. It is called a **flying buttress**. Like hands pressed against a flat surface to keep it from falling, the **flying buttress** pressed against the arches of the cathedral to prevent them from collapsing. You will find them on the exterior of most Gothic cathedrals.

Look again at the interior view of Reims Cathedral (Figure 6.1). Which two art elements do you think are emphasized in the design of this great building. Why? Compare the design of this church to that of Hagia Sophia (Figure 6.5). How are they different?

Some of these cathedrals took hundreds of years to build. As architectural styles changed, so did the cathedrals. Sometimes the style changed before a cathedral was even completed. For example, at Chartres [SHAH•tra] (Figure 6.10), the front of the cathedral or **facade** [fah•SOD] isn't symmetrical. This is because the spires (pointed towers on either side) were built at different times.

The sculptures that decorated the outside of the cathedrals also show changes in style. For example, compare the sculptures shown in Figure 6.11 with those in Figure 6.12. What differences do you notice? Which style do you think is the older of the two? Why?

Both these styles of sculpture can be found on a great cathedral—Chartres. Like a book of art styles, this cathedral, built over so many years, gives us a chance to see and compare these changes. We see how later artists borrowed ideas from earlier artists, changing them to express new ideas.

The sculptures shown in Figure 6.11 are from an earlier period. They are very straight and stiff, looking as if they are part of the columns they stand on. On the other hand, the sculptures shown in Figure 6.12 don't seem as stiff. They are beginning to turn and move their bodies away from the column shape. They are from a later time.

They represent a more "modern" way of sculpting the figure.

THE MIDDLE AGES IN OTHER CULTURES

While the Middle Ages might have been a time of spiritual focus for Europe, other peoples around the world were also expanding and developing. These people were also creating a rich and fascinating art heritage. Let's take a look at what was happening in art in the cultures of China, Africa, and North America during the Middle Ages.

IN HARMONY WITH NATURE—THE ART OF CHINA

Although the culture and artistic traditions of China were as old as those of Mesopotamia and Egypt, it is the period of the Middle Ages that is considered one of the greatest in Chinese art.

Like the history of Europe, that of China, especially during the Middle Ages, was a violent one. Leaders of different groups made war to gain control over areas of land and over people. During this time many beautiful works of art were destroyed. Fortunately, like the ancient Romans, the Chinese liked to make copies. Through these copies we can admire works of art that would have otherwise been lost.

Just as Christianity united the people of Europe and became the main subject of their art, the religion called Buddhism [BOO•diz•um] became the main inspiration for Chinese art. One of the principle ideas of Buddhism is that humankind and nature must exist in harmony. For the Chinese it was the duty of the emperor to maintain that harmony. It became the duty of the artist to express that harmony. Chinese landscape painting expresses harmony between humankind and nature perhaps better than any other art form.

Painting

Figure 6.13 shows a Chinese landscape painting from the Middle Ages. It has all the peace and misty expression of a dream. Line is the art element emphasized the most. In fact, to Western eyes, Chinese painting often seems more like drawing than painting. Even the materials and tools that are used in Chinese painting are reserved for drawing in Western cultures.

Ink and brush are used to apply lines of varying widths onto silk or paper. This is similar to the way the Chinese write. To the Chinese, writing or **calligraphy** is

Figure 6.11. *Jamb Statues,* Chartres Cathedral. Caisse Nationale des Monuments Historiques et des Sites.

Figure 6.12. *Jamb Statues,* Chartres Cathedral. Credit: Caise Nationale des Monuments Historiques et des Sites.

Figure 6.13. Yen Tz'u-yii. *Hostelry and The Mountains.* Ink and light color, 10" x 10 3/16". Courtesy of the Freer Gallery of Art, Smithsonian Institution, Washington, D.C.

Figure 6.14. Chao Meng-Chien. *Narcissus.* 1100-1260. Paper makimono, 12⅜″ x 30⅛″. Courtesy of the Freer Gallery of Art, Smithsonian Institution, Washington, D.C.

Figure 6.15. *Tang Horse.* Ceramic clay horses of the Tang period (618-907 A.D.) are famous for their grace and beauty.

Figure 6.16. *Chinese Ceramic vase.* Yuan Dynasty (1280-1368 A.D.) Jar with cover; decorated with blue under the glaze, porcelain. 17¾″ h. The Metropolitan Museum of Art, Rogers Fund, 1927.

also an art form. They frequently combine painting and writing in one composition (Figure 6.14).

In Figure 6.13 notice how the artist has shown space by putting objects in the foreground (close to the bottom of the picture) and background. The middle ground seems filled with mist. You can almost see through the trees, rocks, and mountains. The artist has made no effort to make these look heavy and three-dimensional. But have you noticed how everything in the painting seems to belong together? There is harmony and unity between all things in this painting, just as the Chinese believed there should be in life.

Ceramics

The Chinese had a long tradition of working with clay to create ceramic containers and sculpture. During the Middle Ages this art form reached new heights of excellence.

Figure 6.15 shows one of the most famous styles of Chinese ceramic sculpture. It is a horse from the T'ang [TANG] period.

These sculptures were found in tombs. Perhaps these spirited horses were needed to carry the dead through the afterlife. What other culture have you read about in this unit that buried images and objects for the use of the dead in an afterlife? Do you think the Chinese artist who created this horse understood his subject? How can you tell?

Most of these wonderful animals (camels were a favorite also), were glazed in beautiful colors. Decorating and adding color to ceramic sculpture and pottery through glazing became very important during the Middle Ages. Glazing was a way to add color and gloss to ceramics. Heated in ovens reaching thousands of degrees, tiny particles of glass contained in the glaze, melted together to form a colorful, shiny coating. Figure 6.16 shows an example of the beautiful patterns and designs that were possible with glazing.

FROM THE SILENT CONTINENT—THE ART OF AFRICA

When African art is mentioned, many people think of tribal masks like those shown in Figure 6.17. African art, however, is much more. During the period known as the Middle Ages, several cultures in Africa developed works of art as varied and beautiful as any ever created. In fact, some of these pieces, when discovered, were thought to be the work of one of the great sculptors of ancient Greece!

Figure 6.18 is an example of a whole group of portrait heads made by artists of the Ife [EE•fay] culture in what is now Nigeria. This head was fashioned during the time of the great cathedral building in Europe. The Ife sculptors worked in both clay and bronze. This particular work is made of ceramic clay.

How lifelike it seems! Surely this is a portrait of a real person—perhaps a queen. The photographic realism reminds us of the portraits from ancient Rome. The serious and dignified expression on her face suggests a life of responsibility. The downcast eyes appear lost in thought.

As wrapped in mystery as Stonehenge or the pyramids of Egypt, is great Zimbabwe [zim•BOB•way] (Figure 6.19). This symbol of past African greatness has become

A.   B.

C.   D.

Figure 6.17. *African Tribal Masks.*
A. Dance Mask, Kete people, Upper Kassai River, "Congo" B. Helmet Mask, Mende people C. Mask, Kuba people D. Dance Mask, Pende people

Figure 6.19. Zimbabwe. *Conical Tower Ruins.* Photograph by Eliot Elisofon, 1959. National Museum of African Art, Smithsonian Institution.

Figure 6.18. *Queen of Ife.* Ife, Nigeria. Museum of Mankind, London. Courtesy of the Trustees.

Figure 6.20. top. Mandan Indians. *Decorated Shirt and Leggings.* Collected about 1850 by Thomas S. Twiss at Fort Laramie, Wyoming. bottom. *Shirt, with Beaded, Blue and Purple Painted Decoration.* Collected from Chief Four Bears about 1880. Mandan Sioux, Upper Yellowstone River, North Dakota. Photo courtesy The Museum of the American Indian, New York.

Figure 6.21. Cliff dwellings of Pueblo Indians. Mesa Verde, Colorado. Courtesy of the National Park Service.

the center of pride for a new African nation that borrows its name from the monument. Look for Zimbabwe on a recent map of Africa. It occupies the area once known as Rhodesia. The monument of Zimbabwe is located seventeen miles from Fort Victoria.

When the remains of this great structure were discovered, they were thought to be the work of some lost civilization that had settled on the continent of Africa and then vanished without a trace. No thought at all was given to the idea that this monument might have been built by the people of Africa themselves. Those who discovered Zimbabwe during the 19th century thought that the native people of Africa had always lived in grass huts and led a primitive existence. The idea that Zimbabwe might have been built by a proud and prosperous people, the native Africans, was not considered. But, Zimbabwe, as we know now, was built by Native Africans.

Zimbabwe was once a rich and important center of trade and culture. Part fortress, part temple, its granite walls enclosed a variety of buildings. One in particular continues to puzzle archeologists. It is a cone-shaped tower that appears to be solid. Was it a watchtower or the tomb of a chieftain? Is there a secret entrance that remains hidden? Is it filled with gold? The truth remains to be discovered.

OVER THE EDGE OF THE WORLD—THE NATIVE ART OF NORTH AMERICA

The cultural heritage and art of the Native Americans, who lived on the continent before the arrival of European settlers remain incomplete and mysterious. We think of the life of the Native Americans as being a nomadic one. People banded together in tribes, traveling with the changing seasons, following the great animal herds of the plains. The art they created had to be as mobile as they were. They decorated the clothes they wore with designs that represented the spirits of the earth and the animals they hunted (Figure 6.20). They didn't settle long enough to build structures, or so we thought.

Figure 6.21 shows the cliff dwellings of the Pueblo Indians at Mesa Verde [MAY • sah VER • day] in Colorado. These amazing brick structures cling to the side of a canyon wall. This community could only be reached by ladders and steps in the rocks of the cliff. This provided the Pueblo Indians with protection from hostile tribes. It is now thought that work on Mesa Verde began during the Middle Ages, about 700 hundred years ago.

The Colors of Heaven

Although the art of stained glass was known long before Chartres and the other great cathedrals of the Gothic period were built, this art form reached its greatest achievements during this time.

From sand, ash, and salt melted together, the glassmakers created the dazzling beauty of Chartres's windows (Figures 6.22 through 6.24). Color was added to the molten glass by mixing in various metallic oxides, such as copper for red; cobalt for blue; iron for gold. The dark lines between each section of colored glass are made of lead. Since lead is soft, it could be formed around the odd-shaped glass pieces.

The designs were assembled and then mounted in the windows of the cathedral. Imagine how the glassmakers must have felt on the day when the great rose window was finally in place. As the morning sun's rays struck the colored glass, they could, at last, see and appreciate the time and effort that had gone into this art form.

Chartres cathedral has most of its original windows still in place and unbroken. Other cathedrals throughout Europe were not so fortunate. Bombing during World War II destroyed many fine windows.

Chartres boasts a total of 176 stained-glass windows. The expense for many of these was covered by wealthy nobles. The royal family of France donated the great rose window known as the "Rose of France" (Figure 6.23). Not to be outdone, the merchants of Chartres, France donated their share of windows. Bakers, shoemakers, and water-carriers all had their own windows. We know this because symbols of their trades were included in the designs (Figure 6.24). The glass artists or **glaziers** [glay • ZEERS] who designed these great windows with infinite care and patience remind us of the work of mosaic artists and manuscript illuminators. Working with flat, two-dimensional designs, they created works that are endlessly varied and interesting.

Figure 6.23. Rose window from Chartres Cathedral. Photo: Giraudon/Art Resource, New York.

Figure 6.24. Stained glass window from guild, Furriers and drapers, Chartres Cathedral. Photo: Giraudon/Art Resource, New York.

Student work.

Did you learn

- The definitions of these words and phrases: Middle Ages; Byzantine; Hagia Sophia; mosaics; manuscript illumination; interlace; Celtic; Gothic; facade; calligraphy; glazier?
- Two things the Roman Pantheon and Hagia Sophia have in common?
- One way in which the art of the Middle Ages was different from the art of Greece and Rome?
- What Chinese artists tried to express in their paintings?
- Why a single cathedral may have more than one style of architecture and sculpture?
- The previous name of the country in which Zimbabwe is located?
- Why much Native American art is found in items that can be carried?
- The name of a great Native American ruin in Colorado?

Understanding and Evaluating

- Write a one-page description of Chartres cathedral for someone who has never seen it. Describe why it is considered an example of Gothic architecture.
- Make a list of differences between the sculptures used on Chartres cathedral and those used on the Greek Parthenon.

Seeing and Creating

- Using any letter from the alphabet, make a manuscript illumination design. Use interlace in your design. Include animals and plants if you like. After drawing your design lightly in pencil on white drawing paper, retrace with India ink. When the ink is dry, add color with watercolor or tempera paint.
- © [CAUTION: India ink stains. Wear protective clothing.]
- Using a brush and India ink, write your name (don't print) on a sheet of white drawing paper. As the ink dries, study the shape of the letters and the shape of the negative spaces between. If you cannot see the design clearly, turn the paper upside down or turn it toward a mirror. Write your name once more, letting some letters touch the letters of the first signature. Continue to fill the paper with your signature. After each writing, study the design.

Many believe the time period known as the **Renaissance** [REN•i•sauns] was unique in all of history. **Renaissance** is a French word which means "rebirth." The 200 or so years known as the Renaissance, from 1400 to around 1600 A.D., was indeed a "rebirth," of learning, exploration, and art.

As the great astronomers Copernicus [co•PERN•i•cus] and Galileo [gal•i•LAY•o] explored and studied the universe, explorers Christopher Columbus, (Figure 7.1) Vasco da Gama, and Bartolomeo Diaz [bar•toe•low•MAY•o DEE•ahz] explored the New World. Sailing ever further from home in their ships, they were changing the face of the world forever.

Artists were also reawakening to the possibilities of this exciting new age. Casting off the dark cloak of the Middle Ages, artists, especially those in Italy, looked back to the grace and realism of Greek and Roman art and found new inspiration.

They saw how proudly the ancient artists had expressed their personal feelings and moods in sculpture, painting, and architecture. More than anything, the Renaissance was the rebirth of the individual artist, creating works for personal pleasure and meaning. No longer would artists have to hide their personal identities and spirits behind the veil of religion. The Renaissance was truly the age of individual human achievement.

A TIME OF GIANTS

You have already met two of the greatest artists of the Renaissance, or of any time for that matter. Leonardo de Vinci (Book One, Chapter 1) and Michelangelo Buonaratti (Book Two, Chapter 1). It is indeed strange that two of the world's most famous artists should have been living and working at the same time, and in the same place—Florence, Italy. In the early part of the 15th century, it must have seemed that the small, but beautiful Italian town on the Arno River was the art center of the world. In many ways it was.

Florence was a city graced with learning, culture, and great wealth. The famous Medici family, led by Lorenzo the Magnificent (see Chapter 1) encouraged the creation of art in all forms, from painting to architecture. And although the giant shadows of Leonardo and Michelangelo stretched far over Florence and this age of "rebirth," there were many others who added their share to the glory of the Renaissance and to our artistic heritage.

Chapter 7

THE GREAT AWAKENING— ART OF THE RENAISSANCE

WORDWATCH
Renaissance
Vatican
linear perspective
Gates of Paradise
Pre-Columbian
obsidian
roof comb
conquistador
Aztec
Maya

Figure 7.1. Sebastiano del Plombo. *Christohper Columbus.* 1519. Oil on canvas, 42" x 34¾". The Metropolitan Museum of Art. Gift of J. Pierpoint Morgan, 1900.

Figure 7.2. Ghiberti. *Baptistry Doors.* Begun 1425, put in place 1452. Bronze gold plate, 17″ h. East Baptistry Doors, Florence Cathedral. Photo credit: Archiv fur Kunst und Geschichte, Berlin. These doors are also known as the Gates of Paradise.

Figure 7.3. Ghiberti. *Baptistry door panel, Joseph in Egypt.* Bronze relief. Baptistry, Florence. Photo credit: Archiv fur Kunst und Geschichte, Berlin.

Lorenzo Ghiberti and the Gates of Paradise

Perhaps it is right and fitting that Renaissance art should have reached its peak in Italy, the ancient home of Rome's glory. From the plowed fields and coastal harbors came the long-buried art treasures of the past. Artists could not help but be impressed and influenced by the beautiful statues and objects that turned up daily from the fertile earth of Italy. How different these ancient sculptures seemed from the rigid figures of the Middle Ages.

Like young people in every age since the beginning of time, the artists of the Renaissance wanted to do something new—something fresh and daring. Rejecting the "old fashioned" art of the Middle Ages, they rediscovered their cultural roots, and a new way of seeing through the art of Greece and Rome.

In the work of one artist it seemed that the best of Gothic and Renaissance art styles was combined. The artist's name was Lorenzo Ghiberti [low • REN • zoe ghee • BEAR • tee].

A citizen of Florence, Ghiberti came to the attention of the wealthy patrons of the city in an art competition. It had been decided by the city council of Florence that a competition would be held to select an artist to decorate the great bronze doors of the baptistry [BAP • tis • tree] of the cathedral. The baptistry is a part of the church where baptisms are performed. The surprising winner of the competition was a very young (age twenty) Lorenzo Ghiberti.

Figure 7.2 shows the completed doors. It took Ghiberti over twenty years to complete the task. But most people, seeing them, think the time was well spent. In fact, they became known as the **Gates of Paradise,** because as one viewer observed, they were beautiful enough to be the gates of heaven!

Cast in bronze and painted with gold (or gilded), each panel is a relief sculpture. The subject matter of the panels comes from the Bible's Old Testament. Figure 7.3 shows one of the panels.

It was Ghiberti's intention to make the reliefs so detailed and life-like that they would seem like paintings. Look carefully at the building shown in the panel. Does ? the style of the architecture look familiar? Where do you think Ghiberti got the idea to use those rounded arches?

Notice also the illusion of space inside the building. Although the relief carving is little more than one inch at its deepest, the space behind the columns of the building seems huge.

Ghiberti, like many other Renaissance artists, became fascinated with the latest invention of the age—**linear perspective**. Linear perspective is a system that was invented to create an illusion of three-dimensional space on a flat surface. Figures 7.4 and 7.5 are examples of drawings using linear perspective.

Notice in the diagrams that all horizontal lines (lines parallel to the horizon) converge or meet at the point called the vanishing point. When these simple rules are followed, objects seem to have three-dimensional form even though they are drawn or painted on a flat surface. Study the diagrams carefully. What other "rules" can you discover about linear perspective?

The discovery of this wonderful system was attributed to another Italian artist named Filippo Brunelleschi [fee•LEE•po Brew•nah•LESS•key]. Brunelleschi was also one of the artists who had competed for the baptistry doors and lost to Ghiberti. Still, Brunelleschi was a fine artist and innovator. And in another competition he beat Ghiberti! This contest was for the honor of designing the dome of the Cathedral of Florence (Figure 7.6).

Although the cathedral had been started in the Middle Ages (1296 A.D.), Brunelleschi departed from the Gothic style. He had carefully studied and measured the ancient buildings of Rome, using his new system of linear perspective to make detailed drawings of the ruins. He was one of the first artists to do this. It is clear by the dome design he created that he admired the work of the ancient Roman architects.

Donatello

Ghiberti had a very talented student named Donatello [don•ah•TELL•o]. Like his teacher, Donatello made relief sculpture of great beauty, such as the one shown in Figure 7.7. It is called the *Feast of Herod*. Compare it for a moment with the panel by Ghiberti (Figure 7.3). What similarities do you see? Do you notice the illusion of space inside the building in Donatello's panel? Do you think Donatello used linear perspective? Now compare the figures shown in both panels. Are they similar or very different? Which seem to you more realistic? More natural?

It is obvious that Donatello learned about relief sculpture from his great teacher, but he wasn't content to just make relief carvings. He wanted to make three-dimensional sculptures. He wanted to make sculptures you could walk around.

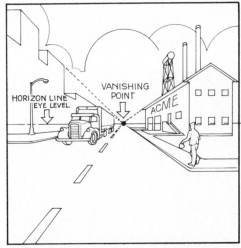

Figure 7.4. The horizon line in a perspective drawing also represents the eye level of the viewer. The vanishing point is the point at which all horizontal lines converge.

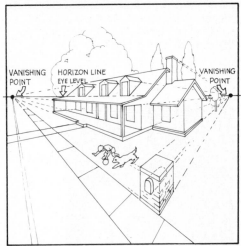

Figure 7.5. Perspective diagram.

Figure 7.6 Bruelleschi. *The Cathedral of Florence.* Photo credit: Archiv fur Kunst und Geschichte, Berlin.

Figure 7.7. Donatello. *The Feast of Herod.* c. 1425. Gilt bronze, 23½″ square. Baptistry, Siena. Photo credit: Art Resource.

Figure 7.8 shows one of Donatello's most famous works. It is a sculpture of Saint George. In legend, Saint George killed a dragon, and rescued a beautiful woman. He became the symbol of knighthood and bravery and the patron saint of England.

Donatello's Saint George certainly looks like a hero! He is young, handsome, and ready for any danger, including dragons. The slight turn in the figure makes him look as if he might raise his shield and draw his sword at any moment. He has the confidence of the Renaissance man, rather than the prayerful posture of a man of the Middle Ages.

Raphael

One young artist who charmed all who met him was Raphael Sanzio [RAF • fy • el SAN • zee • o], known simply as Raphael. He arrived in Florence in 1504 when he was twenty-one years old. What a time and place to be young and filled with a wondrous talent! Michelangelo and Leonardo's works were everywhere to be studied and admired. Small wonder that Raphael was greatly influenced by the art of these two Renaissance titans. For example, the influence of Leonardo can be easily seen in a work by Raphael known as the *Sistine Madonna* (Figure 7.9). Doesn't the face of the Madonna remind you of the Mona Lisa (Figure 1.18 in Book One)? Notice how Raphael has used deep shadows in contrast with bright highlights. Again, this reminds us of Leonardo's style of painting.

Figure 7.8. Donatello. *St. George.* 1415. Life-size marble sculpture. Original in the Museo Nazionale del Bargello. Photo credit: Archiv fur Kunst und Geschichte, Berlin.

Figure 7.9. Raphael. *Sistine Madonna.* 1512. Oil on canvas, 265 cm. x 196 cm. Gemalde-galerie, Dresden. Photo credit: Archiv fur Kunst und Geschichte, Berlin.

It wasn't long before the quiet, well-mannered, talented Raphael came to the attention of the wealthy and important citizens of Florence. He became an important painter in a city of important painters. Soon his reputation reached Rome and the attention of Pope Julius II.

Traveling to Rome in 1508, Raphael was called by Pope Julius to discuss the decoration of the Pope's new apartments in the Vatican. Pope Julius, you may remember from Chapter 1, was the patron and tormentor of Michelangelo. The Pope, a difficult man in the best of times, was still one of Italy's greatest art supporters. He recognized great genius in the young Raphael. He also must have found the painter's polite, respectful manner a pleasant change from that of the gruff, surly Michelangelo.

Pope Julius offered Raphael a commission of great importance. He was to decorate the Pope's private rooms with several magnificent wall murals or frescos. You can imagine the pressures on Raphael to please the most important man in Italy. A man known for his violent temper! Did he please him? Yes he did. Just take a look.

Titled *The School of Athens,* Figure 7.10 is but one of the frescos Raphael completed for Pope Julius. It is considered one of the greatest paintings of the Renaissance. It was important not only as a work of art, but also as a representation of the very spirit and ideals of the times. In 1511, it was considered a very "modern" painting.

First, the subject was typical of the Renaissance. We have the two greatest philosophers and thinkers of ancient Greece, Plato and Aristotle [AIR • is • stah • tul], in the very center of the painting. They are strolling along with great dignity, no doubt speaking in hushed tones of great thoughts and wondrous deeds.

It was scholars of the Renaissance who had "rediscovered" many of the ancient writings of Greece and Rome and translated them. Any individuals or events from Greece or Rome's distant and glorious past were considered perfect subjects for art.

Have you noticed the space? Raphael certainly understood and used the new Renaissance discovery of linear perspective. This painting would have been impossible during the Middle Ages. Look how far back you are able to see into the painting. This gives importance and dignity to the event being recorded.

The composition or visual arrangement of the painting is interesting also. The two main figures are placed exactly under the arch in the center of the painting. All parts seem ordered and balanced. This is a good example

Figure 7.10. Raphael. *School of Athens.* 1508-11. Fresco, 26′ x 18′. Vatican Museum, Rome. Photo credit: Archiv fur Kunst und Geschichte, Berlin.

of a visual composition that is symmetrically balanced.

Of course, Raphael took some liberties with history. The wonderful building he created for the famous philosophers to stroll through was never seen in Greece! It is very Roman in design and feeling. What elements remind you of Roman architecture?

Saint Peter's Cathedral

Raphael's paintings were located in the **Vatican.** This is an area of the city of Rome that belongs to the Catholic Church. The Pope lives there today, just as Pope Julius II did during the Renaissance. Like a city within a city, the Vatican has its own laws and even issues its own stamps.

At the time Raphael was working on the Pope's apartments, Michelangelo was laboring on the Sistine Chapel ceiling next door. Frequently, Raphael would sneak into the darkened chapel to gaze in wonder at the master's work high above his head (Figure 7.11).

There was another great work of art taking shape nearby also. It was the building of the new Saint Peter's Cathedral. When you compare the building painted by Raphael in *The School of Athens* (Figure 7.10) with the interior of Saint Peter's (Figure 7.12) there are many similarities. Do you think Raphael borrowed some of his ideas from Saint Peter's?

The great Michelangelo, now in his seventies, was once again called by a Pope to take on the task of chief architect of Saint Peter's. But, this time it wasn't Pope Julius who called him. Pope Julius had died. Pope Paul III, a much more reasonable and agreeable man, asked his friend Michelangelo to take on what would be Michelangelo's last task. In fact, Michelangelo died before even the dome of Saint Peter's was completed. The church we see today, however, was built largely from his plans (Figure 7.13).

Figure 7.11. Michalangelo. *View of Sistine Chapel.* 1508-1512. Fresco, 13 m. x 36 m. Vatican, Rome. Photo credit: Archiv fur Kunst und Geschichte, Berlin.

Figure 7.12. Interior of *St. Peter's Cathedral.* Rome, Italy. Photo credit: Archiv fur Kunst und Geschichte, Berlin.

Figure 7.13. Exterior view of *St. Peter's Cathedral.* Rome, Italy.

For centuries, Saint Peter's was both the largest and tallest building in the world. Now, of course, many modern skyscrapers have dwarfed this monumental church. However, the influence of its design on future architecture was enormous. Our own national Capitol and the capitol buildings of many states are based on this design. This design of domes, rounded arches, and columns was in turn borrowed from a much older source. ? Where do you think these ideas came from?

THE RENAISSANCE OF THE NORTH

Although it sometimes appears as if Italy were the only country producing great artists during the Renaissance period, this isn't true. In this book and in Book One, you have already met some of the great Northern European artists of the Renaissance. Can you recall them?

Do you remember Jan Van Eyck, the father of oil painting (Book One, Chapter 6, Figure 6.3)? Hans Holbein, who was court painter to King Henry VIII of England during the Renaissance (Chapter 3, Figure 3.4).

A Walk Through *July*

One Northern Renaissance artist you haven't met as yet is Pieter Bruegel [Pe • ter BROY • gul]. Pieter Bruegel lived and worked in Brussels and Antwerp, cities that are now part of Belgium. During the Renaissance, Belgium was known as Flanders. Jan Van Eyck was from Flanders also.

Like many Northern European artists of the time, including Albrecht Dürer (Book One, Chapter 6), Bruegel traveled to France and Italy. As an artist, he could not help but be influenced by the great art he saw there. When he returned home, he used many of the painting techniques he had learned there. For example, he became very interested in landscapes and in how artists like Leonardo could create such feelings of deep space in their landscape backgrounds.

But Bruegel was an artist of the North. The main subjects for his paintings were not the rich and famous, but simple peasants and working people going about their daily tasks.

Figure 7.14 shows one of his most famous works. It is called *July*. It was one painting in a series of paintings representing the months of the year. In each painting the main subject is the land itself and the simple people who work it.

Figure 7.14. Pieter Bruegel. *The Harvesters (July)*. 1565. Oil on wood 36½" x 63¼". The Metropolitan Museum of Art, Rogers Fund, 1919. Photograph by Eric Pollitzer.

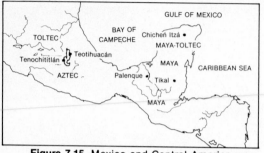

Figure 7.15. Mexico and Central America were the sites of numerous native cultures. The Mayan and Aztec cultures built magnificent buildings and sculptures.

July is a beautiful example of how a skilled artist like Bruegel can turn ordinary activities into great art. When you look at this painting you can almost feel the hot, still air of a late summer's day.

Imagine for a moment you are standing near the tree, looking out over the golden fields towards the sea. It's there in the distance. Can you see where sky and sea have melted together into one, pale color? Take a deep breath of the warm air. Can you smell the fresh-cut hay? Is there any breeze blowing? Take your shoes off. What textures do you feel underfoot. Has Bruegel included these textures in the painting? Do you see the village church behind the trees? Doesn't the cool, green shade of those trees look inviting? In contrast, the other colors in the painting seem very warm. What warm colors has Bruegel used?

If you want to stay in Bruegel's painting, you may have to ask the people sitting at lunch under the tree for a cool drink and something to eat! Don't trip over the fellow stretched out under the tree. He must be so tired he would rather sleep than eat! The man with the red jug seems barely able to drag his feet. How has Bruegel made him look so tired? The nice thing about taking an imaginary walk through a painting is that you can always leave when everyone starts working again!

A painting like *July* invites the viewer to take an imaginary walk-through. You might try this with other paintings you encounter in this book. It is a good way to experience the work and give your imagination a good workout!

LORDS OF THE FEATHERED SERPENT

As Renaissance explorers ventured across the globe in their ships, they came in contact with many strange and wonderful people and places. None, were more amazing than the people and civilizations of Central America and Mexico (Figure 7.15).

Completely unknown to the rest of the civilized world until the 15th century, several great **Pre-Columbian** civilizations had grown and flourished. Pre-Columbian refers to those cultures of the Americas that developed before the discovery of America by Christopher Columbus in 1492. These peoples, although highly accomplished in art, architecture, and astronomy, seemed to the first Europeans as strange and alien as beings from another planet.

The Maya

One of the greatest of all ancient American cultures was that of the **Maya** [MY•yah]. The centers of their civilization were concentrated in the jungles of Central America and the Yucatan [YOU•cah•tahn] penninsula (Figure 7.15). The first European to see the Maya was Christopher Columbus in 1502. But the Maya he met were but shadows of the powerful people they had been many centuries before. Their civilization had reached its height during the Middle Ages. At a time when Europe was still in the grip of the Dark Ages, the Maya were building magnificent cities and creating art and science that would not be equaled for centuries.

The Maya were great mathematicians and astronomers. In fact, Mayan culture seemed obsessed with the movement of the planets, the position of the stars, and with time itself. They could predict with great accuracy the dates of eclipses of the sun and moon. The priests/astronomers would then use this information to direct the planting of crops and to maintain control over the Mayan people. As mathematicians, the Maya excelled the Greeks, Romans, and Egyptians. Their calendar is thought to be the best ever devised by any people. With it, they could identify dates tens of thousands of years into the future!

But, as with so many other cultures, it is in art and architecture that the Maya made their greatest contributions to humankind. Without knowledge of the arch or column, the Maya constructed pyramids to equal those of Egypt and temples to equal those of Rome. But these creative people, so brilliant in some areas, never mastered the use of the wheel! They used it only as part of a child's toy, never as a working tool.

Palenque

Lying in the midst of the Yucatan jungle, like carved ivory ornaments in a green velvet box, the great buildings of the Mayan city of Palenque stand as symbols of a vanished people's achievements (Figure 7.16). Figure 7.17 shows one of the best-preserved structures. It is known as the Temple of the Sun.

The Temple of the Sun is characteristic of Mayan architecture. Most temples were built on raised platforms. Entrance to the buildings was by way of a steep staircase. The tops of the buildings usually have a decoration called a **roof comb.** You can see it in Figure 7.17. Although made of stone, it has a delicate look of lace. Look at the openings in the building. There are no arches or columns.

Figure 7.16. General view of *Palenque.* Photo courtesy of Lee Boltin Picture Library, New York.

Figure 7.17. *Temple of the Sun, Palenque.* Photo credit: Rosenthal Art Slides.

79

Figure 7.18. *Chichen Itza, the Castillo.* Photo credit: Rosenthal Art Slides.

Figure 7.19. The Great Pyramids at Giza. Photo credit: Lee Boltin Picture Library.

Figure 7.20. *Serpent Column of Temple of the Jaguar.* Chichen Itza Serpent Symbol and Temple of Warriors. Photo courtesy of Lee Boltin Picture Library, New York.

The exact purpose of each building at Palenque is unknown. Many were probably temples where various ceremonies were performed by the priests. You can visit the ruins of Palenque today. The government of Mexico maintains this beautiful area for the benefit of the thousands of tourists who visit each year. For Palenque, and many other Mayan sites, cannot simply be left to themselves. They must constantly be won back from the jungle, which threatens to cover them in its smothering, green silence once again.

Chichen Itza

Chichen Itza [chee•CHIN eat•ZAH] was one of the last great strongholds of the Maya. Here, another warlike tribe, the Toltecs would soon overrun and conquer the Maya. But Chichen Itza is filled with many amazing things. Figure 7.18 shows the most important building at Chichen Itza. It is known as the Castle or Castillo [cas•TEE•yo].

Obviously a pyramid, the Castillo is, however, very different from the pyramids of Egypt (Figure 7.19). Can you find the difference? Notice that the roof combs from Palenque are gone. The pyramid is topped with a square-shaped temple. This is the influence of invaders—the Toltecs.

The title of this section—Lords of the Feathered Serpent—might have puzzled you. But, look at Figure 7.20. This is a view of some very unusual columns. They frame the entrance to a temple at Chichen Itza known as the Temple of the Jaguar (not the car, but the cat!). Can you imagine what the elegant Greek architects of the Parthenon would have thought of these columns?

The snake, or more precisely the feathered serpent shown in these amazing columns, represents one of the main gods—Quetzalcoatl [KET•zah•co•OT•tul]. He was the god of knowledge and civilization. Though represented by a feathered serpent, the god himself was thought to be very handsome, with red-gold hair and beard. This image and the belief in the god's return to earth from out of the sun was to have terrible consequences for the last Pre-Columbian civilization of Mexico—The Aztecs.

The Aztecs

Many people visiting Mexico City travel another twenty-five miles outside the city. Here, lying among the

Figure 7.21. General view from the air—Teotihuacan, Mexico.

brown hills, are the ruins of a once great city. It is
believed that at one time over 100,000 people lived there.
Figure 7.21 shows this ancient place today. Its buildings
have been restored by archeologists. Towering above the
site are two great pyramids—The Pyramid of the Sun
and The Pyramid of the Moon. The Pyramid of the Sun,
though shorter, covers more area than the largest
pyramid in Egypt. No one knows who built these
monuments or what they were called.

Even the **Aztecs** [AS • texs], who arrived from Northern
Mexico in about 1168 A.D., found the city deserted.
Impressed by the size of its great pyramids and temples,
the Aztecs called the place Teotihuacan [teh • o • TEE •
wah • can]. It means "Place of the Gods."

If the people of Teotihuacan had been at home when
the Aztecs arrived in the valley of Mexico, they probably
would have had to fight hard to hold onto their city.
Lovers of flowers, color, and costumes, the Aztecs also
loved war and were very good at it. They soon gained
control of a large portion of Mexico and created a culture
that was a strange combination of beauty and horror.

In 1519, the Emperor of the Aztecs was the great
Moctezuma [mock • teh • ZOO • mah]. He commanded
respect from thousands of citizens living in his magnificent capital, Tenochtitlan [teh • NOCH • tet • lan]. The
remains of this capital now lie beneath the busy streets
of modern Mexico City.

Moctezuma was a superstitious man. He had been
having some very bad dreams of late. His dreams were

filled with strange soldiers riding on the backs of monsters that looked something like deer. Maybe the dreams were a message of the return of the red-haired god, Quezalcoatl? After all, he was expected. What else could the dreams mean?

As we now know, it wasn't the return of Quezalcoatl, but a menace far greater. It was the invasion of Mexico by Spanish conquistadores and their leader, Hernán Cortés. Before the invasion was complete, the Aztecs were conquered and their civilization completely destroyed. The capital city, with its great temples, would be totally leveled. And how strange that the invaders would come on horseback.

Neither the Aztecs nor anyone else in the Americas had ever seen horses before. Both horses and riders came jangling through the jungles, gleaming with silver armor. They must have looked like monsters to the natives. Perhaps the strangest coincidence was that Hernán Cortés had red-blond hair and a beard just like Quezalcoatl!

Figure 7.22. Mexico, Aztec. *Onyx vessel in the shape of a Monkey.* 10″ h. Photo courtesy Lee Boltin Picture Library, New York.

Aztec Art

War was not the only skill the Aztecs possessed. They were also fine artists. Figure 7.22 shows an example of their ability to use animal forms in creative ways. Here, the Aztec artist has used a monkey as the subject for a container. The monkey's body is enlarged so it can hold the opening of the pot. What do you think this container is made of? It looks like glass, doesn't it?

It is natural volcanic glass called **obsidian** [ob•SID•e•un]. Obsidian is found in chunks of different sizes, from pieces the size of dimes to baseball size. It is usually dark brown or black in color. When carved into thin sheets, it is like a dark mirror. A truly beautiful material for making many objects. The problem with obsidian is its hardness. Like granite, obsidian is very difficult to carve.

Look again at the monkey pot. What an amazing piece of carving this is! With primitive tools, the Aztec sculptor has fashioned this very hard material into a beautiful work of art. The black, mirror-like surface seems very mysterious. Does the monkey appear playful and friendly? Why or why not? How has the artist given him a personality? What kind of tools do you think were used to carve and polish the monkey pot?

Another Aztec work is shown in Figure 7.23. It is a monumental stone sculpture of the goddess Coatlicue [co•WHAT•lee•que].

Like an alien robot, this strange sculpture seems to be beyond human understanding. But, look more closely.

Can you tell how the goddess's head is made? Two enormous snakes' heads are pressed together to represent her single head. Even her skirt is woven out of snakes. Notice how many different types of textures the sculptor has used. What shapes can you find on the sculpture? This particular goddess represents earth and death. Does knowing this help you understand why the sculptor chose certain objects to place on the goddess? How? What is the basic geometric shape used in the sculpture? A square? A rectangle? A circle?

Although the great Indian civilizations of Mexico and Central America came to an end, they left many remarkable works of art and architecture. Archeologists and art historians are still exploring to find out more about these cultures. There is much work left to do.

If you have an opportunity to visit Mexico City or the Yucatan Penninsula (Figure 7.15), you will be able to see these wonders for yourself. The governments of these countries, especially Mexico, value their heritage and preserve and protect it for future generations. Mexico City now has one of the greatest museums in the world, a museum built especially to hold the treasures of its glorious past. You will read more about this museum, The National Museum of Anthropology, in a later chapter.

The heritage of the Aztecs is also shown in the Mexican flag (Figure 7.24). The image of the eagle devouring a snake comes from an Aztec legend. It seems that the Aztecs, in searching for a site for their new capital, received instructions from one of their gods about where to look. The god told the people that they would come upon an eagle holding a snake in its mouth and perched on a cactus. This would be in the exact place where they were to build their capital. And, so it was. Today, Mexico City is one of the major cities of the world, and the people of Mexico still revere the eagle, snake, and cactus as their nation's symbols.

Figure 7.23. *Coatlicue,* Mother of Gods with Head of Two Snakes. 8′ h. Photo courtesy Lee Boltin Picture Library, New York.

Figure 7.24. Symbol on the Mexican Flag. The eagle devouring a snake appears on the flag of Mexico, a reminder of the country's ancient Aztec heritage.

BORN: 1525
DIED: 1569
BIRTHPLACE:

UNKNOWN

Figure 7.25. Pieter Bruegel. *January*. 1565. Oil on canvas, 46" x 63 3/4". Kunsthistorisches Museum, Vienna.

ARTIST OF THE SIMPLE PLEASURES

There is much that is unknown about this greatest artist of the 16th-century Netherlands. We don't even know exactly where Bruegel was born, or where he got his training in art. What we do know is that he was a master artist in both printmaking and painting.

Around 1551, Bruegel traveled to Italy. This trip influenced his work in landscape painting more than anything else. Apparently, the journey over the Alps was as impressive to Bruegel as the great works of art he saw in Italy. By the time he returned to Antwerp, he had made many wonderful drawings of mountain scenery. Most of his most famous paintings feature detailed studies of a variety of landscapes.

In 1563 Bruegel moved to Brussels with his family. His son Pieter was born the next year. His sons, Pieter and Jan, would both achieve fame as artists, though never as great as that of their father's. Both Pieters are separated by "elder" and "younger" after their names, very much the way we now call a son "junior," if he has the same name as his father.

It was in Brussels that Pieter Bruegel the Elder received an important commission. A wealthy banker wanted a series of paintings made representing the months of the year. *July* (Figure 7.14) is one of five of these works which survive. Another, Figure 7.25, *January* or *Return of the Hunters*, is considered one of the greatest landscape paintings ever created. Like *July*, this painting lets us feel the weather of the scene. Bruegel leads us to experience the cold, biting air of the day by draining the landscape colors down to their basic values—chill darks against frosty whites and grays. The silhouettes of the men and dogs seem carved out of the chill, crystal air. The clear air lets us see for miles across the snow-covered fields. The only sounds are the cawing, circling crows and the whisper of the wintry wind.

Did you learn

- The definitions of these words and phrases: Renaissance; Vatican; linear perspective; Gates of Paradise; Pre-Columbian; obsidian; conquistador; roof comb; Aztec; Maya?
- Why Ghiberti's doors became known as the Gates of Paradise?
- The name of the inventor of **linear perspective**?
- Two artworks Raphael saw while he worked on the *School of Athens*?
- The architect of the dome of St. Peter's Cathedral?
- A favorite subject of Pieter Bruegel's paintings?
- The names of two famous Mayan centers?
- The name of the emperor of the Aztecs?

Student work.

Understanding and Evaluating

- It is 1509 and you have been assigned by Pope Julius II to write a short report on the progress of young Raphael's work on *The School of Athens*.
- See if your library has any books on the Aztecs, Moctezuma, or Hernán Cortés. Read more about the conquest of the Aztecs. Imagine yourself a priest or official at Moctezuma's court *or* a soldier in Cortés's army. Write a letter to a friend about the events surrounding the first meeting between Cortés and Moctezuma.

Seeing and Creating

- Make a pencil drawing in perspective of a building, such as your house or your school. Draw from life, if at all possible. Use one- or two-point perspective (see Figures 7.4 and 7.5).
- Under the instruction of your teacher, make a small clay container using an animal form as a subject. Either glaze or paint your completed container.
- Ⓒ [CAUTION: Some students are allergic to clay or glazes. Use protective masks or gloves, if necessary, when using these materials.]
- Christopher Columbus needs sailors for a second voyage to the New World. Using tempera paint, design a recruitment poster for the captain. Having been on the first trip, you know what wonders and riches await—and what dangers!

Chapter 8

BAROQUE AND ROCOCO ART OF THE 17TH AND 18TH CENTURIES

WORDWATCH
Baroque
foreshortened
Rococo
etchings

Look for a moment at the columns shown in Figure 8.1. The first column, you may remember, is ancient Greek in style. Do you recall what kind of capital (top) is shown? Look at the second column. How is it different from the first column? What words would you use to describe it? Wavy, twisted, flowing? Compared to the Greek column, it seems full of movement and action.

THE BEAUTY OF BAROQUE

The second column is designed in a style called **Baroque** [Bah•ROWK]. The Baroque style of art and design was very popular during the period of time from 1600-1750.

As the great Renaissance artists, like Leonardo and Michelangelo, grew old and died, a new group of artists took their place. Like all young people, these artists had their own ways of painting, sculpting, and designing. Art and artists had become very important during the Renaissance. Kings, popes, and emperors listened to artists and valued their work.

The young Baroque artists took advantage of this respect and position. They ventured into ever more exciting and daring art projects and subjects. The more thrilling, emotional, and dramatic the subject, the better. Painters ignited their canvasses and ceilings with swirling movement, vivid colors, and strong emotions. Sculptors and architects set cold stone and marble in motion. Like the Baroque column, no material was allowed to rest in stately peace. It was as if straight lines had been declared illegal!

Michelangelo da Caravaggio

Along with drama, vivid color, and restless motion, at no other time in the history of art did artists use the contrast between light and dark to greater effect. One the masters of this effect was the Italian artist, Michelangelo da Caravaggio [care•rah•VAGE•ee•o].

Figure 8.2, titled *The Supper at Emmaus*, shows how the quietest subject could, under Caravaggio's hand, take on drama and action. The painting shows two strangers, who, while dining on a simple supper at an inn, find themselves suddenly in the presence of Jesus. This work not only shows characteristics of Caravaggio's style of painting, but also of Baroque painting in general.

The first thing you notice is the light. It shines brightly on the faces of the men and on the white tablecloth. Around this bright core of light lie deepest shadows. This makes Jesus stand out from the other figures. It is as if a spotlight were shining on the group. The contrast between this bright, concentrated light and the deep, surrounding shadows is seen in much of Caravaggio's work. It is also a characteristic of other Baroque paintings. The strong lights and shadows give drama and emotion to the scene. Doesn't it almost appear like a climactic scene from a play?

[?] How has Caravaggio used motion and action to enhance the drama? Have you noticed the position of the hands? None of the figures in the painting are quietly holding their hands. All the hands are in motion—pointing, gesturing, gripping.

One hand, in particular, is worth special notice. The figure on the right pushes his outstretched hand directly at you, the viewer. What skill it takes to draw and paint a hand in that position! If you don't believe it, try it for yourself!

When an object, like a hand, is drawn pointed at the viewer, it is said to be **foreshortened.** The name can be understood by looking at the right figure's hand once more. The hand seems to reach into the *foreground* towards you. Look at the arm. We cannot see its full length because of the position. To make it appear realistic, the artist must *shorten* the length. You may have already realized that foreshortening is a kind of perspective. As you look at other paintings, see if you can identify more examples of foreshortening. Compare them with Caravaggio's. It will be difficult to find an artist who does it better.

Have you noticed the basket of fruit in the foreground? It is about to fall off the table. When it falls it will be another dramatic event in the painting. One small bump against the table leg will send it flying!

At first glance, *The Supper at Emmaus* doesn't really look like a painting of a religious subject at all. The faces and gestures of the men surrounding Jesus look like those of ordinary, hard-working people. And in truth they were. Caravaggio always used real people from the streets for his models.

The leaders of the church, who bought some of his works, objected to this. They felt that religious paintings should use noble, saintly-looking individuals as models. Caravaggio, on the other hand, frequently used beggars, thieves, and other people of the street for models. And he was in a unique position to know these individuals, since he spent much of his leisure time with them.

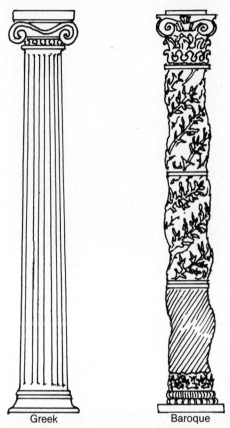

Greek   Baroque

Figure 8.1. Greek and Baroque columns.

Figure 8.2. Caravaggio. *Supper at Emmaus.* 1596/98-1602. Oil on canvas, 143 cm. x 196.2 cm. Reproduced by courtesy of the Trustees, The National Gallery, London.

Figure 8.3. Peter Paul Rubens. *Rubens and Isabella Brant in the Honeysuckle Bower.* 1609. Oil on canvas, 178 cm. x 136.5 cm. Alte Pinakothek, Munich. Photo credit: Artothek.

Figure 8.4. Diego Rodriquez de Silva y Velazquez. *Juan De Pareja.* Oil on canvas, 32" x 27½". The Metropolitan Museum of Art. Fletcher Fund, Rogers Fund, and Bequest of Miss Adelaide Milton de Groot, by exchange, supplemented by gifts from friends of the Museum, 1971.

Not only were Caravaggio's paintings full of drama and action, but his life wasn't exactly dull either! He was known for his arrogance and love of starting fights. He liked nothing better than to swagger around with his sword at his hip, looking for a duel. He had a police file as long as your arm! Enraged over the outcome of a tennis match, Caravaggio killed a man in a duel. He himself was finally wounded by an opponent. He died at the age of thirty-eight. Strange, how this violent and disagreeable individual could also possess such wonderful artistic talent and ability.

Peter Paul Rubens

After spending eight years in Italy, Peter Paul Rubens seemed to combine in his work the best of Northern European and Italian art. Rubens would become one of the greatest, most successful artists of all time.

He has been called the "artist prince," because he was as educated, elegant, and worldly as the royal patrons he worked for. Many of the kings and princes who bought his paintings considered him a friend and equal. His fame and success assured him of a position in society that was unique for an artist. No starving artist here! Rubens lived to see his paintings admired around the world, and himself become rich and famous, with a personal art collection that rivaled those of his royal friends.

Rubens, as much as Caravaggio, was a true Baroque artist. You have only to look at Figure 8.3 to recognize the characteristic Baroque style.

Velazquez

Spanish artist Diego Velazquez [dee • A • go vel • LAS • kez] was one of the greatest painters of the 17th century or of any century. Painting in a very realistic manner, Velazquez combined the drama of Caravaggio with the elegance of Rubens. He, like Rubens, became a treasured friend of royalty. In 1622 Velazquez became court painter to Spain's King Philip IV. From this prized position he was able to observe and paint the people of the Spanish court as no one ever had. Velazquez was one of the greatest portrait painters of all time.

The proud young man pictured in Figure 8.4 is Juan de Pareja [whan day pha • RAY • ha]. He was Velazquez's assistant. Have you noticed the bright light shining on Juan's face? What about the dark shadow above his head? These are similar to the way Caravaggio painted figures in light and shadow. Around the head you can see brushstrokes. As in a sketch, these strokes of the artist's brush add movement and energy to the painting. Don't they seem to make the figure move a little? Surely, if we wait a few more minutes Juan will speak!

Many people believe that Velazquez's greatest work is a painting known as *Las Meninas* or "The Maids of Honor" (Figure 8.5).

Let's look closely at this wonderful painting. It is full of interesting people and mysterious details. You can already tell this painting is from the Baroque period, can't you? There is the bright light streaming in through a window on the right. As we look further back into the room, the light fades into a soft, warm gloom. Shadows cover details.

The movement and position of the figures may remind you of Caravaggio's or Rubens's painting. Everyone is turned in a different direction. Can you pick out the figures that are looking at you? Can you find the artist? Velazquez painted a self-portrait within a royal family portrait. But, let's meet some of the other people.

The beautifully dressed little girl with the silky, blond hair is the Princess Margarita or the "Infanta" [in•fon•tah] as she is known in Spain. The other young ladies are her attendants or "maids in waiting." These elegantly dressed young women were of noble birth themselves and were honored to be servants to the little princess. It was their job to see that she was content and happy. Do you think the maid kneeling at her side is trying to convince her to stand still for her portrait a little longer? Or has the Infanta simply come into the artist's studio to visit and play with his dog?

Can you tell who the artist is painting? Look closely at the mirror on the back wall. Don't you wish you could take a look at the portrait Velazquez is painting?

Las Meninas is special because the figures, though of royal birth and high social standing, are not really posed. It looks as if you, the viewer, have stepped into the room and interrupted the playful conversation of the little princess and her maids.

This was a most unusual type of portrait for Velazquez, as court painter, to paint. He shows the world that the royal family are real people, who play, tease, and laugh just like everyone else. By putting himself in the picture, he shows us something of his position in court. He was obviously accepted as part of the royal family. Like Rubens, Velazquez helped raise the status of artists higher than it had ever been before.

Rembrandt

In Holland the Baroque period also produced a number of fine artists, the greatest of whom was Rembrandt Van Rijn [RIM • brant von rine].

Although a master landscape painter, Rembrandt is best known for his magnificent portraits. He was fascinated by people's personalities and the character he saw in their faces. Even his own face interested him. He used it as the subject of over one hundred self-portraits throughout his long life. Figure 8.6 shows a self-portrait he painted in 1666 when he was 60 years old. He would die three years after this portrait was completed.

Once again, as with most paintings from the Baroque period, light and shadow play an important part. Rembrandt's face seems spotlighted, while the rest of his body dissolves into the dark shadows of the background. Although the face seems very realistic, the surface isn't free of brushstrokes. Rembrandt hasn't tried to smooth them out at all. And yet we somehow know that this is a photographic likeness of the great artist.

Figure 8.7 is another portrait masterpiece by Rembrandt. This time the subject isn't the artist's own face, but a model posing as an ancient Greek thinker. Of course, here the ancient Greek is shown in clothes from Rembrandt's own time. By now you should be able to point out the characteristics of the Baroque style. Compare this portrait with Figure 8.6. How are they similar? Can you tell how Rembrandt has made the gold chain look so shiny? Do you think Rembrandt thought the Greek was a wise man? How would you describe the colors in this painting? Warm or cool?

Before we leave Baroque art and the 17th century, let's look at one other work. Figure 8.8 shows a ceiling painting, *Triumph in the Name of Jesus,* created by Italian artist Giovanni Gaulli [gee • o • VAN • ee GOW • lee]. Can you tell where the painting stops and the building begins? If you can't, don't worry. The artist wanted to create just that kind of confusion. Do you remember the name for this kind of painted illusion? (see Chapter 5, Figure 5.25).

Soaring many feet above the heads of the viewers, this amazing ceiling gives the illusion that the roof of the church has disappeared and that the interior is open to the sky. The scene, filled with floating clouds and the swirling cloth of the suspended figures, is typical of the energy, drama, and excitement of Baroque art.

It is as if the artist wants the viewer to feel a part of the scene, to believe it would be possible to float up into the painting itself. To achieve this illusion, parts of the painting extend into and overlap the actual structure of

Figure 8.6. Rembrandt van Rijn. *Self Portrait.* 1666. Oil on canvas, 31⅝" x 26½". The Metropolitan Museum of Art. Bequest of Benjamin Altman, 1913.

Figure 8.7. Rembrandt van Rijn. *Aristotle with a Bust of Homer.* Oil on canvas, 56½" x 53¾". The Metropolitan Museum of Art. Purchased with special funds and gifts of friends of the Museum, 1961.

the building. So skillful is the artist it takes a very sharp eye to see where the painting ends and the building begins.

ROCOCO ART OF THE 18TH CENTURY

The 18th century, the years 1700 to 1799, included many important and exciting historical events. One, in particular, has special meaning to the citizens of the United States. It was the American Revolution. Do you remember the dates? (1775-1783). The French also had a revolution during the 18th century (1789-1799).

In spite of the turmoil and revolution taking place, the 18th century became known as "The Age of Reason." During this century, many old ideas of how the world worked and how people should be treated were cast aside. In place of the old belief that humans could not understand nature, and were completely at the mercy of natural forces, the idea that science could reveal the workings of nature developed. Human beings could even learn to use science to better their lives.

The second ancient belief to fall was that kings and royal-born people were somehow better than everyone else, and had, by birth, the right to rule and control others. The idea that all people had equal rights to life, liberty, and property was one of the great contributions of this remarkable century. It was this idea that ignited the American and French revolutions.

But, what about the art of the 18th century? What was it like? Well, at first, it wasn't very different from art of the 17th century. It was art created in the Baroque style. There was still movement and drama in paintings. Figure 8.9 is a painting by the French artist Jean-Antoine Watteau [juawn an•TWANE wah•TOE], called *Embarkation for Cythera*. Watteau, who was inspired by Baroque painters like Rubens, gave movement and drama to this painting through, brushstrokes and vivid colors. But there is a difference. It is obvious that a new style of art is about to be born. This style was called **Rococo** [ROW•co•co].

Next to many Baroque paintings, with their bold, strong, active figures, this work seems almost delicate in comparison. Compare it for a moment with Figure 8.2. The Watteau painting seems more like a painting of a stage set and a play than reality. Notice how the light washes over everything. It isn't used as a strong spotlight anymore. The people look more like dolls, than flesh and blood individuals. All is like a beautiful, misty dream.

You can identify the Rococo style in painting in several ways. The subjects are usually people enjoying them-

Figure 8.8. Giovanni Battista Gaulli. *Triumph in the Name of Jesus.* Fresco, ceiling of the nave of the Church of Jesus, Rome. Photo: Alinari/Art Resource, New York.

Figure 8.9. Watteau. *Embarkation for Cythera.* Oil on canvas, 129 cm. x 194 cm. Collection The Louvre, Paris. Photo ©R.M.N.

Figure 8.10. Francoise Fragonard. *The Swing.* c. 1768. Oil on canvas, 31 7/8" x 25 3/8". The Wallace Collection, London.

Figure 8.11. *Rococo Room* from the Metropolitan Museum of Art. Wrightsman Galleries: Room from Hotel de Varengeville, Paris, view looking southwest. Photographed August, 1979. The Metropolitan Museum of Art.

selves in a beautiful landscape. The figures will be elegantly dressed, even though they may be on a picnic in the country. Everything is pastel swirls and golden light. What a beautiful dream these paintings reveal.

One Rococo painting that has all the characteristics of the style is Figure 8.10. It is by one of the most famous Rococo artists, Jean-Honoré Fragonard [juawn on•no•RAY FRAG•go•nar]. It is titled *The Swing.*

Let your imagination wander for a moment through the cool, green shade; among these young, carefree, beautiful people. The trees and bushes twist and billow like green clouds. The warm, pink dress of the young lady in the swing makes a wonderful color contrast to the cool, blue-green background. Movement is everywhere, from the twisted tree branches overhead to the delicately kicked shoe. The forward motion of the swing is frozen in place; the shoe suspended in space forever.

This painting of these rich, privileged individuals enjoying themselves is a good representation of how French royalty and the upper classes wanted to see themselves—perfect people in a perfect setting. However, it is just this rich and careless life that would eventually bring their downfall. For the beauty and grace of this scene hides the terrible poverty and suffering of the common people during the 18th century in France and elsewhere. These same common people would seek a terrible vengence upon these privileged few, but not for a while yet. When this painting was completed the French Revolution was twenty-five years in the future.

Rococo Decoration

The term *Rococo* was originally used to describe a type of decorative style; that is, a way of designing architecture and objects. Elements of this decorative style can be clearly seen in Figure 8.11.

This magnificent room is filled with ornaments and furniture that are Rococo in style. For example, the gilded (gold-covered) wall decorations use delicate, twining vines and flowing ribbons to add movement and interest to the cream-colored walls. The legs of the furniture are gracefully carved. No straight-legged chairs here! And just look at that carpet! Its woven patterns repeat the vines, leaves, and flowers seen throughout the room. Gold is everywhere. One could never mistake this room for that of a poor person's.

If you squint, you can see how the swirling, twisting decoration, gilt, and rich colors give vitality and energy to the room. Your eyes are drawn from one pattern to another in a restless movement. But, there is still a delicate quality about it all. Those chairs were obviously meant for elegant conversations, not for sprawling in to watch T.V.!

The Rococo style of design was more decorative than functional or useful. You may find the Rococo style a bit too fussy for your taste. Modern taste in furniture and decoration tends to be simple and functional. In a future chapter, you will have an opportunity to read more about the differences between decorative and functional designs.

Although painting, architecture, and decoration were the main art forms of the 18th century, sculpture still played a part, though not as it had in the Renaissance. One of the most gifted sculptors of the 18th century was Jean-Antoine Houdon [oo•DON]. Not only did he capture in marble the likenesses of many famous French people, but he gave Americans some of the best likenesses we have of our own leaders.

Figure 8.12 shows Houdon's famous sculpture of George Washington. Houdon was invited to America by Thomas Jefferson. He spent several weeks at Washington's home, Mount Vernon, making sketches and studies of the first president. In 1788 Houdon began work on the full-length sculpture of Washington that now stands in the state capitol in Richmond, Virginia. Like all Houdon's portraits, his portrait of Washington is full of realism and life. Washington stands tall and determined, his hand resting firmly on a bundle of rods that represents the union. He seems to look toward the future—a future that sees the end of the old century and the beginning of the new.

Figure 8.12. Jean-Antoine Houdon. Statue of *George Washington.* Marble, 74″ h. State Capitol, Richmond, Virginia. Photo courtesy Library of Congress.

BORN: 1606
DIED: 1669
BIRTHPLACE: Leyden, Holland

Figure 8.13. Rembrandt van Rijn. *Christ Preaching*. Etching, 6 1/16" x 8⅛". The Metropolitan Museum of Art. Bequest of Mrs. H.O. Havemeyer, 1929. The H.O. Havemeyer Collection.

Figure 8.14. Rembrandt van Rijn. *Presentation of the Temple*. c. 1654-57. Etching, 8¼" x 6⅛". The Metropolitan Museum of Art. Gift of Felix M. Warburg and his family, 1941.

Portraits That Never Lie

Although skilled in several different artforms, including painting and printmaking, Rembrandt is perhaps most famous for his portraits. In capturing in paint the truth of an individual's personality and spirit, he is without equal.

Rembrandt was the son of a miller, who was prosperous enough to have his own mill called the Rhine Mill on the Rhine river. It was from this mill that Rembrandt took his last name. A miller is someone who grinds grains into flour and meal used for baking. Not surprisingly, Rembrandt's mother was the daughter of a wealthy baker. The Van Rijn family was a respectable, middle-class family with great hopes for their son.

At age fourteen, Rembrandt started school. His teachers soon realized that the boy's talents did not lie in learning Latin, math, or history! He was never without a sketchbook and pencil in hand. Rembrandt's interest in drawing soon convinced his parents that he should devote himself to the serious study of art. They found him a teacher, first in their hometown, and later in Amsterdam.

It so happened that his teacher, one Pieter Lastman, was a great admirer of the talented, but infamous Caravaggio (see Figure 8.2). The influence of Caravaggio's style on Rembrandt's art can be seen clearly if you compare the two. Both were interested in adding drama and emotion through strong contrasts between light and shadow.

After completing his studies in Amsterdam, Rembrandt returned home and established himself as a painter. He soon began to receive commissions. As the commissions flowed in, he decided that he should move back to Amsterdam to take advantage of the wealth and culture of the city.

Along with a splendid collection of paintings, Rembrandt has left us some wonderful prints. These prints are all **etchings**. An etching is produced by scratching lines into a metal plate. The plate is then inked and printed. Shading is created by a drawing technique known as crosshatching. Figures 8.13 and 8.14 show two of these etchings. Can you see how Rembrandt used light and shadow just as he did in his paintings? The movement and drama in these etchings identify them as being in the true Baroque style.

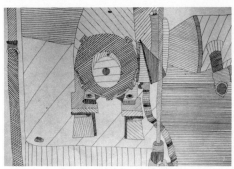

Student work.

Did you learn

- The definitions of these words and phrases: Baroque; foreshortened; Rococo; etchings?
- At least two characteristics of the Baroque style?
- One way Caravaggio added drama to his painting, *The Supper at Emmaus*?
- The meaning of the title *Las Meninas*?
- Why *Las Meninas* is an unusual painting of a royal family?
- Rembrandt's favorite subject for painting?
- Two ways the Rococo style is different from the Baroque? Two ways it is similar?
- The name of the artist who created a famous sculpture of George Washington?

Understanding and Evaluating

- Review the four stages of art criticism in Chapter 3. In a page or two, apply each stage to Caravaggio's painting *The Supper at Emmaus*. (Figure 8.2)
- Write a short story or a play about the scene shown in *Las Meninas*. (Figure 8.5)

Seeing and Creating

- Try your hand at foreshortening. Take an object and place it on the table facing you. If it is a tree branch, make sure some of the twigs point straight at you. A bottle or can could be turned so the end or neck points towards you. Make several pencil sketches of the object. What did you learn about foreshortening? Does knowing the rules of linear perspective help you draw foreshortened objects?
- Using a pen and India ink, make a drawing of figures or objects that are lighted by a spotlight. Use crosshatching to create strong contrasts in light and shadow. [**CAUTION**: India ink is permanent. Wear protective clothing.]

Ⓒ

Chapter 9

A TIME OF CHANGE—ART OF THE 19TH CENTURY

By the end of the 18th century, there had been many changes in both Europe and America. In France the ruling class had been overthrown in a violent revolution. It seems the poor had finally taken their revenge on the rich, careless aristocrats who filled the paintings of Watteau and Fragonard (Figures 8.9 and 8.10). In the United States an independent nation, free of England's rule, was taking shape. Before the end of the 19th century, yet another kind of revolution would take place, affecting the future of the world as much as did the French and American revolutions. This revolution would not be one of cannons and soldiers, but of machines. It would be known as the Industrial Revolution.

REMEMBERING THE PAST— THE NEOCLASSIC STYLE

At the start of the 19th century, as revolutionary wars faded and new nations arose, a style of art became popular that once again drew its inspiration from those amazing ancient Greeks and Romans. This style of art became known as **Neoclassic.**

Think back to what you studied in Chapter 1. You were introduced to another work that contained the preface "neo." Do you remember the word? "Neo," as a prefix to a word, means "new." In the word **Neoclassic,** the new part refers to a revival or rediscovery and appreciation of a former style of art and design. That former style was, of course, the art of ancient Greece and Rome.

France, coming out of a revolutionary period, embraced a style of art inspired by the Greeks and Romans. One of the greatest artists of the Neoclassic style was French artist, Jacques-Louis David [jock lu•ee dah•VEED].

Figure 9.1 shows one of David's most famous paintings. It is called *Oath of the Horatii* [hor•RAY•she•eye]. In this painting, David uses an incident from Roman history as the subject for his work. Three Roman brothers, seen on the left with raised hands, have just taken an oath to defend Rome against a neighboring city's three champions. It is easy to see that David had not only carefully studied the costumes, weapons, and architecture of ancient Rome, but that he also tried to show something of the spirit and determination that built the Roman empire.

Compare this work with Figure 8.10, and you will see how different the Neoclassic style was from the Rococo.

Figure 9.1. Jacques-Louis David. *Oath of the Horatii.* 1784-85. Oil on canvas, 10′8¼″ x 14′. Collection The Louvre, Paris. Photo ©R.M.N.

The strong light entering the scene from the left seems to mold the figures as if they were statues made of marble. Gone are the misty, delicate landscapes and frail figures of Watteau and Fragonard. And notice the brushstrokes. There aren't any! The marks of the paintbrush have been smoothed out. The painting style is clear, photographic, and very different from the painting style of Rembrandt (Figure 8.7), Rubens (Figure 8.3), and Watteau (Figure 8.9). The edges of the figures in David's painting are sharp and clean. This increases the impression that they are made of a hard, solid material like stone.

The three brave Roman brothers are definitely strong and determined. In David's painting they represent the strength and determination of the French Revolution. Look carefully at the painting. See if you can locate the focal point of the composition. Remember, the focal point, or point of emphasis, is the area of a visual composition that catches your eye first. It is the main focus of the work. Does David's focal point help us understand the meaning of his painting?

David was not only a painter who believed in the cause of the French Revolution, but he had also been an active participant in the revolution. In fact, he was at one time imprisoned for his part in the chaos that followed the overthrow of the monarchy (royal family). He narrowly escaped losing his head to the guillotine! However, his luck held, and he was released from prison.

Shortly thereafter, he attracted the attention of Napoleon Bonaparte [nah•POLE•ee•on Bone•a•part]. Napoleon became the new leader of France and had himself crowned emperor. He selected David to record in a painting the occasion of his coronation. Figure 9.2 shows David's completed work. In this beautiful painting we see the newly crowned emperor about to place a crown on the head of his queen, Josephine.

The photorealistic style of painting is still there, but things are changing. For example, there is a richer use of color. The vivid reds that are sprinkled throughout the painting give it the look of a Byzantine mosaic from the court of Justinian and Theodora (see Chapter 6.2, Figure 6.3). Gold and jewels sparkle from every corner. It looks as if the richness of the monarchy has returned. And can you see the crown on Napoleon's head? It is in the shape of laurel leaves made of gold. This is the same type of crown that Roman emperors wore. There is little doubt that the vain and powerful Napoleon saw himself as a ruler as great as the Caesars of ancient Rome.

Figure 9.2. Jacques-Louis David. *Coronation of Napoleon and Josephine.* 1805-7. Oil on canvas, 20′ x 30′6½″. Collection The Louvre, Paris. Photo ©R.M.N.

Figure 9.3. Jean August Dominique Ingres. *Pauline Eleonore De Galard De Brassac De Bearn, Princess De Broglie.* 1853. Oil on canvas, 47¾″ x 35¾″. The Metropolitan Museum of Art. Robert Lehman Collection, 1975.

David soon realized that Napoleon had rescued France from revolution only to become another version of the privileged and powerful ruling class. No longer able to tolerate the deception, David left his beloved France, never to return.

Another French artist who help to spread the popularity of Neoclassicism was David's student, Jean-Auguste-Dominique Ingres [jhun Ah•GUST Dom•mah•NEEK AN•gre]. Ingres was a master at drawing and painting objects and their textures, or surface qualities, realistically. You have only to look at the wonderful portrait shown in Figure 9.3 to appreciate Ingres's amazing skill with a paintbrush.

The elegant, thoughtful young women shown in Figure 9.3 is painted with photographic realism. In fact, the whole painting looks like a polished jewel, with each surface and every detail flawlessly drawn. Be sure to notice the different textures of the woman's dress. From shiny satin to delicate lace, she is the picture of elegance and calm.

When you compare this work with Figure 9.1 by David, you can see how much the student, Ingres, learned from his teacher. In Ingres's painting, titled *Portrait of the Princess de Broglie,* edges are very sharp and clean, and all trace of brushstrokes have been removed. And although the subject isn't borrowed from ancient history, it wouldn't be difficult to imagine the young princess in a toga, the traditional Greek or Roman costume. She seems as cool and reserved as a classical statue.

Neoclassic Architecture

Influenced by the belief that Greece had established the first democracy, many American artists and architects also found inspiration in the art of ancient Greece and Rome.

Figure 9.4 is a fine example of Neoclassic architecture. It is the main building and entrance to the University of Virginia. It was designed by an architect you may know. He was the third president of the United States. The architect's name was Thomas Jefferson. Another Jefferson design was his own home, Monticello (Figure 5.4).

You have only to look back at the Greek and Roman buildings in Chapter 5 to see how they inspired Jefferson in his designs. For example, in Figures 9.4 and 5.4, notice the use of a dome in both buildings. Doesn't this remind you of the Pantheon in Rome (Figure 5.20)? The graceful

Figure 9.4. Thomas Jefferson. *The University of Virginia, Lawn and Rotunda.* 1976 (after restoration of the Rotunda). University Archives, Special Collections Dept., University of Virginia Library, Charlottesville, Virginia.

white columns look very much like the Greek Parthenon, don't they?

The Neoclassic style of architecture became so popular in the United States during the early 19th century that many government buildings, including many state capitols, were built in this style. For this reason it is sometimes known as the **Federal style,** after the federal government.

A PASSION FOR LIFE—THE ROMANTIC STYLE

Not all artists followed the Neoclassic style. Some, like the French artist Delacroix [Del•ah•QUAH], were called romantics. Their vivid and emotional artworks became known as the **Romantic style.**

When you hear the word "romantic," you probably think about love. But, the meaning of "romantic," when used to describe the art style of the 19th century, has a wider meaning.

Art of the Romantic style could usually be identified by its subject matter. Stories, myths, and legends, which were both exciting and emotional, were favorite subjects. If they took place in an exotic location, such as the Middle East or Africa, so much the better. Figure 9.5 by Delacroix is an example of a painting in the Romantic style.

Compare Figure 9.5 with Figure 8.3 Can you find any similarities? What are the differences?

The Romantic View—English Landscapes

While Delacroix traveled to strange, exotic lands in search of ever more exciting subjects for his paintings, several English artists were rediscovering the beauty of their own local surroundings.

John Constable and Joseph Turner established landscapes and seascapes as the most popular subjects for art in the 19th century. Both artists, though using different styles of painting, used the English countryside and seashore for inspiration.

Figure 9.6, titled *The Haywain,* is by John Constable. This wonderful painting seems to cast a spell of calm and quiet over everyone who sees it in the National Gallery in London. The museum has kindly placed a bench in front of this large (50½"x73") canvas, so visitors can linger for a moment and enjoy the beauty and peace of Constable's England.

Like a remembered dream, we see a perfect country scene of golden sunlight warming smooth fields; still, cool water; towering oaks. Time seems to stand still in this painting. All is quiet and peaceful. You have only to

Figure 9.5. Eugene Delacroix. *View of Tangier from the Seashore.* 1858. Oil on fabric, 31 15/16" x 39 5/16". Minneapolis Institute of Arts. Bequest of Mrs. Erasmus C. Lindley in memory of her father, James J. Hill.

Figure 9.6. John Constable. *The Haywain.* 1821. Oil on canvas, 50½" x 73". Reproduced by courtesy of the Trustees, The National Gallery, London.

Figure 9.7. Joseph Mallord William Turner. *The Grand Canal, Venice.* Oil on canvas, 36" x 48⅛". The Metropolitan Museum of Art. Bequest of Cornelius Vanderbuilt, 1899.

compare it with Figure 9.5 to see the contrast in moods between the two paintings. Delacroix's work will leave you out of breath; Constable inspires you to dream. If you listen carefully, you may hear the sound of the horses' hooves splashing the water in the pond. Are there birds singing? Can you hear the ducks?

Paintings like *The Haywain* became famous the world over as representations of the peaceful, quiet, stable life that could be found in the English countryside during the first half of the 19th century. But, is this a painting in the Romantic style? It doesn't share many characteristics with Delacroix's work.

Although the subject is far from the frantic drama of Constable's landscape, it is still very "romantic" in mood. It celebrates and idealizes the beauty and goodness of nature. The man driving the wagon, the horses, the dog, and the ducks are all part of the natural environment. "Ideal" scenes like Constable's were probably found only in the artist's imagination and the paintings he created. Constable's painting is very much a part of the 19th-century Romantic tradition.

Another English painter who specialized in both land-scapes and seascapes was Joseph Turner. Turner's paint-ings are very different in feeling and mood from Con-stable's. Turner liked to paint not only the traditional parts of landscapes and seascapes, such as trees, moun-tains, lakes, waves, and ships, but also people and machines in action.

Figure 9.7, titled *The Grand Canal, Venice,* is character-istic of Turner's style of painting. The city of Venice in Italy is a very special place. In place of streets, the citizens of the city use canals to get from one place to another. Because of the famous canals and the many beautiful buildings in the city, Venice has always been a popular subject for artists. In Figure 9.7 Turner gives us his "impression" of this city on the edge of the Adriatic Sea.

With energetic brushstrokes, Turner gives a sense of movement to everything. Even the buildings appear to shimmer in the afternoon heat.

THE AMERICANS JOIN IN

Although French, English, and Spanish artists seem to dominate the 19th century, there was, in America a grow-ing number of talented artists. Many of these artists, like Thomas Eakins [EE•kins], Winslow Homer, and Mary Cassatt [Cah•SOT], were accepted into the select club of serious artists.

Considered one of the greatest artists of the 19th cen-tury, Thomas Eakins brought an amazing talent to portrait painting. In Figure 9.8, a portrait of Eakins's wife, Hannah, and his dog, Harry, there is a realistic, unromantic quality like that of a photograph. Hannah looks up at us from her book, as if we had disturbed her reading. Harry continues to sleep peacefully. The colors in the painting are soft and quiet. The only bright note is the red sock on Hannah's foot. Like an anchor, it seems to hold the parts of the painting in place.

Winslow Homer was a self-taught artist. He, like many other American artists, visited France and was influenced by the art he saw and the artists he met. However, Homer stayed true to his heritage and subjects. In his later years, he turned to seascapes, such as that shown in Figure 9.9, titled *Northeastern.* In presenting the violence and power of nature in the sea, Homer was without equal. He frequently arranged or composed his paintings so that the viewer feels a part of the scene.

In Figure 9.9, for example, we seem to stand dangerously near the crashing waves, trying to keep our balance on the slippery rocks in the foreground. You can almost feel the spray on your face and the wind in your hair.

A most unique American talent and personality, achieving fame and distinction during the last half of the 19th century, was Mary Cassatt. As a woman trying to achieve recognition in a man's world, Mary Cassatt had to work harder to prove her talent—but prove it she did. In a series of paintings devoted to mothers and children, she proved herself the equal of any artist working at that time.

Figure 9.10, titled *Sleepy Baby,* shows the sensitivity and skill with which she could represent the love and care shared by mothers and children. What is especially interesting is how she shows this affection without becoming sentimental. Her mothers work hard to care for their children. The children are more interesting and realistic than "cute." Notice how you can almost feel the weight of the child on the woman's arm. The figures of the mother and child seem very solid and real. Few artists could equal Mary Cassatt's ability to draw and paint the human figure.

Figure 9.8. Thomas Eakins. *Lady with a Setter Dog.* 1885. Oil on canvas, 30" x 23". The Metropolitan Museum of Art. Fletcher Fund, 1923.

Figure 9.9. Winslow Homer. *Northeaster.* 1895. Oil on canvas, 34⅜" x 50¼". The Metropolitan Museum of Art. Gift of George A. Hearn, 1910.

Figure 9.10. Mary Cassatt. *Sleepy Baby.* c.1910. Pastel, 25½" x 20½". Dallas Museum of Art. Munger Fund Purchase.

ARTIST WITH A CONSCIENCE

Many of the artists of the first half of the 19th century seemed unaware of the problems still faced by the poor throughout the world. Few were using their art to protest the poverty, hardship, and despair they saw everywhere. But, from Spain came an artist who would use his art to show the world the inhumanity of war and the greed and vanity of the ruling family. His name was Francisco de Goya [Fran•CHESS•co de GOY•ya].

Like Velazquez before him, Goya was selected by the Spanish royal family to paint their "family" portraits. They would all pose in their splendid clothes and jewels, while the talented Goya, through his portraits, made them the envy of Europe.

Figure 9.11 shows us how Goya saw the king and queen of Spain and their various children and relatives. The clothes and jewels are certainly rich, but look carefully at the faces. Goya has made no attempt to hide the plain, coarse faces and personalities of these vain, cruel people. You have but to compare them with the royal scene painted by Velazquez (Figure 8.5) to see the difference. The royal couple has been described as looking like a butcher or baker's family who has just won a big prize!

Though Goya is poking fun at the pompous vanity of these people, he also intends to reveal them for what they really are—evil.

Goya, as both a great artistic genius and a man of conscience, was deeply affected by the invasion of Spain by Napoleon's army in 1808.

IMPRESSIONISM

More than any other style of art developed during the 19th century, the style known as **Impressionism,** had the greatest impact on future art movements.

Impressionist paintings were first exhibited in Paris in 1874. French artist Claude Monet [Mo•NAY] had painted an interesting work he called *Impression—Le Harve* (Figure 9.12). There was nothing particularly unusual about the subject of the painting. It showed the sun setting behind sailboats.

What is unique was the way the paint has been applied to the canvas. Instead of brushing on areas of smooth color, Monet uses short streaks and dabs of color everywhere. He seemed not to care whether the viewer could see or recognize the objects in the painting. Monet's concern was for the "impression" of light and color that strikes the eye during those first moments of looking at a scene.

Visitors who attended this historic exhibition failed to understand or appreciate what Monet was trying to achieve. To them, the lack of clear edges and smooth color areas simply meant that Monet couldn't paint—at least not in the realistic way they had come to expect. The exhibition was met with scorn and hatred. The local newspaper ran an article of how certain "sensitive" visitors had actually been driven mad by the sight of these "impressionistic" artworks. One man, or so the story goes, after viewing the exhibit, ran yelling into the street where he started biting passersby!

There is little doubt that the world had not seen works of art like this before. It seemed that both subject and substance had vanished in a maze of dots, streaks, and blobs of paint. But, new movements are often looked upon with mistrust. Before the end of the century, Impressionism would become the main art style of painting and sculpture throughout Europe.

Monet's painting, titled *Bridge Over a Pool of Water Lilies,* (Figure 9.13) doesn't seem strange at all to us. We know how really abstract art can get. In comparison, the works of the Impressionists seem very realistic.

In Figure 9.13 we can clearly see the bridge that spans the peacefully floating waterlilies. In fact, this painting is more realistic than a photograph of the same scene would be. In Monet's painting, everything seems to vibrate and shimmer. Photographs, while they record details, freeze movement. In this painting our eyes take in at once the kalaidoscope of colors. The brushstrokes break up the surface of the painting into a mosaic of colored points.

Have you noticed how skillfully Monet has indicated the surface of the pond? With downward brushstrokes he

Figure 9.12. Claude Monet. *Impression-Sunrise, Le Havre.* 1872. Oil on canvas, 19½" x 25½". Photo ©R.M.N.

Figure 9.13. Claude Monet. *Bridge over a Pool of Water Lilies.* 1899. Oil on canvas, 36½" x 29". The Metropolitan Museum of Art. Bequest of Mrs. H.O. Havemeyer, 1929. The H.O. Havemeyer Collection.

Figure 9.14. Berthe Morisot. *In the Dining Room.* 1886. Oil on canvas, 24⅛" x 19¾". National Gallery of Art, Washington, D.C., Chester Dale Collection.

Figure 9.15. Pierre Auguste Renoir. *The Luncheon of the Boating Party.* 1881. Oil on canvas, 51″ x 68″. The Phillips Collection, Washington, D.C.

Figure 9.16. Pierre Auguste Renoir. *Bal Du Moulin de la Galette, Monmartre.* 1876. Oil on canvas, 4′3½″ x 5′9″. Collection Musee de Orsay, Paris.

makes reflections of the trees in the background. The waterlilies sit on top, just as if they floated on the water. ⟨?⟩ How would you describe Monet's color scheme (Book One, Chapter 3)? What do you think is the focal point of the painting? Compare this work with Turner's seascape (Figure 9.7). How are they similar? How different?

The Impressionist movement was mainly composed of men, as were most art movements in the 19th century. Some women, however, made names for themselves as outstanding artists, you have already met Mary Cassatt (Figure 9.10). Another gifted female painter was Berthe Morisot [Bearth Mo•ree•SO].

Figure 9.14, titled *In the Dining Room,* shows Morisot's skill in using the Impressionistic style of painting. This quiet, little scene is given life and energy by vigorous brushwork and sparkling colors. Background objects are indicated with a few expertly placed strokes. Can you see the lamp and the china cabinet? The impression is one of clear light flooding into a warm, cheerful room, reflecting off many different surfaces.

One of the most popular Impressionists was Pierre Auguste Renoir [pea•AIR auh•GOOST ren•WHAH]. Renoir's paintings show a light-hearted approach to both art and life. Like Watteau and Fragonard before him, he liked to paint happy, carefree young people having a wonderful time. Looking at a Renoir painting is like going to a party.

Luncheon of the Boating Party (Figure 9.15) shows Renoir at his carefree best. Come aboard and join the party! Lunch is over, and the long, sunny afternoon stretches ahead. The relaxed young men and women are pleasantly engaged in conversation or simply daydreaming. A gentle breeze ruffles the striped awning, as waves lap at the boat's side. The subjects are easily recognized, while the quick brushstrokes lend an energy and excitement to the scene. The position of the figures also gives a feeling of motion. Bodies lean and heads tilt ⟨?⟩ at a variety of angles. Can you find places where Renoir has repeated the shape and rhythm of the wooden railing? Notice the figure leaning back at the lower right. Which figure do you think is the opposite balance in the composition?

The colors throughout the painting are bright and clear as if washed by the fresh, afternoon air. Pay particular ⟨?⟩ attention to the areas of white. Are they really white? What colors has Renoir used in the shadows?

We must leave this happy party for now, but we are going to visit another Renoir party through a painting. This one is also filled with happy people and good times. It is taking place at a well-known outdoor restaurant in Paris. There is even room for dancing (Figure 9.16).

Compare Figure 9.15 with Figure 9.16. What similarities can you find? Which painting do you think has the most energetic brushwork? In Figure 9.16 light and shadow play a very important part. Notice how the sunlight filtering through the trees, dapples the ground and people with shadows. Can you find a place where this pattern is repeated? What other patterns can you locate? Look into the distance. How has Renoir given the impression of crowds of people? Can you see details in the distance? In Figure 9.16 there are areas that appear white. Examine these areas closely. What colors are used in these light areas?

Before you leave the party, use your imagination to turn up the "volume" and listen to the sounds in the cafe. What do you hear?

Impressions in Bronze

We have talked mostly about painters and paintings. But sculpture can also be Impressionistic in style. Of course, the main interests of the Impressionists—light and color—are not possible in sculpture. One sculptor, however, managed to use the spontaneity or unplanned quality of Impressionistic subjects. His name was Auguste Rodin [auh•GOOST row•DAN].

One of his most famous works is shown in Figure 9.17. Known as *The Burghers of Calais,* this work illustrates an event in French history. In 1347 the English king, Edward III, conquered the French seaport town of Calais [cal•LAY]. To prevent the English from burning and destroying the city, six burghers (town leaders) offered to sacrifice themselves to save the city. Dressed in rough, ragged cloth, with ropes about their necks, they presented themselves to the king. Rodin was inspired by the sacrifice of these brave individuals, just as David had been with the Horatii (Figure 9.1).

This monumental work is cast in **bronze,** a difficult task for so large a sculpture. **Bronze** is a material composed of various metals, but made up primarily of copper and tin.

What makes this work similar to an Impressionistic painting? There are no bright, fresh colors or vigorous brushstrokes. But there is a kind of "on-the-spot" immediacy and spontaneity about the work. For example, the figures of the men are not posed in the same way we saw figures posed in Greek and Roman sculptures. These figures seem to be captured at a moment when total

Figure 9.17. Francois August Rene Rodin. *The Burghers of Calais.* 1886. Bronze, 79⅜″ x 80⅞″ x 77⅛″. Hirshhorn Museum and Sculpture Garden, Smithsonian Institution. Gift of Joseph H. Hirshhorn, 1966.

despair takes over. Their bent, twisted forms and grim faces speak clearly of their bravery and inevitable fate.

Rodin makes little effort to smooth the surface of the bronze or to pretty it up with polishing. He wants us to feel the sadness and despair of the whole scene.

Another work by Rodin that is equally famous is a portrait of the famous 19th century French writer, *Balzac* [BALL•zak] Figure 9.18. In this work, Rodin's style of working is even more impressionistic than in *The Burghers of Calais.* Can you tell how?

Wrapped in a long cape, like a caterpiller in a cocoon, Balzac seems more like a heroic figure of legend than a writer of romantic novels. Rodin has once again left the surface of the bronze uneven and rough. This breaks up the reflected light in a way similar to that used by the Impressionist painters. Balzac's face is represented just as rough and rugged. It is like a quick gesture drawing in bronze!

OTHER WAYS OF SEEING

Alhough it might appear that Impressionism was the only art style in the last part of the 19th century, this was not so. True, it had an effect on almost every artist who came in contact with it. Artists from around the world came to France during the 19th century, and many

Figure 9.18. Francois August Rene Rodin. *Balzac.* 1898. Bronze, 9'3"h. Collection Musee Rodin, Paris. Photo credit: Rosenthal Art Slides.

Figure 9.19. Vincent van Gogh. *Starry Night.* 1889. Oil on canvas, 29″ x 36¼″. Collection, The Museum of Modern Art, New York. Acquired through the Lillie P. Bliss Bequest.

were deeply affected by what they saw. Some artists, like Rodin, borrowed parts of the Impressionistic style, and rejected others. Other artists, like those you will meet in the next section, made Impressionism into something unique and personal.

In Chapter 9 of Book One and in Chapter 2 of this book, you met one of the greatest artists of the 19th century—Vincent Van Gogh. *The Starry Night* (Figure 9.19) has become almost as well-known an artwork as the *Mona Lisa*.

Now that you have read about Impressionism and know more about the characteristics of the style, you can look at Van Gogh's work with fresh understanding.

[?] How is *A Starry Night* Impressionistic in style? Which painting in this chapter does it remind you of?

Figure 9.20. George Seurat. *Sunday Afternoon on the Island of La Grande Jatte,* 1884-86. Oil on canvas, 6'9" x 10'6". The Art Institute of Chicago. Helen Birch Bartlett Memorial Collection.

Dots, Dots, and More Dots

Another artist who was influenced by Impressionism, but found his own unique way to use it, was Georges Pierre Seurat [soo•RAH]. Figure 9.20 is considered Seurat's most famous work. It is called *Sunday Afternoon on the Island of La Grande Jatte.*

Seurat, like Monet, Renoir, and other Impressionists, was interested in the way our eyes see light, shadow, and color. He shared the belief of other Impressionists that it was more important and more accurate to break color areas into small dabs of different colors. When applied to a canvas, this method of painting would give a realistic "impression" of what we really see when light and color hits our eyes.

Seurat, however, was a very different personality than Monet and Renoir. He was very methodical and patient. Interested in science and color theory, Seurat soon became unhappy with the idea that a first, quick glance at a scene was the best one to paint. He wanted to create paintings that were about the way light and color affect our view of solid forms in the world around us. He decided that the best and purest way to paint was to apply pure hues or colors to the canvas and let the human eye do the rest.

Figure 9.20 is a very large painting, over six feet high and ten feet long! It took Seurat two years to complete. If you look closely at the reproduction of the work shown in this book, the surface seems made up of thousands of dots. If you could stand before the original painting, you would see that is exactly how it is painted.

Over two years time, Seurat carefully applied individual points or dots of pure colors to the canvas. When he [?] wanted green, he put yellow dots next to blue dots. How do you think he made the orange and violet?

107

This painting technique became known as **Pointillism**. Look how solid and round the forms of the objects seem. Everything and everyone is placed as carefully as if Seurat were assembling a puzzle. No random or spontaneous arrangements for him! When you compare Seurat's painting with that of Renoir (Figure 9.15 or Figure 9.16), you can see the difference.

The last great artist we will meet before the 19th century comes to a close is Paul Cezanne [say • ZAN].

Where Monet and Renoir looked at their world and saw quick flashes of light and color, Cezanne looked and saw color and form. Where the Impressionists used color to fracture edges and forms, Cezanne used color to make shapes and forms.

Figure 9.21, titled *Mont Ste. Victoire,* is a typical Cezanne landscape. One glance at this painting, and you realize that this is a new direction for Impressionism. In fact, many art critics, at the time Cezanne was painting, decided that both he and Seurat shouldn't be called Impressionists at all. But, some label was necessary, so they became **Post-Impressionists.**

The prefix "post," like the prefix "neo," tells you "when" more than "what." In this case, "post" means "after." So Seurat, Cezanne, and even Van Gogh, who came after the main Impressionists, are called Post-Impressionists.

Look again at Figure 9.21. Can you tell what time of day is represented in this landscape? What objects do you see? In fact, can you tell where you, the viewer, are standing?

Unlike Monet and Renoir, Cezanne doesn't care what time of day it is or whether the viewer can place him or herself in the scene. He is only interested in how the shapes and forms he sees in the land, mountains, and trees can be made more solid and durable by assigning chunks of color to certain shapes. If you look closely, you can see that Cezanne's brushstrokes are broader and more square than those of Monet or Renoir. This cube-like method of painting will soon be a strong influence on one of the major art styles of the 20th century—Cubism.

Figure 9.21. Paul Cezanne. *Mont Ste. Victoire from the Bibemus Quarry.* ca. 1897. Oil on canvas, 25⅛″ x 31½″. The Baltimore Museum of Art. The Cone Collection, by Dr. Claribel Cone and Miss Etta Cone of Baltimore, Maryland.

A Woman Ahead of Her Time

Mary Cassatt was born at a time in history when few young women even considered the idea of being an artist, much less earning a living by it. She was born into a prosperous Philadelphia family, whose expectations of their talented daughter possibly did not include running off to Europe to study art! Well-to-do young women living during the last half of the 19th century were expected to be polite and gracious and to marry early in order to raise a family.

But, it was obvious that Mary Cassatt was no ordinary young woman. She had an independence and determination that set her aside from her peers. She had great plans and a consuming passion to paint. Fortunately, she also had the artistic talent to make her dreams come true.

In 1875, after studying drawing and painting in Philadelphia, Paris, and Rome, Cassatt exhibited her work at the Paris Salon. Here her paintings attracted the admiration of Edward Degas, a famous painter. Although their friendship had its stormy periods—they were both very strong-willed and opinionated—it was Degas who suggested that Cassatt should paint a series of paintings of mothers and their children. Interestingly, it is this series of paintings that have become Mary Cassatt's greatest achievement.

Although she was frequently asked to exhibit her paintings with those of the Impressionists, she never really shared their love of quick, soft brushwork. One look at her paintings (Figure 9.10 and Figure 9.22), reveals how solid and confidently she could paint the substance of the human form. Not for her broken dabs of color and misty outlines. She understood form and mass and painted them without equal.

A less well-known accomplishment of Mary Cassett's was her influence in getting wealthy American art collectors to appreciate and buy Impressionist artworks. Her efforts were responsible for the creation of some of the greatest collections of Impressionist paintings in the world. Thanks to her, a number of these works now form the core collection in many American museums. This contribution, together with her sensitive and beautiful paintings, are a fitting legacy to a woman well ahead of her time.

Edgar Degas. *Portrait of Mary Cassatt.* Private collection. Credit: Art Resource, New York.

BORN: 1845
DIED: 1926
BIRTHPLACE:
Philadelphia, Pennsylvania

Figure 9.22. Mary Cassatt. *Mother and Child.* c. 1890. Oil on canvas, 35⅜″ x 25⅜″. Wichita Art Museum, Wichita, Kansas. The Roland P. Murdock Collection.

Student work.

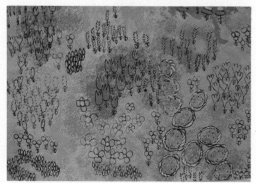

Student work.

Did you learn

- The definitions of these words and phrases: Neo-classic; Federal style; bronze; Pointillism; Romantic style; Impressionism; Post-Impressionism?
- Subjects that were popular with artists of the Romantic style?
- The names of three American artists who achieved success and recognition during the 19th century?
- Why Constable's landscapes are considered "romantic?"
- What Impressionists were interested in painting?
- Two famous Impressionist artists?

Understanding and Evaluating

- Imagine that you have been hired by a museum or art gallery to write a catalogue of an exhibition of 19th-century paintings. Select five artists and works from this chapter and write a brief, one-paragraph description of each work.
- Study Renoir's paintings (Figures 9.15 and 9.16) closely. Imagine yourself as a visitor in either painting. Write a letter to a friend about your visit.

Seeing and Creating

- Make an Impressionistic landscape or still life using watercolor or tempera paint. Begin your painting by washing in various colors in the background. Try to create a particular mood or feeling with your choice of colors. Allow the colors to bleed and wash together. When the paint is dry, add details in water-based felt marker or India ink. [CAUTION: India ink is permanent. Use with care and cover your clothes, if necessary.]
- Think of a particular mood or feeling that you have experienced when you looked at a landscape or sea-scape. It might be "joy," "fear," or another feeling. Using only colored tissue paper, create an Impressionistic mood collage by tearing, cutting, and gluing the tissue pieces to a sheet of white construction paper or posterboard. On the back, name your work and write a brief description of the landscape and mood you were thinking about when you worked on your collage.

At last—welcome to the 20th century! Your journey through the history of art has taken you through many time periods and to many different lands. It has introduced you to artists and artworks from many different cultures. But, at last, you arrive in your own century. And what a century it has been so far!

There have been two world wars, and countless small wars and confrontations. The invention of the electric light by Thomas Edison has not only brightened the night, but also led to numerous other conveniences like television and radio. Cars, airplanes, and nuclear power have been invented and developed.

Women have earned the right to vote, and Neil Armstrong has placed his shoe print on the airless surface of the Moon. As we enter the last decade of this amazing century, we can only wonder at the possibilities and events of the future. Will we travel to Mars? Will we harness the power of the sun for energy? Will humankind finally learn to live in peace and harmony?

And what about visual art? Will drawing, painting, and sculpture be replaced by forms we cannot even imagine? Who can say? What we can say for sure is that art, in all its many forms, will continue to be a vital part of life. For human beings must be able to express their feelings, hopes, ideas, and thoughts in a variety of ways. History tells us that one of those ways has always been through visual art.

Chapter 10
THE MODERN AGE—ART OF THE 20TH CENTURY

WORDWATCH
Industrial Revolution
Cubism
Analytical Cubism
Synthetic Cubism
avant-garde
Fauves
Abstract Expressionism
non-objective
Surrealism

A WORLD OF MACHINES

During the 19th century, there was a revolution that did not involve weapons or armies. This revolution, known as the **Industrial Revolution,** began in England and inspired the invention and development of machines to do many of the tasks that men and women had previously done. These same machines led to many 20th-century industries, such as steel production and transportation. Power sources, such as electricity, were also developed.

Scientific research also took a leap forward, as people demanded a more convenient and safer world. It was only natural that visual art and artists would be affected and influenced by these sweeping changes. After all, art reflects the culture and time in which it is created. One 19th-century invention, in particular, was to have a major effect on art and artists. That invention was photography.

As the 20th century began, many artists were still working in the traditional styles of the 19th century.

Figure 10.1. Paul Cezanne. *Ambroise Vollard.* 1899. Collection of the Petit Palais, Paris. Photo: Giraudon/Art Resource, New York.

Figure 10.2. Pablo Picasso. *Ambroise Vollard.* 1909-10. Oil on canvas, 36″ x 25½″. Collection of the Grand Palais, Paris. Photo: Giraudon/Art Resource, New York.

They still painted scenes and objects realistically, sometimes photographically. Some, however, were beginning to see new possibilities for expression in visual art. After all, why paint with photographic realism simply to record details, when the camera could do it better. Some ideas, moods, and feelings might be better expressed by using only colors, shapes, lines, values, and textures. In other words, the art elements became the subject matter. "Modern" art was about to be born!

AN "ISM" FOR EVERYONE

Look closely, for a moment, at the two works shown in Figures 10.1 and 10.2. The subject of both of these paintings is a portrait of the French art dealer, *Ambroise Vollard.* Figure 10.1 is by Cezanne. You can probably recognize his style by now. Figure 10.2 is by Picasso.

The difference in painting style between the two works is very clear. Although Cezanne has simplified shapes and used his square-like brushstrokes to give a feeling of form, his is still a fairly traditional portrait. In other words, it probably would not cause anyone to go mad if they saw it at an exhibition!

On the other hand, Picasso's version is something quite different. We can still recognize Vollard, but the image seems made up of broken fragments of glass. This painting is obviously concerned with things other than a portrait of a wealthy art collector.

The style of art that we see in the Picasso painting (Figure 10.2), is known as **Cubism. Cubism** was a style of painting that simplified and separated three-dimensional objects or forms into flat, two-dimensional shapes.

There can be little doubt that Picasso studied and learned from the paintings of Cezanne. Where Cezanne used square-like brushstrokes to divide the subject into sections, Picasso took this technique one step further. He didn't even try to make the figure look three-dimensional. We could say that Picasso's painting is more a portrait of the art elements, color and shape and how they work together, than a portrait of a man. By now, you can probably see that **Cubism** was the first big step on the way to "modern" or abstract art.

As the Cubist artists continued to paint, their style began to change once again, giving us two kinds of Cubism: **Analytical** [an•ah•LIT•i•cul] **Cubism** and **Synthetic** [sin•THET•ik] **Cubism.** How can you tell the difference? Easily. Let's make some more comparisons.

Figure 10.3 Pablo Picasso. *Three Musicians.* 1921. Oil on canvas, 80″ x 74″. The Philadelphia Museum of Art: A.E. Gallatin Collection.

Look once more at Figure 10.2 by Picasso. This painting is an excellent example of Analytical Cubism. The painting, as you can see, is made up of fragments or shapes of color and value. Some seem to be part of the head of the subject; some simply float free. Some of the fragments also appear transparent. These are all characteristics of Analytical Cubism.

A good way to remember this style is to think about the meaning of the word *analytical.* When you "analyze" something, you examine it carefully to determine how it is put together. In a way, this is what artists do who work in this style. They examine their subject and break it into more simplified parts. Even the negative or surrounding space is analyzed and shattered into shapes.

Figure 10.3 is a famous example of Synthetic Cubism. Something that is *synthetic* is not natural, but artificial. Synthetic objects are frequently made by combining other objects in new ways.

In this work, Picasso does not fracture the subjects of the painting, the three musicians, into shapes as he did in Figure 10.3. He creates, instead, new shapes that he uses to make up the musicians. In other words, the shapes of the musicians are not natural, human forms, but "synthetic" or created from the imagination of the artist.

Figure 10.4. Pablo Picasso. *La Suze.* 1912-13. Pasted paper with charcoal, 25¾″ x 19¾″. Washington University Gallery of Art. University Purchase, Kende Sale Fund, 1946.

113

Figure 10.5. Georges Braque. *Still Life: Le Jour.* 1929. Oil on canvas, 45¼″ x 57¾″. The National Gallery of Art, Washington, D.C., Chester Dale Collection.

We can still make out the shapes of the musicians in the painting, but once again the main subjects are shape, color, value, and pattern.

Some examples of Synthetic Cubism include pieces of real objects. Figure 10.4 is part drawing and part collage. The collage part is made up of pieces of newspaper and tinted paper. In this work, it is difficult to tell what part is object and what part is background. To the Cubists, background, or negative space, is as important as the positive shapes of objects.

Figures 10.5, 10.6, and 10.7, are examples of Cubist paintings—both Analytical and Synthetic. See if you can identify which is which. Your teacher will share the correct answers with you. If you can identify the works correctly, you should be very proud. Few people can identify a Cubist painting, much less tell whether it is Analytical or Synthetic!

Figure 10.6. Juan Gris. *Still Life Before an Open Window.* 1915. Oil on canvas, 45⅞″ x 35⅛″. The Philadelphia Museum of Art: Louise and Walter Arensberg Collection.

Figure 10.7. Lyonel Feininger. *Arch Tower I.* 1923-26. Oil on canvas, 24⅛″ x 18¾″. Collection Kunstmuseum, Basel, Switzerland.

The Fauves—Wild Beasts of Art

In Chapter 8 you read about the famous exhibition of 1873, in which Impressionist paintings were seen by the public for the first time. As you recall, the paintings were considered so outrageous and experimental that they supposedly drove those who saw them completely mad.

In 1873, Impressionism was considered **avant-garde** [AH•vont]. Avant-garde is a French term which simply means the latest development or style in a field. In the field of art, avant-garde often describes those artworks that are so new and experimental no one understands them. Every art style or art movement you have read about was considered avant-garde by someone at one time or other.

In 1905 another exhibition was held in Paris. Like the previous exhibit, this one also gave a title to a new art movement. Upon leaving the exhibition, an outraged art critic exclaimed that the paintings he had just seen looked as if they had been painted by "wild beasts." The French word for wild beast is **Fauve** [FOVE].

Eager to be considered avant-garde and new, the young artists whose paintings had caused such a stir, happily took the name "Fauve" for the title of their movement. The Fauves wanted to shock people out of their old ways of looking at art. And shock them they did!

Perhaps the greatest representative of Fauvism was Henri Matisse [ON•ree mah•TEESE]. The paintings he exhibited caused a sensation. Figure 10.8, titled *The Green Stripe,* was thought to be particularly outrageous. Viewers and critics were horrified at the wild, strange colors, so unusual for a portrait. Even the background, with its vivid sections of color, was considered ridiculous. But, Matisse knew what he wanted to express, and he believed strong colors and simplified shapes expressed his feelings best.

The Fauves, like the Cubists, were interested in using the art elements of line, color, and shape to express emotions that a realistic picture could not. The Fauves exaggerated color and distorted shapes to achieve their aims.

Figure 10.9, titled *The Red Studio,* shows how far Matisse took his ideas about emotion and color. Although furniture and objects are recognizable inside the room, realistic space and perspective are ignored. Everything is red! The other colors seem to jar and vibrate against the red. It isn't hard to see that another step has been taken toward totally Abstract art. The objects that are shown in *The Red Studio* have no substance, no form, no shadows, no reflections. They are simply flat shapes, used to balance the painting. However, the title of "first

Figure 10.8. Henri Matisse. *The Green Stripe.* 1905. Oil on canvas and partly tempera, 15⅞" x 12⅞". Statens Museum fur Kunst, Copenhagen.

Figure 10.9. Henri Matisse. *The Red Studio.* 1911. Oil on canvas, 71¼" x 86¼". Collection, The Museum of Modern Art, New York. Mrs. Simon Gugenheim Fund.

abstract artist" goes to another painter from yet another "ism"—**Expressionism.** The artist was Wassily Kandinsky [WOSS•i•lee can•DEN•ski].

Expressionism

Artists continued to experiment with new and more challenging ways of expressing ideas and feelings through art. Realism was no longer the only art style. The movement known as Expressionism finally broke all ties to the real world. Expressionist artists felt free to eliminate completely recognizable subjects from their works. They wanted to work only with the art elements. Art had become **Abstract.**

Figure 10.10, titled *Composition 238. Bright Circle,* by Kandinsky is an arrangement or composition of art elements. We can identify shapes, lines, and colors, but no realistic objects. Kandinsky is relying on these elements and their careful arrangement to carry the painting's expressive message.

LOOKING AT ABSTRACT ART

Many people are uncomfortable and frustrated by **Non-Objective** or Abstract art. Unlike a peaceful landscape by Constable or a portrait by Rembrandt, in which we can recognize the subjects of the paintings, abstract artworks like Kandinsky's seems strange and beyond understanding. Some people will never like abstract art. And that is fine. All that is required is an open mind and a willingness to understand. One way to grow in appreciation and understanding of anything is to read about it and, in the case of art, look at as many examples as possible. Right now, you are doing both. You may never "like" Abstract art, but you can learn to understand its purpose and history.

Look once more at Kandinsky's painting. Try not to judge—just look. Notice the range of colors and values he has used. How many kinds of lines can you find? Are they all straight? Look only at the colors, shapes, and lines. How would you describe the mood of this painting? Is it sad? Scary? Cheerful? Why? Does it remind you of music? What do you think is the focal point of the composition?

Abstract Expressionism

As the 20th century unfolded, other art styles developed. Still others, like Expressionism, changed. A new word was added to Expressionism. The art style and movement started by Kandinsky was now called **Abstract**

Figure 10.10. Wassily Kandinsky. *Composition No. 238:* Bright Circle. 1921. Oil on canvas, 54¼" x 70¾". Yale University Art Gallery, New Haven, Connecticut. Gift of Collection Société Anonyme.

Figure 10.11. Jackson Pollock. *Blue Poles.* 1952. Oil, enamel and aluminum paint on canvas, 210.4 cm. x 468.8 cm. Austrailian National Gallery, Canberra.

Expressionism. Many artists were attracted to this art movement, especially American artists.

Abstract Expressionism removed all boundaries and restrictions from what could be painted and how it could be painted. The one word to remember when you want to describe Abstract Expressionism is "individualism." Most artists of this movement created their own way of painting, hardly looking at what had come before or at what other artists were doing. Abstract Expressionists were interested in expressing personal feelings with great intensity, in any way possible, no matter how outrageous it might seem at the time.

American artist Jackson Pollock was one of the most famous Abstract Expressionists. Figure 10.11 shows a typical Pollock painting. Even the geometric shapes of Kandinsky's (Figure 10.10) have now disappeared. We are left with slashing lines and splashes of color. These are created by the drips and swirls made when the artist pours paint directly from a can.

Pollock would tack large pieces of canvas to the floor of his studio. With paint can in hand he would rapidly fling and drip paint over the surface of the canvas. He moved quickly from one side of the canvas to the other, working frantically as he moved.

Why paint this way? Why not use a brush as other artists had done for centuries? Pollock was a true believer in the value of Abstract Expressionism. He felt that by holding the colors in a can in his hand and moving around all sides of the canvas, he could express more intensely his innermost feelings and emotions. He believed this method of working brought him closer to the painting. He could, as he often said, be "in" the painting, not just stand in front of it.

If you look closely at a Pollock work, you cannot miss the energy and movement he used to create these paintings. Your eyes must follow the curving drips and spilled splashes of color. Although, at first, you may think all

117

Figure 10.12. Salvador Dali. *The Persistence of Memory.* 1931. Oil on canvas, 9½″ x 13″. Collection, The Museum of Modern Art, New York. Given anonymously.

Figure 10.13. René Magritte. *Time Transfixed.* 1938. Oil on canvas. 147 cm. x 98.7 cm. The Art Institute of Chicago. The Joseph Winterbotham Collection.

Figure 10.14. Constantin Brancusi. *Bird in Space.* 1928. Bronze (unique cast), 54″ x 54″ x 8½″ x 6½″. Collection, The Museum of Modern Art, New York. Given anonymously.

Pollock's paintings look alike, they don't. Each one has its own mood and feeling. Sometimes bright slashes of red conflict with white and black. Sometimes the mood is quieter, calmer.

The best way to enjoy a Pollock painting is not to look for objects in its tangled lines, but let your mind react to the mood and emotions you feel when you first see the work. As you take more time to study the work—and you should—you can begin to discover why the painting makes you feel the way you do. Is it the color, the movement, or something else?

If you approach all new, avant-garde artworks in this way, you will start to understand and enjoy them more. Your obligation as a viewer isn't to like everything you see, but to give the artist and the artwork a chance to communicate. Looking at art takes both time and patience.

Surrealism

During the 1920s and 1930s, another art movement was established. This movement, known as **Surrealism,** did not reject the realistic painting of scenes and objects, as did the Expressionists. **Surrealism,** which means "super real," uses the dream world of the subconscious and imagination as subject matter. Objects and scenes in a Surrealist painting are usually painted with photographic realism. But, the artist may place these objects in an unexpected environment, as in Figure 10.12, or alter them in some way, as in Figure 10.13.

Surrealism has always been a popular style of painting. We enjoy the strange combinations of objects or tricky changes that the artists create. Surrealism lives on today in science fiction art, on posters, and on record-album covers.

In a later chapter you will read about and see some examples of computer art. Don't be surprised if it reminds you of Surrealistic art. Like the dream landscapes of Dali (Figure 10.12) and Magritte (Figure 10.13), Surrealism is timeless.

20TH-CENTURY SCULPTURE

Let's try an experiment. Look closely at the sculpture shown in Figure 10.14. It is by Constantin Brancusi [CON • stan • teen bran • COO • see]. As you study this abstract work, make a list of descriptive words that you think express the work. For example—"smooth," "curving." What others can you think of?

[?] This sculpture, although abstract, was inspired by a real object. Looking at your list of descriptive words, can you tell what it was?

Brancusi made several sculptures of the original object. Each time he simplified the form a little more. He wanted to reduce the form until it expressed the "essence," or basic nature of the object.

Have you decided what the original object is? It is a bird. The title of this sculpture is *Bird in Space*. Like Abstract Expressionist painters, Brancusi reduced and finally eliminated all realistic form from his work. What remains is a very expressive image of what it means and feels like to soar through space like a bird. It would be difficult to find a sculpture that expressed it better.

Like the painters of this century, the sculptors used a variety of styles to express their ideas. The pure abstract form of Brancusi was but one style.

Figure 10.15 is by Jacques Lipchitz [jock LIP•chis]. What do you think was the inspiration for this sculpture? Compare it with Brancusi's bird. It is not quite as abstract. We identify a head and eyes. We see forms that seem to make up a body. The title of the work is simply *Figure*. If it reminds you a little of a Cubist painting, you are very observant. Lipchitz was greatly influenced by the work of the Cubists.

Figure is over seven feet tall. Its strange, bulky forms tower over the heads of most visitors. Like some alien relic, this sculpture both attracts and disturbs.

Along with the traditional materials of sculpture, like marble, bronze, and wood, 20th-century sculptors began to use materials, such as plastic, that were products of the modern age. Sculptor Naum Gabo [nam GAH•bow] was noted for his "space-age" sculptures made of clear sheets of plastic. Figure 10.16, titled *Space Construction C.*, is an example of his work made from this material. Although this sculpture seems very modern and new to us, it was made in the 1920s!

The transparency of plastic allowed Gabo to take full advantage of the three-dimensional aspect of sculpture. As the viewer walks around the sculpture, he or she is given an ever-changing view of shifting planes and edges. Some planes and edges from one side show through to the other side. This creates the illusion of movement, even though the sculpture itself doesn't move.

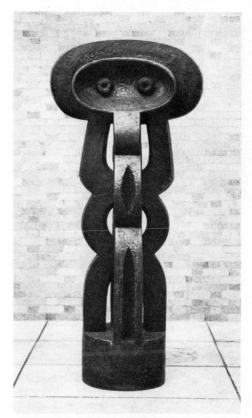

Figure 10.15. Jacques Lipchitz. *Figure.* 1926-30. Bronze (cast 1937), 85¼" x 38⅝". Collection, The Museum of Art, New York. Van Gogh Purchase Fund.

Figure 10.16. Naum Gabo. *Space Construction, C.* Work in plastic, 39" x 40". Yale University Art Gallery. Gift of Katherine S. Dreier for the Collection Société Anonyme.

Pablo Picasso. 1954. Vallauris.
© Arnold Newman, Photographer.

BORN: 1881
DIED: 1973
BIRTHPLACE: Barcelona, Spain

Figure 10.17. Pablo Picasso. *Guitar and Wine Glass.* 1912. College and charcoal, 18⅞" x 14⅜". Bequest of Marion Koogler McNay, Marion Koogler McNay Art Museum. San Antonio, Texas.

Master of Modern Art

Pablo Picasso is considered by many to be the greatest artist of the 20th century. He is as famous in this century as Michelangelo and Leonardo were in the 16th century. Picasso's importance lay not only in his art, but also in his innovation and experimentation. He broke rules, so that new truths could be revealed, new messages communicated through art.

Picasso grew up in a home of art. His father taught drawing. It became obvious at an early date that Picasso was a very gifted young man. He drew and painted like a person of much greater age and experience. By the time he made his first visit to Paris in 1900, he was already a master draftsman.

Like so many other young artists, Picasso went to Paris to learn and to create. It must have been an exciting time to be young, talented, and living in the center of the art world. But, lack of money and social standing caused him to become depressed. Picasso found himself more and more sympathetic to the poor and disadvantaged he saw all around him. This mood of depression is reflected in a series of paintings in which the predominant color is blue. This period in Picasso's life and the paintings he created are known as the "blue" period.

By 1904 Picasso had adjusted himself to the art world of Paris, and his mood had taken a more positive turn. He became interested in circus performers and used them as subjects of his paintings. In these paintings his colors are rose-like and much happier. These works form the "rose" period.

Although Picasso absorbed influences from many artists, one association in particular was most important. This was his friendship with Georges Braque [BROCK], the other "father of Cubism." Their innovative work changed art forever.

Did you learn

- The definition of these words and phrases: Industrial Revolution; Cubism; Analytical Cubism; Synthetic Cubism; avant-garde; Fauve; Abstract Expressionism; non-objective; Surrealism?
- The difference between Analytical Cubism and Synthetic Cubism?
- One characteristic of the Fauve style of painting?
- The name of a Fauve artist?
- Why photography had an influence on modern painting?
- The first artist of abstract painting?
- Why Pollock painted on the floor of his studio with cans of paint rather than brushes?
- The names of two abstract sculptors?
- The two artists responsible for inventing Cubism?

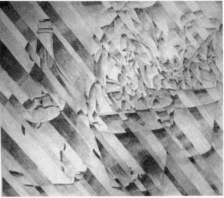

Student work.

Understanding and Evaluating

- In a one- or two-page essay, apply the four stages of art criticism to the Jackson Pollock painting in Figure 10.11. Review the stages listed in Chapter 3.
- Visit your library and research the life of one artist mentioned in this chapter. Write what you have learned in the form of an imaginary "interview" with the artist. Someone reading your interview should be able to learn several new facts about the artist.

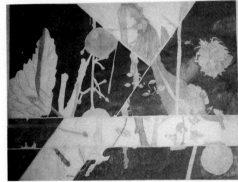

Student work.

Seeing and Creating

- Select several natural objects or plants. Abstract or simplify their shapes and use them to create a new composition. Divide the negative space surrounding the objects into shapes. Use pencils, crayons, or felt markers to make your drawing.
- Draw a still life lightly with a pencil on white drawing paper. With a straight edge, lightly draw vertical, horizontal, or diagonal lines across the entire drawing. Select two colors. You may use colored pencils or watercolors. Begin by filling in a stripe with one color. When you come to a line that is part of the still life, switch colors. You may leave some parts of the stripes white. Your finished work should resemble a Cubist painting. Can you tell which type of Cubism your still life would be?

Unit III
PRESERVING OUR ART HERITAGE

Montreal Museum of Art. Montreal, Canada.
Photograph by John Smithers.

Have you ever visited a museum? If you have, you may have wondered who found all the things in the glass cases, who arranged them, and who decided when other pieces were to be added. Most museums, whether they are filled with artworks or dinosaur bones, have certain things in common. Perhaps the most important is their main purpose—the preservation and display of objects of historical, scientific, or artistic interest and value.

When you consider all the art objects you have read about in this book and the millions of others that have been discovered over the years, it isn't surprising that art museums, whether large or small, play an important part in preserving our art heritage. In the following chapter, you will learn about some very important museums and the roles they play in preserving and exhibiting art treasures. You will also be introduced to some of the jobs that are necessary to maintain a museum and its valuable collections. Much of a museum's business is carried on "behind the scenes," behind those doors you have seen marked "for museum personnel only." You will meet those individuals trained in conserving and restoring fragile artworks, so they can be exhibited and enjoyed by the public.

The people who work in museums take great pride in the many jobs they perform. They want to provide you with many hours of enjoyment and interest and to help you learn more about artworks and artifacts. As you read the following chapter, you might decide that a job in a museum is just what you would like to do. Museums provide a variety of career opportunities for people with an interest in visual art. Maybe one of them is just right for you!

Chapter 11

FINDERS AND KEEPERS—THE ROLE OF ARCHAEOLOGISTS AND MUSEUMS

They had been digging all day in the blazing sun of the desert, stopping only long enough for a drink of water. The young Englishman in charge, after wiping the sweat from his forehead, pulled his hat lower on his head to shield his eyes from the sun's merciless glare. He was becoming more and more discouraged and short-tempered by the lack of progress. There seemed to be nothing here, after all.

Suddenly, one of the Egyptian workmen shouts for the digging to stop. His shovel has struck something hard. The young Englishman rushes to look with the others. Sure enough, as gradually more sand is carefully swept away, a step appears. Then two. Then sixteen!

Descending down to the last step, the young Englishman faces a wall. But there is something odd about this wall. Part of it is covered with plaster. Hairline cracks in the plaster reveal the outline of a door. Stamped on the door is a seal. It is one of the ancient hieroglyphs that the Egyptians used to identify their king, the pharoah. On closer inspection, the Englishman can see that the seal is unbroken. Whatever lies beyond the plaster door has not been seen for thousands of years!

The workmen are jumping with excitement. At last, something to show for months of grueling work in the sun. They are eager to break through the ancient door.

Finally, the plaster and stone of the ancient door give way to let the excited workers peer into the dark of a long tunnel. The air is stale, having been sealed from the outside for centuries. Filled with rubble and sand, the tunnel is cleared at last, only to end in another wall!

Like the first one, this wall shows the outline of a door. Again, it is sealed with the royal symbol of the pharoah. Trembling with excitement, the Englishman breaks open a small hole in the top of the door. He yells for a light. A lighted candle is quickly passed along by eager hands. Taking the candle, he holds it up to the opening in the door. The hot, dry air of timeless centuries rushes out of the hole, as if it had been sealed in a bottle. The candle flickers and almost goes out.

As the light reaches into the opening, the Englishman's eyes adjust to the gloom, and he glimpses objects. From the surrounding dark, emerge the shapes of strange animals and statues— and gold. Everywhere the dim light of the candle reaches, there is the glimmer of pure gold!

WORDWATCH
archaeology
potsherd
museum director
Board of Trustees
curator
conservator
docents

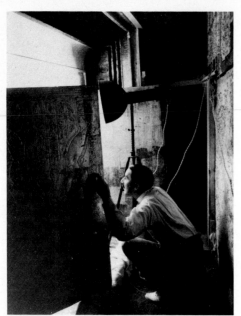

Figure 11.1. Photograph of Howard Carter looking into the second shrine of the Tomb of Tut-ankh-amun, Thebes. Photography by Egyptian Expedition, The Metropolitan Museum of Art.

For minutes he stares, unable to speak. An excited voice asks, "Can you see anything?" Regaining his voice, the Englishman replies, "Yes, wonderful things."

The short story you have just read probably sounds like a scene from a Hollywood movie. There have been many made about the exploits of fearless archaeologists [ar•key•OL•o•gists] and their thrilling adventures in exotic lands in search of buried treasure. But, this story is true—not Hollywood make-believe.

The young Englishman in the story is Howard Carter (Figure 11.1). He was the archaeologist who discovered the tomb of the Egyptian Pharoah Tutankhamun [TOO•tank•ah•mun], or "King Tut," as he is known.

Events like the one you just read about are certainly exciting, and lucky and hard-working archaeologists do make astounding discoveries. But, most archaeologists work long hard hours in difficult conditions without ever finding a treasure like that found by Howard Carter in 1922. The work of archaeology, although interesting, is usually not glamorous.

THE FINDERS—ARCHAEOLOGISTS

Archaeology [ar•key•OL•o•gee] is the science of uncovering and studying artifacts, inscriptions, monuments, and artworks of past cultures and civilizations. Many, if not most, of the ancient art objects you see in museums and reproduced in this book were found by archeologists (Figure 11.2). Working for years at one site in some remote section of the world, these dedicated men and women must be well-trained in their science.

They must have great patience, for archeology is not a science for the quick and careless.

Howard Carter had worked in the area of his great find for almost six years before he discovered the tomb. At times, he must have been so close that he stood on top of it. Before he located Tut's tomb, 200,000 tons of sand and rock had to be removed! No, archaeology is not for the impatient nor for the lazy. Without archaeology, we would know little of our past and our heritage.

At present, throughout the world there are hundreds of "digs" or archaeological sites being investigated. None may yield the treasures of a Tutankhamun tomb, but each will expand in some way our understanding of the past.

Like pieces of a scattered jigsaw puzzle, each artifact, each inscription, fills another space in the puzzle of the past. From these pieces, archaeologists can tell us not

Figure 11.2. *Rosetta Stone.* Reproduced by courtesy of the Trustees of the British Museum.

only what objects people used and treasured, but also what kind of life they led. Were their lives filled with pleasure and joy, or with pain and sorrow?

Archaeology brings the past closer to the present and prepares us for the future. To hold in your hand a simple clay cup made thousands of years ago by some unknown artist is to come as close to time travel as may be possible.

Archaeologists help put dates on objects and events. From a broken piece of pottery, called a **potsherd** [POT • shurd], an archaeologist can tell when the pot was made, the people that made it, and whether it was broken in the past or more recently.

Documenting the location of objects is extremely important to good archaeology. In the past, and unfortunately still today, people plunder archaeological sites looking for treasure. They care little about reconstructing the past from the objects they find. Many of the sacred burial grounds of Native Americans in the Southwest have been destroyed in this way.

These thoughtless individuals steal not only the priceless artifacts, but also the history and heritage of Native American culture. By removing ancient objects without first documenting their locations and their positions in relation to other artifacts, destroys forever a valuable piece of history.

Trained archaeologists carefully plot each artifact on a grid, photograph or draw the object in place, and only then remove it for study. The positions in which objects are found tell archaeologists and historians a great deal about the how the object was used. If you ever find a burial mound or collection of artifacts, don't remove them. Contact a state archaeologist or the Department of Archaeology or Anthropology at the nearest college or university. They will know how to document and investigate the find. To do otherwise, is to be, as the Native Americans say, a "thief of time."

Where to Look?

How do archaeologists know where to look for artifacts? A good question. Most begin by reading and studying. Ancient records and other artifacts sometimes provide clues as to where to look. Even a myth can provide a vital clue.

One of the most interesting stories of another great archaeological find is that of ancient Troy. Heinrich Schliemann [HINE • rick SCHLEE • mahn], a gifted amateur archaeologist, made this interesting find.

Schliemann had read an ancient Greek poem about a war between two kingdoms, one of which was the

Figure 11.3. Portrait of Schliemann. Photo: Giraudon/Art Resource, New York.

Gate at Mycenae. Photo: Foto Marburg/Art Resource, New York.

mythical Troy. Most people thought that the events described in the poem were fiction. Not Schliemann. He felt that though part of the poem might be imaginary, the main events were historical. He set out to find the fabled city of Troy.

Like a good detective, Schliemann matched locations on a present-day map with clues mentioned in the poem. Sure enough, they began to match. Finally, after many years of struggle, Schliemann found a great treasure. He discovered many magnificent and very ancient artifacts from a period in Greek history that had almost been unknown (Figure 11.3).

The hope for a discovery like that of Schliemann's and of Carter's continues to attract people to the science of archaeology. If you don't mind living in very rough conditions in remote and dangerous locations or working long hours on tedious assignments, archaeology might be for you.

There are many archaeological societies that welcome amateurs of all ages. These societies usually have what's called a "field school" during the summer. At this time, all members can explore a site that has been identified as of historical interest. Everyone gets to participate in the various activities of archaeology—from documenting to digging.

THE KEEPERS—MUSEUMS

What public activity do you think attracts the largest number of people every year? Football? Baseball? Rock concerts? You may be surprised to discover that museums attract the most people every year! No longer the stuffy, unwelcoming places they once were, museums have become much more attractive and interesting places to the general public.

Surprisingly, museums are a fairly new idea. For example, the British Museum in London, England, was not established until 1753. Before that time, its magnificent collections of ancient artifacts and artworks were part of private collections. These were simply unavailable for the general public to see and enjoy.

Today, museums of all types are so numerous that we take them for granted. Even small towns and cities usually have at least one museum. Large cities, like New York, Mexico City, and Paris, have some of the greatest museums in the world. Visitors to these cities usually feel that visits to museums are an important part of their trip.

The United States is most fortunate in having some of the greatest art museums in the world. This may be surprising since, compared to Europe, our country is still young. Many of the collections that now form the main exhibits of the Metropolitan Museum in New York, (Figure 11.4), the National Gallery in Washington, D.C., and numerous other museums throughout the country, were once part of private collections. These collections were built by men and women of great wealth and power. Frequently, these collections were left to state governments or national governments for the purpose of starting a museum. Paintings, sculptures, and precious artifacts that once were only for the eyes of a wealthy few can now be enjoyed by thousands of visitors each year.

Museums, especially very large ones, employ hundreds of people in a variety of jobs. Let's meet a few of these people and find out what they do.

Museum Director and Board of Trustees

The **museum director** is the head of the museum. He or she answers only to a Board of Trustees about what should be bought and how much should be paid for it. The **Board of Trustees** is a group of individuals who control the finances or money of the museum. The board is usually made up of outstanding members of the community or those who have made large donations to the museum in the past.

The museum director works with a staff of assistants and secretaries. The director oversees the buying of new works for the museum, as well as organizing special fund-raising activities. Today, museums need a great deal of money to buy important works of art. Fund raising has become one of the most important tasks of the museum director.

Curator

The **curator** [CURE • ray • tor] is the individual who is usually trained in a special area of art history or archaeology. Some museums have such varied collections that they have a curator or curators for each part of their collection. For example, there will be one curator for Greek antiquities [an • TIC • kwah • tees] and another for modern painting. Curators are responsible for the correct evaluation of new works bought by the museum and for the information about the works that will appear in museum catalogues and on exhibit labels. Curators of large collections must have a thorough knowledge of art history.

Conservation and Restoration

Museums of the size of the Metropolitan Museum in New York maintain a large staff of **conservators** [con •

Figure 11.4. *The Metropolitan Museum of Art, New York City.*

SER • vah • tors]. These individuals are trained to conserve and restore old and fragile works of art.

Frequently, when archaeologists uncover a rare object, it is broken into many pieces. Working with a museum's conservation staff, the archeologists can help reassemble the object. If parts are missing, a well-trained staff can reconstruct copies of the missing pieces. When a piece has been reconstructed, the label next to it will identify it as a partial reconstruction.

The preservation and conservation departments of most large museums are incredible places, looking more like hospital operating rooms than museums. There are X-ray machines, vacuum chambers, and numerous chemicals for cleaning and preserving.

A huge clump of corroded metal pulled from the ocean floor can be separated into individual, shining coins by submerging it in the correct chemical solutions.

A painting of questionable authenticity can be X-rayed to determine whether it was painted by the artist who signed it. Sometimes, X-raying can reveal unexpected treasures. Many famous artists, before they become prosperous, save money by painting over old canvasses. Often first paintings can be seen by X-rays.

Figure 11.5. Photograph of the Anthropological Museum in Mexico.

Exhibitions

When you visit a museum, you usually see the exhibits arranged in cases or hung on walls. Small items, or those of great age or value, are displayed in special cases in which the climate is precisely controlled. The temperature in these cases is kept to an exact degree. This prevents changes in temperature and humidity from destroying rare items.

The arrangement of exhibits within a museum is the job of the exhibition staff. This staff makes sure that the art and artifacts are well lighted and can be easily seen by visitors. If large pieces of sculpture are placed in the central spaces of the museum, they must make sure that there is walking space around the works. You have only to imagine the horror of a visitor backing into a priceless work of art to understand how carefully walking space must be considered!

The exhibition staff is also responsible for the attractive design of the entire exhibition. The arrangement of the exhibition should be as much a work of art as the objects, themselves.

In the past, museums were not very imaginative about the way they displayed their treasures. Today, museums, like the Anthropological Museum in Mexico City (Figure 11.5) exhibit artworks in more exciting and unusual ways. These exhibitions are more like dramatic stage sets than museum exhibits.

Education Programs

A very recent trend in museums is the development of special education programs for the public, especially for children. Most museums are interested in reaching as many members of the public as possible. An excellent way to do this is to offer special guided tours and education programs. Specially trained tour guides for the museum's exhibitions are called **docents**. Education programs can take many forms. They may be a series of films and lectures offered at special times, or demonstrations and workshops in which visitors watch and participate.

A number of museums offer special programs for children. These museums even send docents into the public schools to talk about the museum's exhibitions (Figure 11.6). They also give special guided tours to classes when they visit the museum on a field trip. You, yourself, might have had a chance to see an exhibit at your local museum.

Along with these education programs, museums frequently publish books and catalogs just for children. These are usually very interesting and entertaining. They are filled with games and activities that help students understand the museum's exhibitions.

Figure 11.6. Museums have programs designed especially for students. Docents, or trained guides give tours and educate visitors about the exhibits.

Security

Filled with wonderful, priceless works of art and objects of great historical value, museums must be very careful about how people view these treasures. As much as we might like to hold an ancient Egyptian necklace in our hands or touch the expressive surface of a Rodin sculpture, museums cannot allow us to do this. While one person touching artworks and artifacts might not cause damage, thousands would! And remember, visitors to museums every year number well into the thousands.

Museums must set restrictions to protect their valuable resources, so that everyone has a chance to enjoy them for many years to come. For that reason one of the most important jobs in a museum involves security. The security staff, including the director and museum guards, must be constantly aware of what is going on at all times.

Most museum guards are not there to prevent your visit from being enjoyable, but to see that the museum exhibits are protected from theft and vandalism. The guards are usually very friendly and helpful in answering questions about the museum and the exhibits. But, if they tell you not to touch something or not to stand too near a work, you must follow directions, or you might be asked to leave.

HOW TO VISIT A MUSEUM

Here are a few basic suggestions for visiting a museum. If you follow these suggestions, your visit will be more enjoyable.

Before visiting a particular exhibit, try to find out something about its history or what kinds of objects will be displayed. Are they works of art from the Renaissance or ancient coins from Rome? If the visit is part of a school field trip, your teacher will probably give you special materials to help you understand better what you will see. This lets you spend more time looking and enjoying.

A visit to a museum can be an exciting event, especially if your classmates are going too. But, museums, like libraries, are special places. Loud talk, laughter, and rough behavior are not appreciated by other visitors who have come to enjoy the exhibits. You should always be considerate of others when you visit a museum.

Follow the museum rules and the directions of the guides and guards. If your behavior should cause damage to a work of art, you and your parents would be responsible. Courteous behavior will avoid accidents and make your visit a pleasant one.

Many museums have excellent gift shops where they sell books, catalogs, posters, postcards, and slides of the artworks and exhibits. Ask your teacher and parents beforehand whether you may purchase a souvenir of your visit to the museum. These reminders of your visit can be enjoyed for many years. You might create your own collection of souvenirs from museum visits.

Whether you purchase something or not, there is little doubt that you will remember your visit. Museums are wonderful places where you can see with your own eyes the fabulous treasures of lost civilizations. We can gaze into the faces of dead kings and marvel at the good fortune that allowed an ancient Roman glass cup to remain unbroken for thousands of years. Best of all, you can see and appreciate the continuing importance of art to human beings.

The Rewards of Patience

Howard Carter was the youngest son of an artist who specialized in the painting of animals. He had eight brothers and sisters. However, it was young Howard who showed talent for drawing.

His father's friend and patron, Lord Amherst, saw young Carter's drawings. Lord Amherst thought that Carter might be able to help make copies of Egyptian drawings for a professor of ancient Egyptian history. The drawings so pleased the professor that he invited Carter to accompany him to Egypt on his next expedition. Carter was eighteen years old.

Of course, Howard Carter took to the life of an archeologist like a fish takes to water. Besides making dozens of detailed drawings of wall paintings and artifacts found during the excavations, he took the time to learn all he could about proper methods of archaeology and documentation. He also learned to speak Egyptian and to understand the customs of the country. By the age of twenty-six, Carter was expert enough to be hired as Inspector-in-Chief for the Monuments of Egypt and Nubia.

In 1917 Carter met Lord Carnarvon, an Englishman of great wealth who was also a passionate amateur archaeologist. At Carter's suggestion, Lord Carnarvon agreed to finance the search for the tomb of the Pharoah, Tutankhamun.

Carter and his team of diggers moved tons of earth for many years before they finally located the tomb of the nineteen-year-old pharoah. What made the find so remarkable was that it was almost completely undisturbed. Most of the other tombs in the Valley of the Kings in Egypt had been robbed centuries ago. This was the first one ever found that was filled with fabulous artifacts, including a solid gold sarcophagus [sar COF ah gus] or coffin weighing several tons!

The tomb was filled with so many wonderful objects that Carter and his crew took another ten years just to record and pack all the items for transfer to Cairo. "Tut's" tomb still stands as the single greatest archaeological find in the world.

BORN: 1874
DIED: 1939
BIRTHPLACE: London, England

Figure 11.7. Photo of King Tut's tomb as found by Carter. Photo credit: The Metropolitan Museum of Art, New York.

Student work.

Did you learn

- The definitions of these words and phrases: archaeology; potshard; museum director; Board of Trustees; curator; conservator; docents?
- Why it is important not to move artifacts until they are photographed, drawn, and documented in place?
- What the Native Americans call people who steal artifacts from the burial ground? Why?
- Where many museums get their first collections?
- Why conservation is important to museum collections?
- What role docents play in a museum?

Understanding and Evaluating

- Congratulations! You have just been appointed curator of a new museum collection of 20th-century painting. You must prepare a short catalog of three works which you have selected. Your catalog must describe each work and present some information about the artists. It is your job to convince the Board of Trustees and the museum director to purchase these works. You may choose your works from those in this book.
- Imagine yourself a worker with Howard Carter in Egypt. Write a short story about an event you witnessed during the expedition. You may wish to read some other accounts of this famous find. The important thing is to use your imagination. Did you know that there was a rumor that the tomb had a curse on it?

Seeing and Creating

- Make a painting in the Egyptian style, using tempera or acrylic paint. Study the images of Egyptian gods and pharoahs and the way in which they are painted. [CAUTION: Acrylic paint is permanent. Use protective clothing, if necessary.]
- Select a three-dimensional object and make an ink illustration of its shape and decoration for a museum catalog. Be as accurate as possible in your drawing. You may use water-based felt-tip pens.

Part Two
COMMUNICATING WITH ART

Human beings have used visual art as a method of communication for a very long time. In fact, the use of images for communication is older than the use of words.

Part of learning about visual art is learning to use it as a tool for communicating. Just as we improve our understanding and use of language by reading, speaking, and writing, we improve our ability to communicate with art by looking at a wide variety of artworks expressing a range of emotions, moods, and ideas.

We also learn about communicating with art by making art. By trying out for ourselves the various ways to express a feeling or impression, we can learn to use visual art for our own purposes. In some cases, it is easier to express personal emotions or moods with art than with language. This is both the mystery and wonder of visual art.

Just as knowledge of words and grammar is essential to the proper and expressive use of language, so knowledge of the art elements and principles of design is essential to effective and expressive communication through visual art.

In Book One of this series you were introduced to both art elements and design principles. A review of these elements and principles will help you to understand Part Two of this book.

Unit Four covers the main themes or ideas of visual art and how you may use them in your own artworks. You will have an opportunity to see how other artists, using a wide variety of materials and techniques, have expressed these universal themes in art. We will also examine how artists use the art elements and design principles to express and arrange their themes.

REVIEWING THE ART ELEMENTS

The art elements are the ingredients of art. They are what artists use to put together a work of art. They are rarely used alone, but frequently in combination. The elements of art are line, color, value, shape, form, space, and texture.

Line

A line is the trail left by a moving point. Lines are human-made inventions; they do not appear in the natural environment. What we see as lines in nature are really edges, cracks, ridges, or scratches. Because as human beings we like to name things, we call these natural marks—lines.

Lines come in many different forms—thick, thin, jagged, smooth, curved, fast, slow, or broken. They also can go in different directions—up and down (vertical); side-to-side (horizontal); any other way (diagonal).

Lines serve many purposes in art:

They can
- be expressive
- enclose space
- show direction
- show movement
- make shapes
- make textures
- make values

Color

Color is an optical sensation created by light. Color can be organized. Primary colors cannot be mixed from other colors. They are red, blue, and yellow. Secondary colors are made by mixing together the primary colors—green, orange, and violet. The intermediate colors are those colors between a primary and a secondary—blue-green; yellow-orange; red-violet. Another word for color is hue.

When either white or black is mixed with colors, they create tints and shades. Tints are colors mixed with white; shades are mixed with black.

Many artists use color schemes to organize their paintings and give unity to their compositions. Color schemes also help to create a particular mood or feeling.

The main color schemes include monochromatic, analogous, and complementary. A monochromatic color scheme is made with one color plus various tints and shades of the same color. An analogous color scheme is made by using colors next to each other on the color wheel. This range can extend between a primary and secondary color. A complementary color scheme is made by using colors that are opposite each other on the color wheel—red/green; blue/orange; yellow/violet. This scheme can create a mood of tension and energy.

Value

Value is the degree of lightness or darkness in a space, form, or shape. Black-and-white drawings can have value, as well as paintings. Value is important for showing contrast and creating an illusion of a third dimension in a drawing or painting. The modulation of value is called shading.

Shape and Form

A shape is a two-dimensional image of an object. Shapes have only height and width. Shapes can be either geometric or organic (freeform). Shapes can be combined to create new shapes. Shapes can be either positive or negative. Negative shapes are created when the background is divided by positive shapes.

Forms are three-dimensional shapes. Forms can be walked around. Houses, furniture, people, and animals are all forms.

Space

Like shape, space can be positive or negative. Negative space is sometimes called background. There are many different ways to create the illusion of space on a flat or two-dimensional surface—overlapping; position (foreground, middleground, background); size change (linear perspective); aerial perspective.

Texture

Texture is the surface quality of objects. It is the way something feels. Everything has texture. Every object is rough, smooth, bumpy, or scratchy. There are two kinds of textures in art. Actual or tactile texture can be experienced through both sight and touch. Visual or simulated texture is created and can only be seen.

REVIEWING THE PRINCIPLES OF DESIGN

The principles of design act as guides for the artist. They help artists put together the composition or arrangement of a work of art. The principles of design are unity, balance, variety, repetition, emphasis, rhythm, movement, and proportion. Like the art elements, the principles of design are often used in combination.

Unity and Balance

A work of art that has unity appears to be whole. The art elements, subject matter, and materials appear to belong together.

A balanced art composition appears to have an equal arrangement of elements. There are two kinds of visual balance: symmetrical (formal) and asymmetrical (informal). Symmetrical balance is an arrangement that is the same on both sides of a central line or axis. Asymmetrical balance is not equal in proportion of elements. There will be no central axis.

Variety—Repetition—Emphasis

Variety of art elements, subjects, or materials is used to create interest and contrast in a work of art. The opposite of variety is repetition, where an element, subject, or material is repeated. When variety and repetition are balanced, they are complimentary.

Emphasis calls attention to a certain part of a visual composition. This area of emphasis is called the focal point or point of emphasis. Artists create focal points in a variety of ways.

Rhythm and Movement

In a two-dimensional artwork like a painting or drawing, an illusion of movement and rhythm can be created through the repetition of art elements. Art works that display actual or real motion are called **kinetic**.

Proportion

The relative size of objects is an important consideration for artists. Proportion refers to the size of one part to another part. Scale, on the other hand, is a size comparison made against a common standard. For example, a chair designed for the average-size human. Proportion and scale can be altered in artworks to create particular moods and emotions.

We often speak about the universal quality of visual art. Human beings, from every time and from every culture, have felt the need to express themselves through some form of visual art. Interestingly, the subjects of this expression can be organized into certain basic topics or **themes**.

Human beings, working, playing, and relaxing, are themes which have attracted the attention and interest of artists throughout the ages. There are a number of other popular art themes which you will explore in the following chapters. You might want to use some of these themes in your own artworks. You will see examples of how these themes have been expressed by a variety of artists using a range of art forms and art media.

Unit IV
ART THEMES

Chapter 12
THE HUMAN CONDITION

WORDWATCH
brayer
folk art
slip
woodcut
stucco

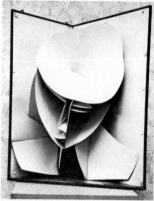

Figure 12.1. Naum Gabo. *Head of a Woman.* 1917-20. Construction in celluloid and metal, 24½″ x 19¼″ x 14″. Collection, The Museum of Modern Art, New York. Purchase.

Figure 12.2. Mary Cassatt. *Head of a Girl.* c.1904. Watercolor on paper, 17″ x 13½″. Marion Koogler McNay Art Museum, San Antonio, Texas. Bequest of Marion Koogler McNay.

One theme that artists return to time and again is that of the life and activities of human beings or the human condition. Working, resting, laughing, crying, playing, fighting—all are part of the human condition, and all have provided inspiration for artists.

THE EXPRESSIVE FACE

Portraits carry a special power. Whether we recognize someone in a portrait is not as important as that we recognize a human face. There is something about the face that is more fascinating than any other subject in art. Throughout the centuries, artists have represented that unique combination of shapes, edges, spaces, and textures that make up a human face. They recreate the human face in an endless variety of materials and techniques. Even when abstracted to its most basic elements, we recognize that familiar symmetry (Figure 12.1).

Perhaps more than any other subject, a portrait can express a wide range of ideas, moods, and feelings. In this chapter you will discover the work of some artists who have used the human face for expression and communication. As you read about and study these works, pay close attention to the art form used (drawing, painting, or printing) and to the choice of media (watercolor, pencil, or charcoal).

Many artists, especially those interested in portraits, sketch people all the time. They never leave their studios without taking along a small sketchbook. This is a very good habit for you to remember. If you really want to improve your drawing, you must practice. Having a small sketchbook with you allows you to catch expressions, scenes, and objects that can provide information and inspiration for later works. The quick sketch can be more successful in capturing a fleeting expression than a drawing that takes much longer.

Figure 12.2, *Head of a Girl,* is just such a sketch. Artist Mary Cassatt has captured, with a few quick strokes of her watercolor brush, the thoughtful expression on a little girl's face. And although the artist might later wish to make a more detailed portrait study in oils, it is doubtful that it could be more expressive and charming than this spontaneous sketch. Can you see the outline of the large hat? How would the portrait change if Cassatt had finished all the details of the hat? In your opinion, would it improve the drawing? Why, or why not?

138

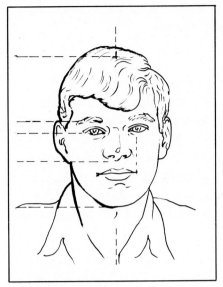

Figure 12.3. Full face.

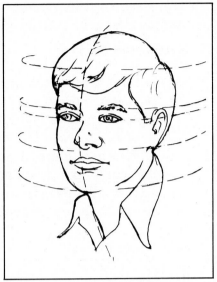

Figure 12.4. ¾ view of the head.

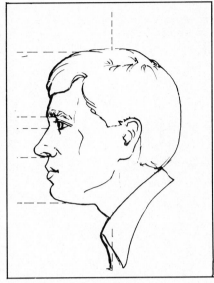

Figure 12.5. Head in profile.

Something to Try:

- Make quick portrait sketches of friends or family members, using watercolor or India ink and a brush ©️ in place of a pen. [CAUTION: India ink is permanent. Wear protective clothing if necessary.] Don't be too concerned with achieving an exact likeness. This takes practice. Try to capture the person's expression. This means paying close attention to the following:

- The position of the head. Is your subject looking straight at you (full face); slightly turned away (¾ view); or in profile? The drawings in Figures 12.3, 12.4, and 12.5, give you an idea of each of these positions. Practice drawing the face from each position. Notice on the diagrams how the center or axis of the face changes for each view.

- The position of the features. Are the edges of the mouth tilted upward? What is the position and shape of the eyebrow line? Is the nose bunched with laughter?

One artist used the human face and form as a design element in a series of posters. The artist was Henri Toulouse-Lautrec [on • REE too • LOOSE • lah • TREK]. Figure 12.6 is a famous example of his work. Although the subject is obviously a portrait, it is secondary in importance to its use as a shape in a design. Notice, for example, how all shading and textures have been reduced. Everything is made into a flat, two-dimensional shape.

Figure 12.6. Henri de Toulouse-Lautrec. *Ambassadeurs: Aristide Bruant.* 1892. Color lithograph, 53″ x 36¾″. Marion Koogler McNay Art Museum, San Antonio, Texas. The Mary and Sylvan Lang Collection.

Figure 12.7. Stuart Davis. *Self-Portrait.* 1919. Oil on canvas, 22¼" x 18¼". Amon Carter Museum, Fort Worth, Texas.

The lettering, like a pattern, adds interest to the overall design. What kind of balance is used in this composition? ? Is it symmetrical or asymmetrical? What mood is expressed by this poster? Does the facial expression of the portrait add to this mood? How?

Something to Try:

• Design a poster, using a portrait as part of the composition. Try to express a particular mood in the poster. Include lettering. Design the lettering so that it helps express the mood or message of the poster. Use either tempera or acrylic paint. You may also use cut paper to create a collage. If you use paper, add small textures or details with water-based felt-tip pens. Keep your shapes flat and two-dimensional.

SELF PORTRAITS

In Chapter 8 you learned that Rembrandt used his own face in over one hundred portraits. Many artists have been inspired by the form and expression of their own features.

The popularity of self-portraits may have to do with the fact that no matter how hard we try, we can never see ourselves as others see us. Yet, we keep trying. Perhaps the self-portrait allows artists to search for answers to the mystery of their own personalities.

Figure 12.7 is a self-portrait by American artist Stuart Davis. Davis has made little effort to idealize his face. We see the face of an ordinary man, neither handsome, nor particularly ugly. What is interesting about the portrait is the way in which it is painted. Notice the heavy brushstrokes on the face and in the background. They give the face life and vitality that it wouldn't have if the artist had smoothed away the marks of the brush.

The colors used in the portrait are interesting, as well. The yellowish tint to the face completes the use of the three primary colors—red, blue, and yellow. An unusual choice for a portrait. Notice the bright green shadow around the edge of the face and along the side of the nose. Do you remember another portrait in Chapter 10 that used bright green on the face?

The use of such pure, bright colors, together with the strong, dark outline, gives this portrait great intensity and vitality.

You may recognize the individual pictured in Figure 12.8. It is the artist Vincent Van Gogh (see Chapter 9). ? Compare Van Gogh's portrait with that of Stuart Davis's. How are the brushstrokes different? Are the colors the same? How do they differ? What other similarities and differences can you find? How would you

Figure 12.8. Vincent van Gogh. *Self Portrait.* 1887. Oil on canvas mounted on wood panel, 13¾" x 10½". Detroit Institute of Arts. City of Detroit Purchase.

describe the mood in each portrait? Do you think these two artists are happy?

Something to Try:

- Using a small, hand mirror, create a self-portrait, using crayons or oil pastels. Select a color scheme that expresses something about your personality. Use the colors not only in the background, but also on the face. Don't be afraid to exaggerate the colors of the shadows and skin tones to increase your expression. As you apply the crayons or oil pastels, try to use an expressive stroke, rather than smoothing out the marks. Look again at Van Gogh's portrait or Stuart Davis's.

Figure 12.9 is a woodcut print by German artist Erich Heckel. It too is a self-portrait. A **woodcut** print is made by cutting away from a block of wood those parts of the print that you want to leave white. The parts that you want black are left raised above the background. These areas catch the ink and transfer the print to paper. When you look at this print, how has the artist used line to express a mood or feeling? How would you describe the kinds of lines used? Straight, curving, jagged? What can you tell about the artist's personality from looking at this portrait?

Something to Try:

- Create a woodcut or linoleum print using a portrait as subject. Try to express one of the following moods: grief, joy, boredom, awe, or thoughtfulness. When your print is complete, print it on a variety of papers, including newspaper, magazine, or a grocery bag.

Block Printing: Hints and Pitfalls

- Always use the proper cutting tools for woodcut or linoleum. Your teacher will supply these. [CAUTION: Never cut towards your hand or body.] Figure 12.10 shows the proper way to hold the printing block for safe carving.
- Make several practice sketches of your portrait before beginning. Keep your portrait simple. Small details are difficult to execute and are usually lost in printing.
- For added interest and expression, vary the width and direction of lines. Use both straight and curved lines.
- When your block is complete, apply water-base printing ink to the surface of the block with a **brayer**. A **brayer** is a small roller with a handle attached. It

Figure 12.9. Erich Heckel. *Portrait of a Man.* 1919. Woodcut, printed in color, block: 18 3/16″ x 12¾″. Collection, The Museum of Modern Art, New York. Purchase Fund.

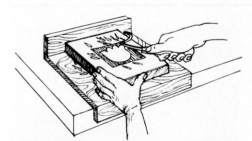

Figure 12.10. Correct way to hold a wood or lineoleum block when cutting. Hand is placed so that hand holding cutting tool cuts away from the body.

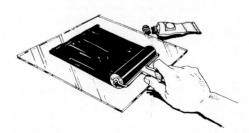

Figure 12.11. Diagram showing how to properly roll out ink with a brayer.

allows you to roll a thick, even covering of ink over the surface of your block (Figure 12.11).

- At the printing stage, work as quickly as possible. Water-base printing ink dries fast and will not make a good print if not used fairly soon after applying. It sometimes helps to dampen your printing paper with a sponge, beforehand.
- Place the block face down on the printing paper. Flip the paper over and carefully press it against the block with the heel of your hand or a clean brayer. Gently pull print from block and allow to dry. Re-ink block for another print.

PORTRAITS IN THREE DIMENSIONS

Figures 12.12 and 12.13 are both examples of portraits from Pre-Columbian Mexico (see Chapter 7). Figure 12.12 is a mask made of pieces of jade, a hard, greenish stone favored by native artists for carving and decoration. This particular mask was placed over the face at death. It is likely to represent a stylized portrait of a dead person's features. Notice how the forms of the features, especially the nose, have been exaggerated to create a design, as well as a face. The pieces of jade create a texture over the surface of the mask. What art technique uses small pieces of glass or stone to create a design? (see Chapter 6).

Compare this portrait with the one pictured in Figure 12.13. Figure 12.13 is a portrait head in **stucco**. **Stucco** is a type of plaster that can be molded, carved, or applied to the surface of other materials.

One of the main differences between the two portraits is the mask was meant to be seen from only the front. The portrait shown in Figure 12.13 is a full, three-dimensional sculpture. You would be able to walk around all sides of this portrait. What other differences do you notice between the two? Are there any similarities in how the artists have sculpted the features? What are they? What art elements do you think are most important in Figure 12.12? In Figure 12.13?

Something To Try:

- Try making a mask from clay. You may use your own face as a model or someone else's. Study the face of your subject closely. Try to determine which features are the most unique to that particular face. Exaggerate these features for more expression. Pay particular attention to the shape and expression of the eyes. [CAUTION: Some people are allergic to clay dust. Wear a protective mask, if necessary.]

Figure 12.12. *Pre-Columbian Jade Mask.* Mayan Mosaic Jade Death Mask with Shell Eyes. Palenque, c. 7-8th Century A.D. Photo credit: Lee Boltin Picture Library, New York.

Figure 12.13. *Pre-Columbian stucco head.* Mayan Stucco Head. 17¼″ h. Photo credit: Lee Boltin Picture Library.

Hints and Pitfalls:

- Begin your mask with a clay slab. With a rolling pin or cardboard cylinder, roll out a slab of clay about ½" thick. You will make your mask lifesize, so roll out enough clay to cover the face.
- Mold your clay slab over a mound of newspapers covered in plastic. This will help round the shape of the face, while supporting it from beneath. The plastic will prevent the clay from drying out too fast.
- Once your slab is shaped, begin adding features using pieces of clay. If the underlying slab is still wet, the features may be pressed into the clay of the slab. If the clay has dried, **slip,** a mud-like glue made from dried clay and water, should be used on both surfaces to attach the features. Carefully press the edges of all features to secure.
- Add texture to make hair or as decoration. Experiment with a variety of tools to create new and interesting textures.

LIVING AND WORKING

Another popular art theme is that of human beings engaged in various kinds of work. For most of us, a good portion of our lives will be spent working at some job or profession. Sometimes this work brings us pleasure and satisfaction; other times it brings only sore backs and aching muscles. Both the pleasure and misery of work have been explored as an art theme for centuries.

One of the most famous artworks using the theme of work and leisure was the *Tres Riches Heures of the Duc de Berri,* or the *Very Rich Hours of the Duke de Berri.* Painted by the Limbourg Brothers in 1413-16, it is a series of beautiful, miniature paintings that served as both a prayerbook and a calendar. Using a painting for each month of the year, the artists were able to show the wide variety of work that was done during different times of the year.

Figure 12.14 is *October* of the series. In the foreground are two peasants, plowing and planting seeds. By contrast, in the background we see a huge castle around which the rich can be seen going about their leisure activities. The paintings of each month of the series show this contrast between the honest, hard labor of the peasants and the carefree, luxurious life of the wealthy.

During the 19th century, as the Industrial Revolution (Chapter 9) gave rise to more factory jobs in which people worked all day inside buildings, some artists saw the honest, hard work of the out-of-doors as a natural subject for art.

Figure 12.14. Limbourg Brothers. *October from Tres Riches Heures of the Duc De Barri.* 1413-16. Musee Conde, Chantilly, France. Photo credit: Giraudon, France.

Figure 12.15. Jean Francois Millet. *The Sower.* Oil on canvas, 40" x 32½". The Museum of Fine Arts, Boston. Shaw Collection.

Figure 12.16. Emma Lee Moss. *Talking Farm.* 1988. Oil on canvas, 30″ x 24″. Collection: Southwest Gallery, Dallas, Texas.

Figure 12.15, titled *The Sower,* is by French artist Jean Francois Millet [juahn fran•SWAH mee•LAY]. The artist has given the peasant the power and grace of a heroic figure. Millet has raised the work of farm and field to a new importance.

The activities of simple people going about their everyday tasks is also a favorite subject of American primitive or **folk art.** **Folk art** is art that is created by individuals with little or no formal art training. Though sometimes referred to as "primitive" art, it is more childlike than primitive.

Favorite themes of folk art are activities that take place on farms, in the neighborhoods, and in the homes of ordinary people. Part of the charm of folk art is its childlike simplicity. It shows the pleasure in the humble, but honest work and play of ordinary people.

Emma Lee Moss is a black, folk artist. Her beautiful paintings (Figure 12.16) in some ways remind us of the miniature masterpieces of the Limbourg Brothers (Figure 12.14). In both paintings, the artists have used a sharp, clear painting style. Notice how sharp the edges of figures and objects stand out against the background of Moss's work.

Talking Farm (Figure 12.16) shows farm workers working in the fields. The little figures are very simply drawn. They are no more than shapes or colors. She has used little value or shading to make objects appear three-dimensional. In fact, it isn't too difficult to imagine this painting as a collage or perhaps the design for a wall-hanging made of fabric and yarn.

What kind of space has been used in this painting? Do you think the artist used linear perspective? Why or why not? Has overlapping been used? Compare it to Figure 12.14. What kind of space has been used here?

Of course, not everyone works on a farm. Artists began to see new subject possibilities in the work of modern society. Some artists, like Fernand Leger [fur•NAN lay•zhay], used the shapes and spaces of skyscrapers under construction to create interesting visual compositions. Leger's paintings also show the variety of new jobs that people of the 20th century perform.

Figure 12.17, titled *The Builders,* is typical of Leger's style of painting. Using a primary color scheme (red, blue, and yellow) the artist has simplified the shapes of steel girders and construction equipment into cartoon-like images. Once again, the art elements of shape and color are more important than realistic detail. Where has the artist used shading? Where has value or shading created new shapes?

The workmen lifting the beam in the foreground of the painting don't seem to be struggling with the weight or

Figure 12.17. Fernand Leger. *The Builders.* 1950. Oil on canvas, 300 cm.x 200 cm. Museum Ferdinand Leger, Biot, France.

the task. Like the rest of the painting, there is a light-hearted mood about them.

Have you noticed the tree branch beneath the feet of the men? This natural object seems strangely out of place in this scene of human industry. But, it serves a purpose.

It is traditional for construction workers to place a branch or small tree on the top floor of a new building as soon as the framework is in place. You may have seen this in your own city and wondered about it. In Leger's painting, it appears as if more building is going on beyond the last floor. What do you think this means?

Something To Try:

- Observe people as they work. Notice whether they work at active jobs or outdoors. Do they do construction work? Do they work in an office? In your sketchbook, make gesture drawings of the position of people's bodies as they move about their work. Remember, gesture drawings are quick sketches that are meant to capture the motion and position of a figure. Don't worry about details. But, observe your subjects closely. Are they bending over? Do they sit at a desk? How do they use their hands?
- Instead of pencil, try using water-based felt markers for sketching. These won't tempt you to erase and will sharpen your observing eye.
- Make wire sculptures from your gesture drawings. Attach a piece of flexible wire to a small block of wood by nailing or taping it. Wrap other wire to it to represent the lines of your gesture drawing. Pay close attention to the negative spaces you create.

AT REST AND AT PLAY

People not only work, but they also rest and have fun. They play sports, vacation, and work with their hobbies. These and other leisure activities are also favorite themes for art.

American artist Winslow Homer painted one of the most famous works using the theme of people at play. His painting *Snap the Whip* (Figure 12.18) shows eight young boys playing a game. Holding hands, the boys run in a circle until the end boy is unable to hold on. Can you find him in the painting? Which boy is the anchor of the whip? Notice the positions and actions of the boys' legs. How do they change from the boy on the right to the boys on the left?

This painting manages to represent all the carefree fun and joy of childhood in one canvas. The mood is light-

Figure 12.18. Winslow Homer. *Snap the Whip.* 1872. Oil on canvas, 12″ x 20″. The Metropolitan Museum of Art. Gift of Dr. and Mrs. Robert E. Carroll, 1979.

Figure 12.19. Ben Shahn. *Handball.* 1939. Tempera on paper over composition board, 22¾″ x 31¼″. Collection, The Museum of Modern Art, New York. Abby Aldrich Rockefeller Fund.

hearted, with no hint of worry. What season of the year do you think it is? Why?

Compare *Snap the Whip* with the painting shown in Figure 12.19. It is by American artist Ben Shahn. Again we see the theme of boys at play, but the location is quite different. So is the mood. All the figures are separated. They also have their backs to us, so we cannot see their expressions. Do you think they are smiling? Do they look as if they are having fun like the boys in Figure 12.18? Why or why not? How has the artist created a special mood in this painting?

Figure 12.20 is a drawing by artist Tim High. In this drawing the mood is not so easy to pinpoint. We see a man with a camera watching what looks like a ride at a carnival or fair. The realism of this work makes it hard to believe that this is a drawing at all. The bright lights of the ride have been stopped in motion, just as a camera would do. This makes us wonder whether we are looking at a real scene or at a photograph.

Pay close attention to the strong, vivid colors and smooth texture of the drawing. It reminds us more and more of a photograph rather than a drawing. What do you think is the mood of this work? Does the mood match the theme—a person at a fair or carnival? Why or why not? What other elements help create the mood?

Something To Try:

- Make some sketches of your friends or family playing sports or involved in other leisure activities. Compare your sketches with those you made of people at work. Can you see any differences between the way people move their bodies when they work and the way they move them when they play?

- Using charcoal and a large sheet of paper, make some quick sketches of figures at rest, as well as at play. Take particular notice of the positions of arm and leg muscles in each figure. Use a variety of lines to change the mood of the drawings. For example, use heavy, thick lines for someone sitting or resting. Use quick, thin lines for someone running or catching a ball. Experiment with lines to alter the meaning of your drawing. [**CAUTION:** Some people are allergic to charcoal dust. Wear a protective mask if necessary. Always work in an area with plenty of ventilation.]

- Use soft charcoal to shade areas of your drawings, giving the figures a three-dimensional appearance. You can use paper towels or a soft cloth to smooth your shading.

Figure 12.20. Timothy High. *Placebo.* 1984. Prismacolor and enamel drawing, 26″ x 40″. Private collection.

146

Painting What She Likes

Emma Lee Moss grew up in a small town in Tennessee, the third of eight daughters. She soon found a job working for a family and caring for their son. When the family moved to San Angelo, Texas, Emma Moss moved with them. She could not stand the thought of being parted from the family's son, Tommy.

About 1950, Moss began to paint, using young Tommy's brushes and paints. Tommy's mother thought Emma had talent and encouraged her to take private art lessons. These lessons helped introduce her to a wider variety of materials and techniques. However, she was encouraged by all who saw her work to remain true to her folk art style of painting and drawing.

Ever the inventive artist, Emma Lee Moss has used an interesting variety of art materials for her work, including shoe polish and department store boxes, wallpaper, window shades, and cloth. However, most of her works are painted and drawn with more traditional materials.

Emma Lee Moss has always found inspiration for her work in her memories of childhood scenes and simple activities like *Let's Rest* (Figure 12.21). In this work she uses the busy life of a farm as her subject. The use of simple shapes and bright colors increasess the mood and joyful memories.

Today Emma Lee Moss continues to paint and to reach an ever-widening circle of admirers. Her work has been compared to that of the best American folk artists.

BORN: 1916-
BIRTHPLACE:
St. Bethlehem, Tennessee

Figure 12.21. Emma Lee Moss. *Let's Rest.* 1987. Oil on canvas, 32″ x 22″. Southwest Gallery, Dallas, Texas.

Student work.

Student work.

Did you learn

- The definitions of the following words and phrases: brayer; folk art; slip; woodcut; stucco?
- Why watercolor and brush are a good medium for quick drawing?
- How to make a woodcut print?
- How to hold properly a woodblock while cutting?
- Two uses for a brayer in printing?
- Two kinds of human activities shown in the *Tres Riches Heures of the Duc de Berri* (Figure 12.14)?
- The art style represented by *Talking Farm* (Figure 12.16)?

Understanding and Evaluating

- Compare Figure 12.16 by Emma Lee Moss with Figure 12.14 by the Limbourg Brothers. Make a list of similarities and differences between the two works.
- Write a short scene or story to accompany either Figure 12.20 by Tim High or Figure 12.21 by Emma Lee Moss. Try to include in your writing the mood or feeling you experience when you look at the work.

Seeing and Creating

- Make a linoleum-block print of a person involved in any sport or hobby. Experiment with various colors of water-based printing ink. Number each print you pull in the bottom left margin. Sign your name in pencil in the bottom right margin. [CAUTION: Always use cutting tools properly. Never cut toward your hand or body. (See Figure 12.10 for correct position.]
- Make a drawing or painting of someone sitting or lying down. How do you have to adjust your point of view? Is foreshortening necessary to make a convincing drawing?
- On a wire armature, create a paper maché figure in motion. Use a sport or other activity in which parts of the body, arms, and legs stretch out into the negative space around them. Add bright colors in tempera or acrylic to your action figure. [CAUTION: Acrylic paint is permanent. Wear protective clothing if necessary. Never let acrylic paint dry in brushes.]

Perhaps next to painting the human face and form, artists love best to paint objects. For thousands of years, human beings have been acquiring objects. From the first primitive spear points of prehistoric hunters, to the new pair of sport sneakers you just bought at the mall, we love objects!

It is therefore little wonder that the art of objects, or as it is more commonly called the **still life**, has had a long history. It should also not come as a surprise that many still lifes combine objects with that other all time human favorite—food. Figure 13.1 shows that even the pleasure-loving, but doomed, citizens of Pompeii and Herculaneum were just as fond of a well-designed still life.

Figure 13.1 was part of a wall painting. In the complete work, there were probably even more luscious fruits and delicate containers to admire.

Can you identify the type of fruit shown here? Notice the technique the artist has used to paint a convincing glass container. Can you tell how the illusion of transparency has been achieved?

The 17th century saw artists reach new heights in painting still lifes. Never have artists lavished such attention on the humble pleasures of the dining room.

Figure 13.2 by Willem Heda [WILL•lum HEAD•ah] shows how great realism was achieved in both painting and arranging. This wonderful work shows the partially eaten food and tipped goblets of a just-finished dinner. It

Chapter 13

A CELEBRATION OF LIFE— THE ART OF STILL LIFE

WORDWATCH
still life
Photorealism
decorative
toned paper

Figure 13.1. Roman Wall Painting. *Still Life with Glassbowl and Fruit.* National Archeological Museum, Naples. Photo credit: Archiv fur Kunst und Geschichte, Berlin.

Figure 13.2. Willem Claesz Heda. *Still Life.* c. 1648. Oil on panel, 34¾″ x 27½″. Fine Arts Museum of San Francisco. Mildred Anna Williams Collection.

Johannes Vermeer. *A Girl Asleep.* Oil on canvas, 34½″ x 30⅛″. The Metropolitan Museum of Art. Bequest of Benjamin Altman, 1913.

149

Figure 13.3. Lubin Baugin. *Still Life with Checkerboard.* Oil on canvas, 55 cm. x 73 cm. Collection The Louvre, Paris. Photo: ©R.M.N.

Figure 13.4. Arthur G. Dove. *The Lobster.* 1908. Oil on canvas, 25¾" x 32". Amon Carter Museum, Fort Worth, Texas. Acquisition in memory of Anne Burnett Tandy, Trustee, Amon Carter Museum, 1968-1972.

Figure 13.5. Paul Cezanne. *Still Life with Apples.* 1895-98. Oil on canvas 69 cm. x 93 cm. The Metropolitan Museum of Art, New York. Photo credit: Rosenthal Art Slides.

is as if the diners had hurriedly left the table, and we the viewers are left to clean up the mess!

Study the painting for a few moments. Let your eyes take in the casual arrangement of the objects and the photographic realism of the painting technique. How has the artist made you think the meal was interrupted? What kinds of foods are being eaten here? Do you think this is the table of a poor or a wealthy person? Why, or why not? Notice the variety of textures that has been included in the painting.

Still lifes, like Figure 13.2, were designed to appeal to all the observer's senses. If they can make you feel hungry, all the better. These wonderful paintings, perhaps better than any other art form, celebrate the fullness and pleasures of life. Beautiful things to see! Delicious things to eat!

A painting like the one in Figure 13.3 includes objects that represent the five senses: sight, hearing, touch, smell, and taste. Study the painting for a few minutes. See if you can tell which object represents which sense. Pay close attention to the chessboard on the right. What Renaissance invention helped the artist paint the board so convincingly? Is the composition of this still life symmetrically balanced? Why, or why not?

Figure 13.4, titled *The Lobster,* is a still life that also pictures food. But notice how differently the artist paints the objects. American artist Arthur Dove has painted a still life filled with color, shape, line, and pattern.

The red of the lobster spilling from the plate in the foreground leads our eyes into the composition. We then notice the vivid yellows, oranges, and greens. The colors in this still life are as rich and juicy as the fruits and vegetables on the table!

There is great variety in the shapes and lines used in the flowered cloth and around the objects themselves. That black edge seems only to intensify the colors and emphasize the shapes.

The pattern of the cloth or paper backdrop makes an interesting play of shapes and colors against the objects on the table. The shapes and colors in this still life are simplified. Realistic details are reduced. This is, however, a very **decorative** still life. **Decorative** art or design, as you will read in a later chapter, is usually ornamental. It will have intricate patterns and fancy details. If you compare it with the still life by Cezanne in Figure 13.5, you will see how decorative the still life in Figure 13.4 really is.

Cezanne, whom you read about in Chapter 10, not only loved to paint landscapes, but also to paint still lifes. Like his landscape paintings, Cezanne's still lifes are not about realistic detail, but form. The peaches, the fabric, and the bottles all have weight and form. In contrast, the dark outline around the objects in Figure 13.4 does more than intensify the colors. Although some shading is used to give a three-dimensional quality to the objects, the dark outline flattens the shapes. Outlining flattens shapes and makes them appear cartoonlike. In contrast, the objects in Cezanne's work have no dark outlines.

Compare the colors in the two paintings. The colors in Figure 13.5 are quiet in comparison to the still life by Arthur Dove. The pattern on the cloth is the same color, although a darker value than the cloth itself.

What other differences do you notice between the two still lifes?

You would expect Henri Matisse, one of the founders of modern art to have a unique way of painting still lifes, and so he does.

Figure 13.6. *Still Life A Sivigilia, II* by Matisse is a charming painting. The mood is cheerful, celebrating the beauty and joy of nature. How would you describe the brushstrokes in this painting? Would you describe this work as decorative? Why, or why not? What kinds of shapes are used in this work? Geometric? Organic? Or both?

Compare Figure 13.6 with Van Gogh's *Sunflowers* in Figure 13.7. What kind of shapes does Van Gogh use? How would you describe the color scheme in this painting—monochromatic, analogous, or complementary?

While some contemporary artists continue to abstract still lifes, others return to the realism of the 17th century. The work pictured in Figure 13.8 is a good example. This painting by Donald Wilson was painted in 1984. Many people, seeing this work in the museum for the first time, believe it is a photograph. So perfect is the technique, with every brushstroke removed, that it is difficult to believe it is a painting.

Take some time to look at this amazing work. You don't want to miss a thing. The first thing you may notice is the lighting. Does it seem natural to you, or is it like a spotlight on a stage? Why would the artist use such a strong, direct light? What does it do to the objects on the table? What kind of mood does this painting represent? Can you describe it? Compare this painting with Figure 13.2 by Heda. Are there any similarities?

Figure 13.6. Henri Matisse. *Still Life A Sivigilia, II.*

Figure 13.7. Vincent van Gogh. *Sunflowers.* 1888. Oil on canvas 92.1 cm. x 73 cm. Reproduced by courtesy of the Trustees, The National Gallery, London.

Figure 13.8. Donald Roller Wilson. *Mrs. Jenkins' Late Night Dinner in her Room Alone. (While out in the Hall Leading to Her Room, Her Small Friends are Sleeping).* 1983-84. Oil on canvas, 50 3/16″ x 72″. The Archer M. Huntington Art Gallery. The University of Texas at Austin. The 1985 Friends of the Archer M. Huntington Art Gallery Purchase.

There are some other unusual things about this painting. For one, the title. It is as detailed as the painting— *Mrs. Jenkins' Late Nite Dinner in Her Room Alone (While Out in the Hall Leading To Her Room, Her Small Friends Were Sleeping!)* Does knowing the title of this work change the mood for you? Does it make it more understandable?

This painting has been cut into an unusual shape. You can see this by looking at the edge of the frame. Why do you think the artist did this? Does the shape of the frame remind you of anything? Where is Mrs. Jenkins?

By now you recognize the art style of Figure 13.8. It is **Photorealism** [fo•to•real•ism] A Photorealistic painting imitates the look of photographs. Can you recall other photorealistic painters you met in Book One?

A well-known Photorealist is Janet Fish. Her *8 Vinegar Bottles* (Figure 13.9) is a remarkable still life. This painting which hangs in the Dallas Museum of Art overwhelms the viewer with its technical skill and size (53″x72 1/8″)!

But there is more than technical skill here. The arrangement of the simple, clear vinegar bottles creates a complicated pattern of shapes, lines, and spaces. The labels on the bottles are turned so that they can be glimpsed around and through other bottles. What happens to the lettering of the labels when it is seen through glass? Have you ever noticed this before?

Something To Try:

- Still lifes don't have to be dull subjects. As you have seen in the works shown in this chapter, the subjects for still lifes are endless. Make a list of objects that would be unusual in a still life, such as automobile parts, blue jeans, sneakers, or grocery bags. Next to this list make another list of different kinds of food and drink—pizza, cotton candy, or pineapples. Draw lines between the two lists, matching objects to food. Select one of the pairs to use as subjects in a still life. Try mixing media. For example, combine watercolor with collage or tempera paint with India ink. Try to create a special mood in your still life.
- If you want to practice drawing realistically like Donald Wilson and Janet Fish, the following suggestions will help:
- Always work from a real object or objects, not from a photograph. This is harder to do, but will give you much better results.

- Examine the object or objects carefully before beginning your drawing. Make some practice sketches beforehand. Observe how highlights and shadows define the shape of the object.
- Try to draw what you see, not what you know! We all think we know how familiar objects look, but drawing realistically takes some special observing.
- It is easier to achieve the illusion of transparency in glass if you draw on **toned paper. Toned** or tinted paper allows you to use white crayon, oil or chalk pastels, or white ink to highlight the reflections that are so important in drawing transparent glass.

Figure 13.9. Janet Fish. *8 Vinegar Bottles.* 1972-73. Oil on canvas 53″ x 72⅛″. The Dallas Museum of Art, gift of The 500, Inc.

You can buy tinted drawing paper at art supply stores, or you can make your own. Try crushing small pieces of charcoal or chalk pastels into a powder. With a cloth or paper towel, rub a smooth coating of the chalk dust onto your drawing paper. Don't get your paper too dark. You will also want to use dark colors for shadows. They won't show up if your paper color is too dark. [CAUTION: Some people are allergic to charcoal and chalk dust. Wear a protective mask, if necessary. Use materials in a well-ventilated room.]

- Practice shading smoothly from one value to another. Observe carefully the shadows on objects that give them a three-dimensional appearance. Avoid heavy outlines. It is very difficult to draw three-dimensional objects convincingly if you outline them heavily. Outlines flatten objects. But, by all means, use line when you want to express a mood or you want to create flat shapes.
- The next time you are at the supermarket, look carefully at the fruits and vegetables. Notice their different shapes, colors, and textures. Put together in your imagination a still life from fruits and vegetables that have unusual colors, shapes, and textures. One fruit that meets all of these requirements is a fresh pineapple. If you have permission to buy one, use it to make a drawing. After sketching lightly in pencil, use water-based felt markers or India ink to outline. Complete your drawing by adding color with a watercolor wash.

MEET PAUL CEZANNE

BORN: 1839
DIED: 1906
BIRTHPLACE:
Aix-en-Provence, France

Figure 13.10. Paul Cezanne. *Still Life.* 1877. Oil on canvas, 23⅞″ x 29″. The Metropolitan Museum of Art, Harris Brisbane Dick Fund, 1956.

The Form of Things

Paul Cezanne came later to art than most artists. The son of a banker, he began his career as a lawyer. Unhappy with the profession he had chosen and wealthy enough to pursue a more interesting career, Cezanne went to Paris to paint.

Like many other artists of the late 19th century, Cezanne first fell under the spell and influence of the Impressionists. His first paintings in this style, however, did not satisfy him. He felt that the sparkling effects of light and color, so loved by the Impressionists, lacked substance. He wanted to give form and weight to Impressionism.

One of Cezanne's beliefs that guided his style of painting, was that geometric forms, such as cubes, cones, and cylinders, should be used to show the structures of nature. It was the development of his solid, block-like style that had such an influence on Cubism.

Cezanne loved to paint landscapes and still lifes. In his paintings he tried to express the emotions he experienced when he looked at a scene or group of objects. In order to do this more accurately, Cezanne made a careful study of color. He soon began to use changes in color, instead of light and shadow, to model his forms.

Both Cezanne's landscapes and still lifes have very little shading of darkened areas and edges. The mass and weight of the forms are achieved through color and brushstroke.

Where the Impressionists were concerned with the immediate, fleeting changes of light and color, Cezanne was concerned with permanence and solid form. And though Cezanne's own paintings were never abstract, they inspired many of the abstract artists who followed. Some consider him one of the fathers of modern art.

Did you learn

- The definitions of these words and phrases: still life; decorative; Photorealism; toned paper?
- Why still lifes have always been popular subjects for artists?
- How to recognize a decorative design?
- Two art elements that Cezanne was most interested in?
- What Photorealism art tries to imitate?
- The names of two Photorealistic painters?

Student work.

Student work.

Understanding and Evaluating

- In your school or public library, read more about the customs and costumes of people in Europe in the 17th century. In a one-page paper, write how you think the still life shown in Figure 13.2 does or does not represent the tastes of people living at that time. What was happening in America during the time this still life was painted?
- Write a short story about Donald Wilson's still-life painting (Figure 13.8). Try to imagine what is going to happen next in the painting.

Seeing and Creating

- Set up a still life using a variety of natural objects. Lightly sketch the objects onto a sheet of white drawing paper or painting paper. Using tempera or acrylic paint, paint your still life with strong, bright colors. Try to create a mood or feeling in the work. Like Cezanne, try to use colors to separate shapes and create an illusion of form in place of shading. Keep small details to a minimum.
- On a sheet of newsprint, simplify flowers or other plants to basic shapes and lines. When you have an interesting and balanced composition, transfer it to a plaster printing plate (Prepare these ahead of time under the direction of your teacher). Using gouging tools, carve away those parts of the design you want to be light. Prepare the plate for inking (see Chapter 12) and print your design. [CAUTION: Use gouges with care. Never cut toward your hands or body.]

Chapter 14

ART AND ANIMALS— THE LONG PARTNERSHIP

WORDWATCH
symbol
attribute
mixed media
diptych
minotaur
centaur
unicorn
tapestry

Figure 14.1. Sakkarah. *Egyptian Statue of a Cat.* Late dynastic period. Bronze, 11″ h. The Metroplitan Museum of Art. Bequest of Mrs. H.O. Havenmeyer, 1929. The H.O. Havemeyer Collection.

Consider the cat. Silent, mysterious, jealous, independent, cruel, playful, and clever. All these words have been used to describe cats, either by their admirers or by their enemies. The cat, like many other animals, has been used as a constant theme throughout the history of art. Animals, whether feared or loved, have inspired some very great artists and many art masterpieces.

But, back to the cat. The cat as a subject in art is interesting because it has been used as much for a **symbol,** as for its image. A **symbol,** you may recall, stands for or represents another idea or feeling. For example, in the 17th century, the sun represented or **symbolized** the French king, Louis XIV.

Figure 14.1 shows one of the earliest uses of the cat as a symbol. This sculpture is ancient Egyptian. In the Egyptian religion, cats were sacred creatures and symbolized or represented a goddess named Bastet. Like the pharoahs, cats were mummified and buried with great ceremony.

The figure of the cat shown here gives a hint as to why the Egyptians used this animal to symbolize a goddess. Just look at the regal, aloof bearing! The graceful body and noble head are beautiful forms for sculpture.

From what you know of cats, how well do you think the Egyptian sculptor captured the personality of this animal?

Figure 14.2 is a painting by Goya, an artist you met in Chapter 9. In this painting, we see a little boy posed quietly for his portrait. But, in the lower left corner we have something really interesting.

Look at those cats! With staring eyes and bodies ready to pounce, they glare at the pet bird in the foreground. The expression on their faces is so realistic and intense that we can hardly tear our attention away to look at the main subject of the painting—the little boy.

When you consider the number of other ways the artist could have painted the cats in this work, it is surprising that he chose to show them this way. It is as if there is a drama going on behind the scenes. Could it be that the cats and bird represent or symbolize something else? Is the artist trying to tell us that the innocent, little boy is in danger? What do you think the cats symbolize? The pet bird holds a piece of paper with the boy's name and the date.

Artists cherish animals as themes for art because of their symbolic power and their **attributes** [AT • trah • butes]. An **attribute** is a characteristic or quality an

156

animal or person possesses. For instance, at the beginning of this chapter, we listed some of the attributes of cats. A lion, although a member of the cat family, doesn't have exactly the same attributes as a house cat. The attributes of lions are thought to be courage, pride, and nobility. The lion, because of these attributes, is frequently used in art to symbolize those qualities.

The cat family's attributes of physical grace and cunning obviously inspired the artists who created Figures 14.3 and 14.4.

Figure 14.3, *Royal Tiger*, is by Delacroix. Delacroix, like many artists of the Romantic style of painting, loved to use animals in his paintings for the color and drama they supplied. On his travels to exotic lands, Delacroix encountered many wild animals that were both strange and beautiful. His painting of an alert, but resting tiger makes good use of the animal's unique beauty.

Stretched out in lazy grace, this tiger appears to be waiting—maybe for his next meal to stroll along. The dramatic pattern of the tiger's orange- and black-striped coat contrasts vividly with the background. Compare the eyes of this tiger with the eyes of the cats in Figure 14.2. Are there other similarities in the way the animals are painted?

Figure 14.4 by sculptor Anna Hyatt uses the feline (catlike) attributes of power and grace to inspire this beautiful sculpture of a panther. Unlike Delacroix, who positions the tiger in a wary, but relaxed pose, Hyatt shows the panther reaching over a cliff. This allows her to show the immense strength contained in those bulging muscles. Although the sculpture is balanced, it still leaves us with an unsettling feeling. We feel the animal strain to keep its balance on the rocky ledge. You want to tense your own muscles when you look at this work.

Something To Try:

- Select two or three animals with which you are familiar. Make a list of attributes for each, both physical (graceful, strong, flexible) and personal (wise, silly, sneaky). Make a drawing or painting of one of the animals and try to indicate both physical and personal attributes. You may want to exaggerate textures, colors, shapes, and lines to achieve your goal.

- In your sketchbook, make gesture drawings of animals. Make additional studies just of the different textures and patterns found on animals. Don't overlook birds, insects, and undersea life as themes for art.

Figure 14.2. Francisco de Goya y Lucientes. *Don Manuel Osorio Manrique de Zuniga.* Oil on canvas, 50″ x 40″. The Metropolitan Museum of Art. The Jules Bache Collection.

Figure 14.3. Eugene Delacroix. *The Royal Tiger.* 1829. Lithograph, 19⅜″ x 25″. Courtesy Museum of Fine Arts, Boston. Otis Norcross Fund.

Figure 14.4. Anna Vaughn Hyatt Huntington. *Reaching Jaguar.* Bronze, 45″. The Metropolitan Museum of Art, New York. Gift of Archer M. Huntington, 1925.

157

Figure 14.5. *Greek Octopus Vase.* Courtesy Archeological Museum, Crete.

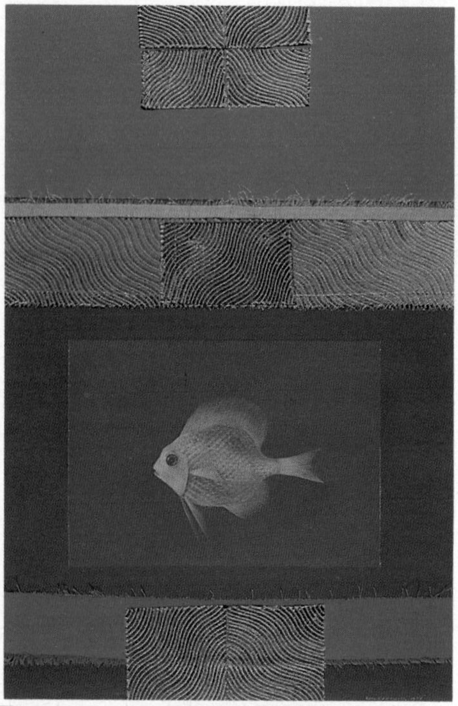

Figure 14.6. Kelly Fearing. *Recapitulation on a Fish Motif, #4. Opalescent Green, Blue, Blue-Green and Blue-Purple.* 1977. Collage with prismacolor pencil drawing, 17¼" x 11½". Collection of Rebecca Brooks.

BENEATH THE WAVES

So many past civilizations depended on the sea for food and transportation, it was natural that the artists of these cultures would be fascinated by the range of creatures, shapes, textures, and colors they saw caught in the nets of fishermen. Like the animals of the sky and land, sea creatures have played an important role in art.

The ceramic pot shown in Figure 14.5 is Greek. It was found on the island of Crete [kreet]. Made by an artist from an ancient culture that flourished there, this container uses a wide-eyed, many-legged octopus for decoration. Even today, Greek fishermen catch octopi (the plural form of octopus) in their nets. In Greece, as well as in many other Mediterranean countries, the octopus is used for food and considered a great delicacy.

The ancient potter who made this charming work obviously had studied the characteristics or attributes of octopi. He carefully records the correct number of legs (eight) and the large, balloon-like head. He also adds the suckers that line the legs of the creature that allow it to grab and hold its prey.

Have you noticed how the head has been placed to one side of the opening? This is a more interesting arrangement than placing it in the exact center of the container. This creates an asymmetrical balance to the composition. The rounded form of the pot is repeated in the coiled legs of the octopus, as well as by the circular handles. What do you think the other painted objects represent? Do you ? think the artist has represented a dangerous creature? Why, or why not?

Artist Kelly Fearing also uses undersea life for inspiration. Using a combination of materials and techniques or **mixed media,** he creates collage/drawings of great beauty and sensitivity. Figure 14.6 shows one of these works.

The fish, drawn in colored pencil, seems to float in the deep, blue waters of a calm sea. Above and below the drawing, pieces of silk material have been attached. Notice the pattern and color of the material. The wavy lines of blue and green seen in the silk remind us of the movement of waves, as well as the delicate coloring and textures of fish scales. Looking at this work is as soothing as watching fish moving soundlessly through the water of an aquarium.

Sculptor Constantin Brancusi [BRAN • ku • see] has used the sleek form of a fish to inspire a modern work of art. Figure 14.7, titled *The Fish*, is made of polished marble. Balanced on a light-colored base, the heavy stone appears weightless, like the floating creature it represents.

When you examine Brancusi's work, what physical attributes or characteristics of fish does the sculptor [?] emphasize? Which does he leave out? Why?

ANIMALS AND THEIR ENVIRONMENT

Many artists use animals to symbolize the mystery and danger of the natural environment. They see animals as much a part of the natural environment as trees, rocks, or mountains.

Artist Oskar Kokoschka [OS • car ko • KOSH • cah] in *The Mandrill* (Figure 14.8) makes the viewer of this painting search for the elusive ape among the greenery of the jungle, just as we would probably have to do in the wild, if we went looking for a mandrill. The artist is conscious of the need of animals to blend into their surroundings, to camouflage themselves against predators.

Kokoschka uses rapid brushstrokes to add energy to [?] his work. What painting style does this remind you of? What color scheme has the artist used?

The painting shown in Figure 14.9 also uses animals in their natural environment. Can you find the animals? [?] What are they? The artist Marc Franz has hidden his animals so cleverly that at first you don't see them. Unlike the Kokoschka mandrill, the deer in this painting are drawn with simple outlines and smooth shapes. With a few, well-chosen strokes, the artist has managed to convey the shyness and frailty of deer. Do they seem at rest or are they on the alert? How can you tell? Have you noticed how the rounded shapes of the deer are repeated in the shapes made by the vines and leaves in the background? This helps create a peaceful unity in the work.

Chinese and Japanese artists are particularly skillful in expressing moods of peace and quiet. You may remember that their landscapes were painted to show the harmony that should exist between all things—between people and nature and animals and nature.

Figure 14.10, titled *Deer, Pine, and Bat,* is a beautiful example of the delicate balance and mood of calm that can be found in Japanese art.

As you can see, this painting is in two parts. This type of two-panel painting is called a **diptych** [DIP • tick]. Many examples of Asian or Oriental art are painted in this manner. Sometimes the connected panels are used as screens to hang on the wall or divide areas in a room.

Compare the deer in Figure 14.10 with those in Figure 14.9. How are they similar? How different? The Japanese artist has added many realistic details, such as the spots

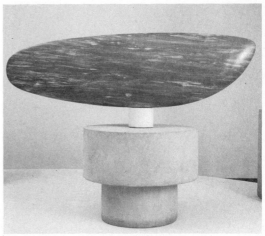

Figure 14.7. Constantin Brancusi. *The Fish.* 1930. Grey Marble, 21″ x 71″. On three-part pedestal of one marble and two limeston cylinders. 29⅛″ h. x approx. 65″ diameter at widest point. Collection, The Museum of Modern Art, New York. Acquired through the Lillie P. Bliss Bequest.

Figure 14.8. Oscar Kokoschka. *The Mandrill.* Oil on canvas, 23½″ x 18¾″. Collection: Rotterdam, Museum Boymans-van Beuningen.

Figure 14.9. Franz Marc. *Deer in the Forest I.* 1913. Oil on canvas, 39¾″ x 41¼″. The Phillips Collection, Washington. Bequest of Katerine S. Dreier, 1953.

Figure 14.10. Kyoto School. *Pine, Bat and Deer Screen.* Screen. Courtesy of Museum of Fine Arts, Boston. Fenollosa-Weld Collection.

on the deer's coat and the needles on the pine branch.

Have you noticed how your attention follows that of the deer? He looks over his shoulder toward the bat in the first panel. This causes you to do the same. You then can take in the details of the first panel, as well as those of the second. This technique helps to unite the two panels into one composition. It also shows how artists direct viewers to look at their works in certain ways. By arranging objects on the surface of your paper or canvas in a particular way, you too can control and direct how people will look at your work.

Something To Try:

- Create a painting of an animal in its natural habitat. Use a monochromatic or analogous color scheme for both background and animal. See if you can make the animal seem a part of the natural surroundings.
- Make drawings of a variety of animals. Simplify their forms into flat shapes. Cut the shapes out of posterboard or thin cardboard. Paper maché over the shapes and allow them to dry. Paint with acrylic paint. Use colors that are not ordinarily found on these animals. Use contrasting colors to simulate fur, scales, and other animal textures. Attach a safety pin on the back and wear the animal as jewelry. For your jewelry pin designs, you might use animals that are on the endangered species list. Besides paper maché pins, you can also make pendants and necklaces.

Paper Maché: Hints and Pitfalls

- To paper maché a small object like a pin, tear (never cut) the newspaper into very small pieces. If your animal shape is complex, be sure all the edges of the newspaper is smoothed.
- For such a small project, mix the art paste in small, plastic butter containers. If paste is left over, the plastic lid will keep it fresh until the next class.
- Use at least three to five complete layers of paper maché to harden the shape of your pin. The last layer can be made out of paper towels. This will create a good, one-color painting surface.
- Textures and small details can be added in paper maché by rolling pieces of newspaper into little balls and applying them to the surface of the cardboard.

160

- Be sure all paper maché is dry before painting.
- Use a small brush to apply painted textures and details.

ANIMALS OF MYTH—ANIMALS OF LEGEND

Long before there were zoos to show the general public exotic animals from all parts of the world, people had their own ideas about what beasts lurked in the heart of the darkest jungles. From these images have come the animals of myth and legend. These animals of the imagination have been popular themes in art for thousands of years.

The ancient Greeks were particularly enchanted with the theme of mythological beasts. Many are still part of our own vocabulary and story-telling traditions. We can thank the inventive Greeks for the **minotaur** (half man/ half bull), the **centaur** (half man/half horse), and the winged horse (Pegasus). All have been represented hundreds of times in every possible art form.

One mythical animal that captured the imagination of the people of the Middle Ages was the **unicorn**. Ancient writers declared that there had been sightings of this magical creature in India. Described as a white horse, with a single horn growing out of its forehead, the unicorn was very illusive.

The myth of the unicorn appears in many examples of medieval art, but nowhere more beautifully than in the *Unicorn Tapestries.* Figure 14.11 shows the last **tapestry** (woven wall hanging) in the series. The complete set details the hunt and final capture of the magical unicorn. In Figure 14.11 the unicorn is shown quietly resigned to his fate.

When you look at these works, it is difficult to believe they were woven, rather than painted. All of the flowers you see are perfect in every detail and can be identified by name. What a remarkable achievement!

Another popular mythical creature was the dragon. His snake-like image was embraced in both Europe and China, although in China he was not the symbol of evil that he was in medieval Europe.

Figure 14.12 shows a fearless St. Michael slaying a dragon, whose head seems to sprout more heads as it is chopped off! Although the unknown artist has used shading to give a three-dimensional appearance to the dragon's body, the background is a flat curtain of gold paint. This leaves little room for the body of St. Michael

Figure 14.11. Franco Flemish. *The Hunt of the Unicorn.* VII, The Unicorn in Captivity. c. 1500. 16th century. Tapestry of silk, wool, silver and silver gilt threds, 12'1″ x 8'3″. The Metropolitan Museum of Art. Gift of John D. Rockefeller, Jr. The Cloisters Collection, 1937.

Figure 14.12. Spanish, Valenciean. *Saint Michael and the Dragon.* 1400-25. Tempera on wood, gold ground 41⅜″ x 40¾″. The Metropolitan Museum of Art, Rogers Fund, 1912.

and the dragon to continue their fight. It does, however, create a very decorative and rich image.

In Figure 14.13, the inside of a Chinese ceramic bowl is decorated with the twisting shapes of dragons and clouds. The artist has carefully designed the bowl's decorative interior so that the dragons follow the contours of the bowl. This, together with the single color, gives harmony and unity to this piece.

Something To Try:

- Try your hand at designing a "new" mythological beast. You might begin by combining, in pencil sketches, shapes and details from several different animals. Be careful to use reasonable combinations. For example, the animals, if they existed, could move about. You wouldn't want to put the body of a hippo on the legs of a stork!
- Once you have a combination you like, make a more finished drawing in water-based felt marker or India ink. [CAUTION: India ink is permanent. Wear protective clothing if necessary.]
- Design a wall hanging using pieces of cloth, felt, plastic, or paper cut in the shapes of animals. Add other shapes that are part of the animal's natural environment, such as trees, rocks, or mountains. Attach the pieces onto a large piece of cloth or

Figure 14.13. *Bowl* with Dragon designs carved in relief. Far East-Ceramics, Chinese 907-960, Shang-Lin, Hu, Chekiang Province. Porcelaneous stoneware with carved and incised design under cedalon glaze. Diameter 1'⅝". The Metropolitan Museum of Art, Rogers Fund, 1917.

Figure 14.14. Charles Russell. *Powder Face Arapahoe.* 1903. Watercolor, 12″ x 9″. Amon Carter Museum, Ft. Worth, Texas.

Figure 14.15. Raymond Duchamp-Villon. *The Horse.* 1914. Bronze (cast c. 1930-31), 40″ x 29½″ x 22⅜″. Collection The Museum of Modern Art, New York. Van Gogh Purchase Fund.

Figure 14.16. *Tang Horse.* Ceramic clay horses of the Tang period (618-907 A.D.) are famous for their grace and beauty.

burlap with white glue or stitchery. Use yarns and other materials to add details and textures. If needed, refer to sample stitches in Book One, Chapter 19.

A PASSION FOR HORSES

Few animals can compete with the horse for the honor of being the most popular animal in art. Every culture and civilization that has known the horse has used it as an art theme.

Its beauty and strength, together with its great value as a means of transportation, have made the horse the focus of artists throughout the centuries. Whether as the faithful companion of the Native Americans of the American West (Figure 14.14), or the inspiration for abstract forms (Figure 14.15), images of the horse fill the museums of the world. Figures 14.16 to 14.18 give you some idea of the variety of art ideas these wonderful creatures have inspired.

Some artists celebrate the spirit and nobility of the untamed horse, while others acknowledge the horse's contribution to history and the progress of civilization. Horses are an art theme so common to most cultures of the world, that we have few problems understanding the meaning of the works. As familiar as the form of the human face, the elegant grace of the horse is recognized by all.

Figure 14.17. Peter Paul Rubens. *The Duke of Buckingham.* 1625. Oil on canvas, 17½″ x 19½″ Kimbell Art Museum, Fort Worth, Texas.

Figure 14.18. Lubeck. *St. George of Cappodocia and the Dragon.* c. 1520. Wood with polychrome and gilt, 28½″ h. Marion Koogler McNay Art Museum, San Antonio, Texas. Dr. and Mrs. Frederic G. Oppenheimer Collection.

B. Frontview.

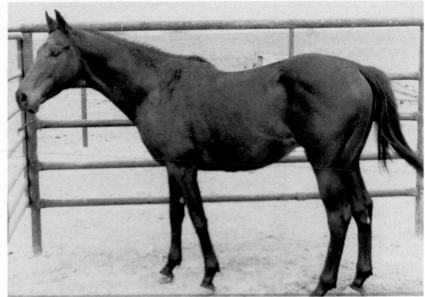

A. Side view.

Figure 14.19. Horses.

C. Rearview.

Something To Try:

- Try to locate some horses to draw from life. Make gesture drawings of their various positions. For more detailed drawings, study their proportions—legs to body; head to body. Use the head as a measuring standard for the other parts.

Measuring Proportions

With your pencil in hand, hold your hand at arm's length. Sight the pencil point on the edge of the object you are measuring. With your thumb, find another sight point. The space between the pencil point and your thumb is now a length of measurement you can use.

Firmly holding the first measure, find another shape or line that is equal or nearly so. For example, the length of the horse's head is similar in length to that of the neck from the base of the head to the shoulder. Figure 14.19 will help you to understand how to use this simple, useful way to measure and compare shapes and forms. After a while, your eye will be able to see more clearly the correct proportions of the subjects you draw. This measuring method can be used on any subject.

Figure 14.20. Kelly Fearing. *Night of the Rhinoceros.* 1968. Oil on canvas, 40″ x 30″. Collection of William Negley, San Antonio.

Artist of the Inner Vision

Photograph by Hans Beacham.

Artist Kelly Fearing has devoted his life to two important tasks—the creation of beautiful works of art and teaching art. Both are ways of sharing our inner thoughts and visions.

After graduating from college, Kelly Fearing worked as a junior-high art teacher in Louisiana. Because he was as enthusiastic about his student's work as his own, he was an exciting and inspiring teacher.

He eventually moved to Texas, where in 1949 he joined the faculty of the then new art department at The University of Texas in Austin. Once again, his lively personality and enthusiasm for art and teaching won him praise and the devotion of his students. During this time, he was also working hard at his own art.

Kelly Fearing has long been interested in the philosophy and religions of a number of cultures. He is particularly interested in India. The thoughtful and mystical world of Hinduism inspired many of his paintings and drawings. Another important influence was the world of animals. Their varied forms, colors, and textures were a never-ending source of ideas and themes for his work.

Figure 14.20 is a fine example of the skill with which Kelly Fearing can create mood in a work of art. With amazing attention to small details (he sometimes paints looking through a magnifying glass!) he convinces us of the reality of the scene—and something more.

The wandering rhino pursued by his avian attendants (they clean his wrinkled hide of insects) seems part of a dream. The only landscape we see is in the foreground. Hundreds of rocks and pebbles, like those found on a beach, are painted in great detail. The texture of the rocks is repeated in the texture of the rhino's bumpy hide. Both are in contrast to the smooth wash of color above. We want to peer through that cool, blue-grey mist into which the birds and rhino will soon depart.

BORN: 1916
BIRTHPLACE:
Fordyce, Arkansas

Did you learn

- The definitions of these words and phrases: symbol; attribute; mixed media; diptych; minotaur; centaur; unicorn; tapestry?
- Some animals that have been favorite subjects of artists for centuries?
- How the Japanese artist of Figure 14.10 encourages us to look at both panels of the diptych?
- A mythological animal favored by medieval artists?

Student work.

Student work.

Understanding and Evaluating

- Make a comparison of Figure 14.6 and 14.7. What attributes of the fish does each artist emphasize? Do both artists feel the same about their subjects? Why, or why not?
- Research in your school or local library an animal on the endangered species list. Your science class may have already studied some of these animals. With water-based felt markers, design a poster featuring this animal.

Student work.

Seeing and Creating

- On your next visit to a zoo, marine park, or farm, take along your sketchbook. Spend time studying the forms and movements of the animals. Make gesture drawings of the animals in different positions.
- Use insects as subjects for drawing. Draw them large, filling an entire page. Indicate the various textures on their bodies. You might try frottage for the textures. Place your drawing paper over a textured surface and rub with the side of your pencil or crayon.
- Under the direction of your teacher, make a plaster-block carving of an animal. Your teacher will instruct you in the preparation of the plaster block and in proper carving techniques. Be sure to select an animal that has a fairly solid form. Once the form of the animal has been carved, add interesting details and textures. Try to emphasize the main attributes of the animal you have chosen. [CAUTION: Plaster mixing and carving must only be done under the direct supervision of your teacher. Never pour or wash off plaster into a sink. If you are allergic to plaster dust, wear a protective mask.]

The natural environment includes all those surroundings and objects that are not made by humans. Trees, grass, mountains, lakes, oceans, deserts, jungles, animals, insects, and humans are all part of the natural environment. And while we all stop once in a while to admire a beautiful sunset or a field of flowers, the technology and conveniences of our modern world separate us more each year from the natural environment.

Sometimes when you are separated from a friend, even a very old and close friend, you forget about them. You start taking them for granted. Like an old, cherished, but absent friend, we have stopped being as close to the natural environment as we once were. We know it's there, but we don't always take the time to enjoy it or care for it the way we once did.

In recent years, various threats to our environment from pollution and the overuse of natural resources, have made people aware of the importance of cherishing and saving this unique and beautiful planet. People are searching for ways to protect our natural home. They are recycling materials and preserving endangered species. Being aware of the wonder and inspiration of the natural environment can help, as well. When people take the time to look, study, and marvel at the remarkable natural scenes that are a daily part of our lives, they are far less likely to waste and pollute those resources. The natural environment and the human place in it have inspired artists and other creative individuals for centuries. This is an added benefit for all people.

Chapter 15
A PLACE IN NATURE

| **WORDWATCH** |
| chiaroscuro |
| viewpoint |
| vanishing point |
| thumbnail sketch |
| picture plane |
| symmetrical composition |
| asymmetrical composition |
| visual composition |
| media |
| linear perspective |
| eye level |
| horizon line |
| panorama |
| etching |

STOP, LOOK, LISTEN, SMELL, TOUCH

There was a time, probably less than one hundred years ago, when you could not pass a day without seeing a tree. They were everywhere, even in many of the largest cities. Today, it is very possible to pass a day, maybe more than one, without seeing a tree or any natural object at all.

"But, I saw trees this morning on the way to school," you reply. Yes, you probably did see trees, but did you really "look" at them? If you were given a test right now, could you describe the trees you saw?

If you have learned to be observant, you might do quite well on the test. If you are used to drawing what you see, you might do even better.

Artists not only show us new ways of seeing and thinking about the world, but they, themselves, must learn to look closely at the subjects they use. They have

to learn to see differences and similarities in shape, form, line, color, and texture. For example, look at the trees in Figure 15.1. Begin by noticing their overall shapes. Are they rounded, long and thin, or shaped like a triangle or circle? In Figure 15.2 we may take a closer look at two trees. Notice the branches. Are they mostly straight and smooth or twisted and bent? One way to decide is to look at the patches of sky seen between the branches. This is the negative space. The branches of different trees will make different negative spaces and patterns against the sky. How do the trees in Figure 15.1 compare?

What about the leaves? The bark on the trunk? If you were going to use one of these two trees in a painting or drawing in which you wanted to create a mood of anxiety or fear, which would you use? Why?

Your eyes are only one of five senses. You have four others that help you to understand and to appreciate your environment. Do you know what they are? The more senses we use to experience the world, the more we learn about it and the better we can express our personal ideas and feelings with art.

Of course, no one expects you to taste a tree! In fact, it isn't recommended at all. But, have you ever smelled one? Do they all smell alike? What about touch? Do all parts of a tree feel the same? You might be surprised how much more information you can learn by using all of

Figure 15.2.

Figure 15.3. Rembrandt van Rijn. *The Three Trees.* 1643. Etching with drypoint and burin, on thin brown paper. National Gallery Art, Washington, D.C. Gift of Horace Gallatin.

Figure 15.4. George H. Hallowell. *The Tree.* 1910-20. Water color, 26" x 18¾". Courtesy The Museum of Fine Arts, Boston.

your senses. Even hearing can help. Trees don't make sounds, or do they? A tall tree on a breezy day will moan and creak like a haunted house. If trees don't all smell the same, do they sound the same?

For some artists, trees and the way we see and use them are an interesting art theme. As you look at the following artworks, pay close attention to how each artist views trees. Can you tell from these paintings how each artist felt about the trees and their place in the natural environment?

Silhouetted against a bright sky, three trees stand watch over a peaceful Dutch valley in this print by Rembrandt (Figure 15.3). Notice how the artist has paid close attention to the outline or contour of the trees. He has also studied carefully the proportion of the top or leafy part of the tree to the trunk and branch size. A common mistake is to make the tree trunk too large in proportion to the leaves and branches at the top. Rembrandt's trees seem realistic and well-proportioned.

This work is an **etching,** a print made by scratching lines into a metal plate. The plate is then inked and printed. A print made by this technique must rely on line to create value. Do you remember the name of the technique for creating value (lights and darks) with lines? (See Book One, Chapter 3).

As you can see, this beautiful print also makes dramatic use of the contrast between light and dark. This is called **chiaroscuro** [key • ah • row • SKOO • row], an Italian word that means light (chiaro) and dark (oscuro). You will find other artists who use the contrast between light and dark to add drama and expression to their artworks. Few were more successful at it than the great Rembrandt. Look at his works shown in Chapter 8. Compare them with his use of chiaroscuro in this landscape.

Large, very old trees have always had a special fascination for artists. Their massive, twisted branches and enormous trunks that seem to defy the passage of time make us all wonder at the human events and history that have passed beneath them. In many cases, very old trees, like animals, are given the attributes of human beings. We speak of them in terms such as, steadfast, caring, and courageous. Some artists make them the main theme of landscape paintings. More than landscapes, these works are portraits of trees.

Consider the watercolor shown in Figure 15.4. It is by the American artist George Hallowell. The artist has used a gigantic, old tree as the main subject of the painting.

Can you tell where you, the viewer, are standing in the painting? In other words, what point of view has the artist used? Are you level with the tree or looking up at it?

In this particular work, the **viewpoint**, or the angle or direction from which a scene or object has been drawn or painted, affects the mood and meaning of this work. ⟨?⟩ What do you think Hallowell is trying to tell us about this tree? How is the point of view in Figure 15.4 different from that in Figure 15.3 by Rembrandt?

Something To Try:

- Practice drawing a variety of trees in your sketchbook. The best way to begin is to start with a light sketch of a simple shape that is close to the shape of the tree. Figure 15.5 shows a variety of shapes that can be used. Pay attention to the size of the top of the tree, made up of branches and leaves, and the size of the trunk.
- Make some small detailed drawings of the various parts of different trees—the shape of the branches, the shapes of the leaves and the texture of the bark. Try making your studies with felt markers. This will help sharpen your observation skills since you cannot erase ink.

Figure 15.5. Trees come in a variety of shapes that can be simplified for drawing.

PLANNING A LANDSCAPE COMPOSITION

As you have learned, the *way* objects are placed on the **picture plane**, the area of paper or canvas used by an artist, is as important as the objects themselves. Artists use the principles of designs to guide their **visual compositions** or the arrangements of objects or art elements on the picture plane. Artists strive for a visual composition that is both balanced and interesting. Let's look at some of the many possibilities for landscape compositions.

Dutch artist Meyndert Hobbema [MINE•dart HOB• eh•mah] in Figure 15.6 has arranged a **symmetrical composition** using landscape. The road in the center and the line of trees on either side create a mood of order, calm, and peace.

This work also makes use of the illusion of deep space that can be achieved through **linear perspective**. Do you ⟨?⟩ remember the name of the Italian Renaissance artist who invented linear perspective?

In this work, we can easily locate the main parts of a linear perspective drawing or painting. The **eye-level** line, or **horizon line,** can be seen in the distance. In the center of our point of view and on the horizon line is the

Figure 15.6. Hobbema. *Middleharnis Avenue.* 1689. Oil on canvas, 103.5 cm. x 141 cm. Reproduced by courtesy of the Trustees, The National Gallery, London.

173

Figure 15.7. Alfred Sisley. *The Loing River at Moret.* 1891. Oil on canvas, 21½″ x 28¾″. Marion Koogler McNay Art Museum, San Antonio, Texas. Gift of Dr. and Mrs. Frederic G. Oppenheimer.

Figure 15.8. Fedelia Bridges. *Milkweeds.* 1876. Watercolor, 17¼″ x 12⅞″. Munson, Williams, Proctor Institute, Utica, New York.

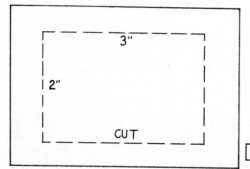

Figure 15.9. Viewfinder.

vanishing point. Hobbema uses this point to draw our eyes to the distant horizon and the lone figure walking along the road.

Can you locate the vanishing point? If you follow the lines created by the tops of the trees and along the sides of the road, you discover that these lines meet or converge at the vanishing point. Can you find other lines that meet there also?

In contrast to the symmetrical arrangement of the landscape in Figure 15.6 is the **asymmetrical composition** of Figure 15.7. This landscape was painted by the English artist Alfred Sisley.

This painting, though a balanced composition, is not equal on both sides. Close to the left is a large tree, while across the river are a number of trees and houses. Linear perspective has been used here, as well. Can you find the vanishing point? The horizon or eye-level line?

The asymmetrical arrangement of this work gives it a more informal, spontaneous feeling than the work by Hobbema (Figure 15.6).

Compare the painting style of the two works. Do you recognize the style in Figure 15.7? Look closely at the brushstrokes. Another hint. The Sisley work was painted in 1891.

Both of the works pictured in Figures 15.6 and 15.7 are examples of views called **panoramas.** A **panorama** is a view that takes in a wide area. The panorama, however, is but one way to view and arrange a landscape.

Figure 15.8, titled *Milkweeds,* by Fedelia Bridges, is a landscape planned from a very different viewpoint. No distant hills or far horizons here! The viewer might be the size of a small animal peering through the tangle of weeds and grass.

This kind of close-up view draws our attention to the variety of shapes, textures, and colors found in the smallest part of the natural environment. Why do you think the artist chose this point of view? What do you think she was trying to say about the natural environment?

Something To Try:

• Use a viewfinder to find landscape views that create symmetrically or asymmetrically-balanced compositions. You can make a viewfinder by folding a three-inch square of paper in half. Cut within one-half inch of the edge around three sides. When opened, your paper should have an open square in the middle (see Figure 15.9). Be sure not to cut your viewer too large.

- Hold the viewer at arm's length and sight your landscape through it. It helps to shut one eye and concentrate on looking through the viewer. Make some **thumbnail sketches** (small, quick gesture drawings) of the different views you see. You can use these sketches later as ideas for compositions.

Selecting a Medium

As you know, **media** are the various materials used to create works of art. Selecting the correct medium to express a certain theme, emotion, or mood is an important task for any artist. The natural environment has been portrayed in every **medium** from oil paint to pen and India ink.

Figure 15.10 is a drawing by Leonardo da Vinci. Titled *Storm Over an Alpine Valley,* it was drawn in red chalk. Chalk is a very free and flexible medium. You can draw quickly with it, as Leonardo has done in this work. Chalk also lets you use a wide variety of values. Here you can see how Leonardo has used darker values to represent the gathering storm clouds and lighter values to represent the distant landscape. Do you remember the Italian word for contrasts between light and dark?

Another drawing medium that creates a very different effect is India ink and pen. Figure 15.11 by Van Gogh is drawn in pen-and-ink. Using a wide variety of lines and marks, Van Gogh shows us all of the interesting textures he found along a village street. Does he use the same marks for human-made and natural objects? How is an illusion of space created in this drawing? Can you find the vanishing point?

Similar to the work by Van Gogh is one by Charles Burchfield, titled *Dandelion Seed Balls and Trees* (Figure 15.12). As you can see, the artist is interested in emphasizing the variety of textures seen in nature. This time, instead of pen and ink, Burchfield has used watercolor. How does this work differ from the one by Van Gogh? Do you think both works represent the same mood? Why, or why not? Which work appears more cheerful? Why?

Paul Cezanne, in *Houses on a Hill* (Figure 15.13), uses oil paint as if it were a drawing medium, such as oil pastels or crayons. He has made a quick sketch using paint. Can you tell how light values have been indicated? Did he use white? From what you know of Cezanne's painting style (See Chapter 9), how does this work represent that style?

Figure 15.10. Leonardo da Vinci. *Alpine Valley in a Rain Storm.* 1506. Red chalk on white paper, 8.7 cm. x 15.1 cm. Copyright reserved to MH the Queen. Royal Library, Windsor Castle.

Figure 15.11. Vincent van Gogh. *A Street in Saintes-Maries.* 1888. Brush, reed pen and ink, traces of pencil on paper, 9⅝″ x 12½″. Collection, The Museum of Modern Art, New York. Abby Aldrich Rockefeller Bequest.

Figure 15.12. Charles Burchfield. *Dandelion Seed Balls and Trees.* 1917. Watercolor on paper, 22¼″ x 18¼″. The Metropolitan Museum of Art, Arthur Hoppock Hearn Fund.

175

Figure 15.14. Chiaroscuro can be used in photography as well as drawing and painting to create a dramatic mood.

Figure 15.13. Paul Cezanne. *Houses on the Hill (River Bank)*. 1900-06. Oil on canvas, 23¾" x 31⅜". Marion Koogler McNay Art Museum, San Antonio, Texas. Bequest of Marion Koogler McNay.

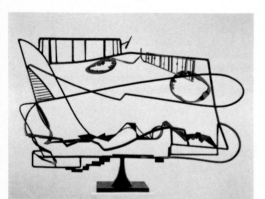

Figure 15.15. David Smith. *Hudson River Landscape*. 1951. Welded steel, 125.73 cm. x 190.5 cm. x 42.55 cm. Collection of the Whitney Museum of American Art, New York. Purchase.

The photographer has chosen photography as the medium for expression in Figure 15.14. Using a tree, a [?] landscape, and the glare of sunlight as subjects, he has created a magical image of shapes and values has been created. Compare this work with the etching by Rembrandt (Figure 15.4). What similarities do you notice? How has the photographer made his work like a painting or drawing? Why do you think this photograph would be called a work of art?

Although most artists of the natural environment work in a two-dimensional medium, such as a painting, a drawing, or a print, artist David Smith decided to try a landscape sculpture!

Figure 15.15, titled *Hudson River Landscape*, is constructed of welded steel. This work is an abstraction of a landscape. The elements of the landscape—trees, hills, rivers—have been reduced to shapes, spaces, lines, and textures. In this work, as in other wire sculptures, the negative space creates shapes as important to the composition as the positive shapes. As you look at this work, what parts of the landscape do you think are represented? Is there an illusion of space in this sculpture?

Something To Try:

- Practice drawing the same landscape with a variety of drawing materials—pencil, chalk, charcoal, ink, or watercolor. Compare your drawings. Decide which medium best allows you to express texture, value, line, or color. Choose a mood to express with a scene from the natural environment. Experiment with different media to see which one best expresses the mood.

- If you have a camera, try your hand at taking photographs with the natural environment as your theme. Try both panoramic views and closeups. Try to capture a variety of textures and values in your photographs. You might want to refer to Book One, Chapter 20 for directions about making a simple pinhole camera (see Figure 20.4).

Selecting a Style

Just as artists use many different materials and tools to express various themes using the natural environment, they also use a variety of art styles from Impressionism to Expressionism.

John Marin [MAR • ren] was a well-known painter of seascapes. Figure 15.16, titled *Sun, Isles, Sea*, uses quick, slashing brushstrokes of watercolor to indicate the constant movement and shifting light and shadows of a seascape view.

In contrast, Piet Mondrian [PEET MON • dree • on] paints with block-like brushstrokes and opaque (not transparent) color to reveal the patterns created by the

Figure 15.16. John Marin. *Sun, Isles and Sea.* 1921. Watercolor on wove paper, 415 mm. x 495 mm. The Baltimore Museum of Art: Edward Joseph Gallagher, Jr. Bequest Fund, in memory of his son Edward Joseph Gallagher, III.

Figure 15.17. Piet Mondrian. *The Tree.* c. 1908. Oil on primed linen, 43" x 28½". Marion Koogler McNay Art Museum, San Antonio, Texas. Gift of Alice N. Hanszen.

Figure 15.18. Joseph Mallord William Turner. *The Burning of the Houses of Parliament.* 1834. Oil on canvas, 36½″ x 48½″. The Cleveland Museum of Art. Bequest of John L. Severance.

limbs of trees against the sky? Look at Figure 15.17. Does this artist's work remind you of the style of another artist you have read about in this chapter? What kind of art style would you call this work? (See Chapter 9).

Do you remember seeing the work of Mondrian before? (Book One, Chapter 7, Figure 7.5). Compare Mondrian's two styles of painting. Without looking at the dates of the paintings, see if you can tell which style came first.

In Chapter 9 you met English artist Joseph Turner. His painting, *The Grand Canal, Venice* was an example of the way he used vigorous brushstrokes and vivid colors to express the excitement and action of the scene. When Turner visited a new place, like Venice, he always made plenty of sketches. He would draw the same scene at different times of the day and in different whether. These sketches from life helped Turner create paintings that allow a viewer to almost feel the climate of a particular day.

Figure 15.18 is another work by Turner. *The Burning of the Houses of Parliament* has even more movement and excitement than *The Grand Canal.* Here Turner uses the same style of painting, but adds a mood of danger by using a wild splash of brilliant color for the fire. Notice the surrounding colors and values. How do they intensify the colors of the fire? It is said that Turner stayed up for several nights in a row studying the action of the flames and smoke, as they engulfed these famous government buildings in London. He frequently recorded his impressions in quick, watercolor sketches.

In complete contrast to the emotional movement of a Turner painting, is a work by Neil Welliver. Figure 15.19, titled *The Birches,* is an amazing example of the Photorealistic style of painting. As you recall, this style of painting mimics the detail and appearance of a photograph. This work by Welliver is five feet square and painted with absolute realism.

The confusion of textures and patterns created by the tree trunks, branches, and shadows seems almost like an abstract painting. If you squint your eyes, you might even be reminded of a work by Abstract Expressionist, Jackson Pollack (Chapter 10, Figure 10.11).

Something To Try:

Select a painting style that you have read about in this book. You might want to experiment with Cubism, Surrealism, or Impressionism. Create a landscape or seascape painting using the style you have selected.

Figure 15.19. Neil Williver. *Birches.* 1977. Oil on canvas, 60″ x 60″. The Metropolitan Museum of Art. Gift of Dr. and Mrs. Robert E. Carroll, 1979.

MEET JOHN MARIN

"The Moving of Me"

John Marin began his artistic career not as a painter, but as an architect. He soon realized that painting was the art form he wanted to use for expression and communication. Like so many other young American artists who lived during the exciting start of the 20th century, John Marin went to Europe to study art.

However, the avant-garde movements of Cubism and Expressionism didn't influence his work as much as the misty, atmospheric style of Impressionism.

Marin was interested in capturing the restlessness of the world of nature and humans he saw around him. He was especially attracted to both the city of New York and the coast of Maine. The ever-changing play of light, shadow, cloud, and wave inspired him for years. For Marin, even the buildings of the city were alive,

> . . . the whole city is alive; buildings, people, all are alive; and the more they move me, the more I feel them to be alive. It is this (moving of me) that I try to express. . .

Figure 15.20, titled *Lower Manhattan*, shows how he tried to give the impression of life and movement, even with objects as static and solid as skyscrapers.

Marin worked mostly in watercolor, liking the quick sketching that is possible with this medium. In this painting, he also combines charcoal with watercolor, creating a mixed-media work. Charcoal also allows quick, expressive strokes and wide contrasts in values.

Photograph by Paul Strand. 1945. Gelatin Silver Print, 5⅜″ x 5¾″. National Portrait Gallery, Smithsonian Institution.

BORN: 1870
DIED: 1953
BIRTHPLACE:
Rutherford, New Jersey

Figure 15.20. John Marin. *Lower Manhatten.* 1920. Watercolor and charcoal on paper, 21⅞″ x 26¾″. Collection, The Museum of Modern Art, New York. The Philip L. Goodwin Collection.

Student work.

Did you learn

- The definitions of these words and phrases: chiaroscuro; etching; viewpoint; vanishing point; thumbnail sketch; picture plane; visual composition; symmetrical composition; asymmetrical composition; media; linear perspective; eye level; horizon line; panorama?
- What two parts of a perspective drawing can be found in Figure 15.6?
- The kind of space that can be created with linear perspective?
- Subjects that were of interest to John Marin?

Understanding and Evaluating

- Practice using your senses of smell and hearing. Walk around your neighborhood or school and record not what you see, but what you hear and smell.
- Write a short story about one day in the life of a tree. Write your story from the viewpoint of the tree. Try to imagine that you are a tree. What would you see and notice about the world around you?

Seeing and Creating

- Try the process of carbon printing to begin an idea for a landscape. Take inexpensive carbon paper, an old iron, and some white construction paper. Begin by tearing the carbon paper into pieces of any size. Wrinkle it in your hand and then smooth it out. Place carbon side down on your construction paper. Begin your first print by placing the pieces in any arrangement you like.
  When the pieces are in place, cover with a sheet of newsprint. Press over the pieces with an iron for 30 to 60 seconds. More pressing may be necessary if the iron isn't hot enough. When the pieces of carbon paper are removed, a print of each piece should be left on the construction paper. Using water-based felt markers or India ink and pen, create an imaginary landscape from the textures and shapes you have printed. Draw in parts you need with markers.
- © [CAUTION: Irons can burn. Keeps hands out of the way while ironing. Never leave iron sitting flat on paper. Replace each time in an upright position. Unplug iron when not in use.]

Everyone loves a good story. A well-told story—whether truth or fiction—can grab and hold our attention for hours. If the scenes and characters are real enough, we can actually lose ourselves in the story, imagining that we are a part of the action and drama.

Artists have long realized the power of stories and have used them as inspiration for works of art. Art that is based on a historical event, story, myth, or legend is called **narrative art**. In this type of art, the artist is using a real or imagined event as the theme of the artwork. You have already read about and looked at some examples of narrative art. Look through this book again and find the ones you think fit the definition.

TELLING A GOOD STORY WITH ART

When we read, listen to, or watch a story unfold, we are following events that take place over a given period of time. Stories have a beginning, a middle, and an end. This would seem to mean that a story, or a series of related events, could not be told in a painting, drawing, print, or sculpture. These are, after all, single works, not movies or videotapes in which movement and the passage of time can be shown with great realism.

However, this lack of motion and time has not stopped artists from exploring stories as themes for their artworks. In the following examples, you will see that there are numerous ways around this problem. Some paintings are so full of action, characters, and details that they can occupy our attention just like a written story. Let's look at some famous examples of narrative art.

The Lure of History

Historical events have always offered artists ideal subjects for art. The drama and crisis of great events that shape the world provide an irresistible theme in a variety of art forms. Great historical battles have been a favorite theme since ancient times.

In Book One, Chapter 19, you were introduced to a famous tapestry called the *Bayeux Tapestry* (Figure 19.1). Over 230 feet long and 20 inches high, this embroidered tapestry records the main events of the Battle of Hastings, during which England was invaded by William the Conquerer. Like the scenes of a motion picture, we follow the images of the tapestry with fascination as the fateful events of 1066 A.D. unfold (Figure 16.1).

Chapter 16
NARRATIVE ART

WORDWATCH
narrative art
illustration
graphic device

Figure 16.1. *The Bayeux Tapestry.* 1073-83. Wool embroidery on linen, 20"h. Bayeux Museum. Photo credit: Archiv fur Kunst und Geschichte, Berlin.

But, you don't always need 230 feet to visualize a historical event. Sometimes, the story can be told with both drama and action within the space of a single picture frame.

Figure 16.2 is a Roman copy of a Greek work, titled *Victory of Alexander over Darius III.* Covering over ten feet of wallspace, this work is a mosaic. Found in the ruins of Pompeii, this magnificent example of ancient mosaic art illustrates the defeat by Alexander the Great of the Persian army led by Darius III.

For hundreds of years, Greece had been threatened by the armies of Persia. Finally, a true Greek hero, Alexander the Great, and his army were able to defeat and conquer Persia, bringing new glory and riches to Greece. The famous battle, which occurred in 333 B.C., became a favorite subject in Greek art.

To the right, we see the fast retreat of Darius as he turns to see his bodyguard trampled underfoot. To the right, just above the damaged part of the mosaic, we see the victorious Alexander. Doesn't he look every inch the hero?

Both the action and the realism of this work make it remarkable, but there are other interesting elements that make it a great work of art.

The artist has created a feeling of deep space, even though the background is painted white. Look how convincing the horses and soldiers are. There appears to be plenty of room for them to move about. Even the limitations of the mosaic process (colors and values formed with pieces of colored stone) have not prevented the skillful use of shading and light. The horses and figures appear three-dimensional; the metal armor appears to glisten and gleam.

Figure 16.2. Roman mosaic. *Alexander's Victory over Darius.* 356-323 B.C. Mosaic from the House of Fauno in Pompeii, 10'3¼" h. National Museum Naples, Italy. Photo credit: Archiv fur Kunst und Geschichte, Berlin.

The composition, or arrangement of the figures, is worth noting also. The artist has created a feeling of motion through the use of the many directions and positions of the men and horses. Waving swords and flailing legs keep our eyes busy. There is also the use of foreshortening. Do you recall another artist in this text who used foreshortening? (See Chapter 8). Can you find examples of foreshortening in this work?

Have you noticed the spears? Most are pointing in one direction, calling our attention to the victor and hero of this historical event.

The ancient battle between Alexander the Great and Darius continued to be a popular subject. Renaissance patrons and artists were especially taken with the heroic events described in this historical account.

During the Renaissance, the appeal of ancient history was intensified as more objects of antiquity were uncovered. Historical accounts like that of the battle between Darius and Alexander encouraged both heroism and fame.

Duke William IV of Bavaria loved great battles. In 1528, he decided that he wanted to have eight paintings created that depicted great battles of ancient times. The battle between Darius and Alexander was, of course, to be the subject of one of these paintings. For this work, he employed Albrecht Altdorfer [AL•breck ALT•dor•fur]. Little did Duke William know what he would get for his money! (Figure 16.3)

Within the picture plane space of 5 x 4 feet, Altdorfer crowded hundreds, perhaps thousands, of fighting soldiers. There is so much to see that it is impossible to grasp it all in a single viewing. This painting is like watching a three-hour movie! Considered one of the greatest battle scenes ever painted, there has never been a painting like this one—there probably never will be.

This is the same historical event represented in the Roman mosaic (Figure 16.2), but instead of a single scene

Figure 16.3. Albrecht Altdorfer. *The Battle of Alexander and Darius.* 1529. Oil on wood panel, 5'2" x 3'11". Alte Piankothek, Munich.

from the battle, Altdorfer shows us the whole battle. So much is happening we must move our eyes over the picture plane, taking in bits of action here and there. We almost feel as if time is passing, and we are watching the battle in slow motion.

Altdorfer also makes other changes not seen in the Roman work. Have you noticed the armor of the soldiers? They are dressed like medieval knights, not like Greek soldiers. This lapse from historical accuracy didn't seem to bother Altdorfer or his patron. Many Renaissance paintings use contemporary dress in scenes from ancient history. This may have had the added benefit of letting the Renaissance viewer feel more a part of the action. You may feel greater sympathy with people dressed the same as yourself.

Can you tell which soldiers are fighting for Alexander and which are part of Darius's army? The brave knights in armor are Alexander's soldiers. Darius's wear turbans and are mostly on foot. Can you find the figures of Darius (he's still fleeing in his chariot) and Alexander?

At the top of the painting, above a beautiful and peaceful Bavarian landscape, you see a rising sun and a setting moon. The sun represents Alexander; the moon, Darius. The strange plaque which hangs from the top of the painting describes the battle and points out the center or focal point of the action. Just let your eye travel down the cord hanging from the tassel, and you will find both Darius and Alexander.

Photographing History

With the invention of the camera, came a new way to create narrative art. Along with portraiture, the documentation of historical events attracted the attention of more and more artists/photographers. One of the most famous American photographers was Mathew Brady. He and his dozens of assistant photographers recorded both the people and events of the American Civil War. In fact, the Civil War became the first war in history to be so fully documented.

Figure 16.4 shows an example of Brady's work. We see a Civil War scene of a steam engine crossing a trestle bridge, as Union soldiers look on.

Some photographers used general scenes to represent or symbolize a whole historical period. Figure 16.5, titled *Steerage*, was taken in 1907 by Alfred Stieglitz [STEEG • leets]. It is a sensitive reminder of the hardships endured by many immigrants who came to America during the first part of the 20th century.

"Steerage" is a term that refers to the lower areas of a ship, where both cargo and the poor often traveled

Figure 16.4. M.B. Brady. *Fire Fly.* Photograph. The Metropolitan Museum of Art. Harris Brisbane Dick Fund, 1933.

Figure 16.5. Alfred Stieglitz. *The Steerage.* 1907. Chloride print, 11 cm. x 9.2 cm. © The Art Institute of Chicago. Alfred Stieglitz Collection.

184

together. Like the plot of a short story, this photograph tells us, in a single view, the differences between the traveling and living conditions of the upper-class passengers and those "below deck." The passengers on the second level watch the steerage immigrants as if they were part of an exhibit.

Storytelling and Illustration

You probably had a favorite book as a child which you liked as much for its pictures or illustrations as for its story. In fact, some stories are forever set in our minds through the images of the events and characters created by the illustrator of the story.

An **illustration** is the depiction of events in a story through visual art. Sometimes, the art itself makes the story.

English artist William Hogarth was both a fine narrative artist and a witty commentator on 18th-century life. Many of the people who populate his paintings are exaggerations, rather than real people. The themes of his works are the rewards and pitfalls of society as it was in 18th-century England.

Through a series of paintings, Hogarth told a visual story of how youth, money, and ill luck (or plain laziness) could ruin the most hopeful life. Each painting in the series is filled with visual clues and symbols which turn the viewer into a detective searching for answers among the characters and objects of the painting.

Figure 16.6 is scene one, or the first painting, in the series titled *Marriage a' la Mode.* "A la mode" is a French phrase that means "in the manner of the time." By the title of this series, we know that we are going to be told a visual story of the manners and customs of marriage in 18th-century England. Let's look at scene one.

The first painting is titled *Signing the Contract.* We see to the right, the fathers of the bride and groom arranging the terms of the marriage. The bride's father is offering a large sum of money, or dowry, as well as pointing out the importance of his family tree. The elegant and vain groom is found on the far right, admiring himself in a mirror. The bride sits nearby, but she is completely absorbed, not in her future husband, but in her lawyer. Clearly, this is not a marriage made in heaven. In fact, it seems doomed from the start.

Hogarth was a humorous, but cynical artist. He disliked many things about the society in which he lived and used his art to criticize, as well as entertain. His personal dislikes are never far from view. For example, the walls of the room shown in this painting are covered

Figure 16.6. William Hogarth. *Marriage a la Mode: Signing the Contract.* 1743. Oil on canvas, 28" x 35⅞". Reproduced by courtesy of the Trustees, The National Gallery, London.

185

Figure 16.7. Roy Lichtenstein. *Whamm!*. 1963. Oil and magna on canvas, 68″ x 160″. Collection, The Tate Gallery, London. Photo credit: Leo Castelli Gallery, New York.

by paintings by old masters. Hogarth was known to dislike the pretense of the rich, "showing off" their wealth by collecting these works.

Look through the window. You will see a building under construction. The style of this building, somewhat classical in form, was another of Hogarth's dislikes. Why does he put it into the painting? It belongs to the vain, young bridegroom who has wasted his fortune trying to pay for it. That is why he is forced to marry someone he doesn't love!

The details of a Hogarth painting can be fascinating, but a little frustrating. Like an elaborate computer game, the viewer must constantly search for more keys to unlock the action and meaning of the scene. But, if you enjoy puzzles and good stories, Hogarth's works can provide great enjoyment.

Perhaps the modern version of a Hogarth series is a comic book. Each frame of the comic, whether it has words or not, adds a little more information to the visual narrative. One contemporary artist found the style of comic-book illustration a source for his large-scale paintings. His name is Roy Lichtenstein [LICK•ten•stine].

Figure 16.7, appropriately titled *Whaam*, is painted on two panels. Do you remember what a two-panel painting is called?

Just as a comic-book drawing moves the action from one section to another, so does Lichtenstein's painting. The style of the painting is also an exact copy of the black-outlined, bright-colored drawings of a comic book.

Notice how movement is represented. How has the artist illustrated an explosion? These are **graphic devices** that we also see used in advertising. A **graphic device** is simply a way an artist has of showing, through drawing, painting, or printmaking, a movement, expression, or idea. In cartoons, comics, and some advertising, realistic details are reduced to graphic devices. Devices include quickly drawn, repeated lines to represent movement or radiating, overlapping shapes to represent an explosion.

Lichtenstein not only uses the graphic devices of cartoons and comics, but he also adds words. When you look at Figure 16.7, do you think words are necessary to understand the painting? What purpose do you think the words serve?

Artist Norman Rockwell is probably the most famous American visual storyteller or illustrator. For over thirty years his works decorated the covers of *The Saturday Evening Post* magazine.

One of the reasons people like Rockwell's illustrations so much is the story they tell. With photographic detail and the use of real people for his models, Rockwell painted scenes that were as familiar and American as a

Figure 16.8. Norman Rockwell. *Girl at Mirror.* 1954. (Saturday Evening Post: March 6, 1954, cover). Norman Rockwell Art Collection Trust. The Norman Rockwell Museum at Stockbridge.

Thanksgiving dinner. Like Hogarth, Rockwell filled his works with interesting details that the viewer could examine to learn more about the visual drama taking place.

Figure 16.8, titled *Girl at Mirror,* is one of the most famous and popular magazine covers he painted. As we look at this painting, we begin to imagine a narrative or story to go along with it. Like a detective, we start making connections between them and their actions.

Legends and Mighty Deeds

Legends and deeds of valor also play an important part as themes for narrative art. In the world of fantasy and mythology, the imagination of the artist is given complete freedom to invent and to exaggerate for added meaning and expression.

Figure 16.9 is by the Renaissance artist Raphael. It is a painting of a popular medieval and Renaissance legend, titled *St. George and the Dragon.* Do you remember another Renaissance artist who used a character from this legend as inspiration for a work of art?

Raphael's painting reminds us of an illustration in a fairytale. The brave knight on the white horse is slaying the fierce dragon to save the prayerful maiden kneeling in the background. Although there is movement and action, it isn't very violent. The entire conflict seems to be elegant and polite, as if played out by dancers in a ballet.

Figure 16.10 shows a page from an East-Indian manuscript, showing a legendary event from the life of the Hindu god, Krishna. In this detailed painting, we see the god hold up, with effortless grace, an entire mountain like an umbrella, over the heads of the astonished crowd. Notice the style of painting. The edges of all the figures and objects are painted with precision. Brushstrokes are completely eliminated. All parts of the work are painted with the same degree of realism.

Something To Try:

Try your hand at telling a story with art. Select an event, real or imaginary, and visualize it in a painting or drawing. Like Hogarth, add details, that help the viewer uncover more information about the characters or events.

Read a myth or legend. Design on paper a monument representing the legend. Plan the monument to be erected in a public place. Try to select a critical moment from the story to represent. Add enough details to reveal other parts or characters in the legend.

Figure 16.9. Raphael. *Saint George and the Dragon.* 1506. Oil on wood, 11⅛″ x 8⅜″. National Gallery of Art, Washington, D.C., Andrew W. Mellon Collection.

Figure 16.10. *Harivamsa* (The Geneology of Hari): Krishna Lifts Mount Govardhan. Produced in the Imperial Studios of Akbar, probably by Miskin. Opaque watercolor on paper, 11⅜″ x 7⅞″. The Metropolitan Museum of Art, Purchase. Edward C. Moore, Jr. Gift, 1928.

Portrait—William Hogarth. *The Painter and his Pug.* 1745. Tate Gallery, London. Photo: Tate Gallery/Art Resource, New York.

BORN: 1697
DIED: 1764
BIRTHPLACE:
London, England

The Lessons of Life

Perhaps William Hogarth's need to use his art to teach people the results of leading a wasted or wicked life came from the fact that his father was a schoolteacher.

Hogarth's cynical view of life was also influenced by his father's imprisonment for debt, when William was still a boy. Visiting his father in prison gave Hogarth realistic, but depressing material for his paintings. He saw first hand how debtors were treated in 18th-century England. And it was not a pretty sight!

Although trained as an engraver or printmaker, Hogarth soon turned to painting as his main means of expression. He adopted a new kind of painting, called moral, narrative art. By telling a story with paint, a moral lesson could also be taught for the benefit of the viewer. He became famous for this kind of painting and produced several "picture-story" series. Each series usually contained from six to eight paintings. Each painting represented one more episode or chapter in the story.

The success of the paintings encouraged Hogarth to copy them as engravings. In this way, many copies could be sold, making them available to the general public. With the public's love of stories and gossip, these engravings made Hogarth a great deal of money. They helped establish Hogarth's reputation as one of the most important English artists of his time.

Figure 16.11 is yet another episode in the *Marriage a' la Mode* series. In this painting, we see the bride is now a wife, one Lady Squanderfield. She is entertaining a group of her elegant, but worthless friends. The husband is nowhere to be found. What a marriage!

Figure 16.11. William Hogarth. *Marriage a la Mode: Scene IV Coutness' Levee.* 1743. Oil on canvas, 27" x 35". Reproduced by courtesy of the Trustees, The National Gallery, London.

Did you learn

- The definitions of these words and phrases: narrative art; illustration; graphic device?
- The historical event that inspired the creation of the *Bayeux Tapestry?*
- Two works that were inspired by an ancient battle between Alexander the Great and Darius III?
- A "pointer" that directs attention at Darius and Alexander in Altdorfer's famous painting?
- The first war to be fully documented with photography?
- A famous American photographer of the Civil War?
- An example of a graphic device?
- Why Hogarth's paintings are called "picture-stories"?

Student work.

Understanding and Evaluating

- See if you can discover more information about Alexander the Great in your school or local library. Make a list of other historical events from Alexander's life that might make an interesting theme for a work of art.
- Examine Figure 16.8 closely. Write a short story about the scene you see. In your story answer the following question: Why is the young girl sitting in front of the mirror?

Student work.

Seeing and Creating

- Select a favorite adventure story to illustrate. Use a style of drawing like that of a cartoon—strong colors and black outlines. Try to pick one moment that represents the main point or action of the story.
- Choose a historical event from American history to illustrate. Try to call attention to the main character or action through an art element. For example, make the colors around the main figure more intense. Use the directions of lines to point to the action (see Figure 16.2), or lighten or darken the focal area to create contrasts with surroundings.
- Write a short story about a lost treasure. Create a tempera or acrylic painting to illustrate your story. Use a color scheme that adds a mood of mystery or danger.

Unit V
ART FOR TODAY

Art is as important in today's world as it was in centuries past. The difference today is that many people still believe art is found only in a museum or on the walls of a wealthy person's home. This is, of course, not true. Like the threads of a tapestry, visual art is woven into the very fabric of the modern world. The products we use, the cars we ride in, the magazines we read, and the movies we see all make use of the talent and creativity of artists.

No longer confined to museums, art is everywhere and available to everyone. In the not too distant past, most great works of art were rarely seen by ordinary citizens. Shut away in the private collections of the wealthy, average people had little or no opportunity to view the great works of art.

How lucky we are! The whole world of art is now gathered into books or reproduced as prints, on postcards, and in dozens of other visual forms. These reproductions allow everyone to admire, compare, and evaluate works of art.

For the price of a book or postcard, you too can wonder about the meaning and mystery of Mona Lisa's smile, just as the king of France once did.

Of course, a photographic reproduction, no matter how well done, can never replace the wonder of seeing these great works in their original form. Visits to museums and galleries are an important part of learning about art.

The following chapters will explore some of the uses modern society makes of art and artists, as well as some of the new directions artists are exploring today. You will also have an opportunity to read about art careers, and whether you might want to consider a future in one of the many art-related professions.

The future holds exciting possibilities for art and artists. Whether human beings travel to distant planets or into space, you can bet that art will go with them. Artists will be there too. After all, who is going to design all those new space cars for the 22nd century!

Although you have several years yet to plan your future career, you probably have already thought about what you might want to do and have discussed careers with your friends and parents. If you have thought about art as something you would like to do, you will be pleased to know that you have a wide selection of careers to choose from.

But, how do you know if you should seriously consider art as a career? Your grades in art may be very good, but you make good grades in other subjects, as well.

For some people the need to express themselves through visual art is so powerful they cannot even consider another line of work. If you are one of these people, you are lucky. You already *know* you have to be an artist. If, on the other hand, you have a sincere liking for art activities, but are not sure if you have what it takes to be an art professional, the following traits or qualities might help you in your search for a career.

HOW TO RECOGNIZE AN ARTIST

Many artists share certain characteristics of personality and skill. If you don't recognize yourself in these traits, it doesn't mean you can't be an artist! Talent in art and a desire to succeed are difficult to measure. But, if any of these traits sound familiar to you, you probably should at least consider an art-related career.

Artists Are Observant

Artists are very observant. They see more than most people and often see in different ways. Artists are able to discover new information or ways of looking at an object or scene. Artists see creatively.

Artists Feel Strongly About Things

Artists will often react strongly to a scene, object, or event that others find uninteresting. Artists can get very excited about the color of the sky, the shape of a tree, or the texture of a leaf. To an artist, these sensations have great intensity and meaning.

Artists Like To Work With Their Hands

When an artist sees something that is interesting or inspiring, he or she will have a need to express his or her feelings about it by making something with their hands, such as a drawing or sculpture. They like to design and redesign the world around them. People who are truly interested in art make art all the time. They draw in the margins of notebooks, in math class, and in their spare time at home. They build models, collect all manner of

Chapter 17

CAREERS IN ART

WORDWATCH
freelance
portfolio
fine art
applied art
graphic designer
layout
interior designer
architect
urban designer
industrial designer
Post-Modern

ADVERTISING
  Graphic Designer
  Art Director
  Layout Artist
  Illustrator
  Paste-Up Artist
  Display Artist
  Package Designer
  Calligrapher
  Type Designer
  Window Decorator
  Researcher
  Photo Retoucher
  Sign Painter
  Color Consultant
  Photographer
  Publicity Director
  Printer
  Advertising Agency Director
ARCHITECTURE
  Architect
  City Planner
  Model Maker
  Lighting Consultant
  Landscape Architect
  Draftsman
  Architectural Illustrator
  Stained-Glass Designer
  Woodworker

odds and ends to build imaginary structures, and restore the old, the broken, and the useless. Artists love to work with their hands.

Artists Work Hard

Some people don't consider art to be work at all. They think that artists just sit around all day mixing paint and sketching with pencils! This is a mistaken idea. Creating art is some of the hardest work you can do.

To create art means to be constantly solving problems. Art means using your brain and creative instincts to their maximum capacity. Few artists work only an eight-hour day. Most work far into the night, on weekends, and on holidays. And that's when you work for yourself, or **freelance. Freelance** artists work from their own homes or studios. Even though they don't go into an office every day, they are under great pressure to seek out **clients** (customers for your artwork) and commissions. Like all artists, they are under pressure to come up with new ideas and new images. Yes, art is very hard work!

Artists Like to Experiment

Artists like to try new things. They are not timid about being the first to try a new dance or taste an unusual food. Most artists enjoy traveling because it takes them to new and different places where they can see new things and experience new sensations. These experiences and sensations are then used to come up with creative ideas and images.

Artists like to experiment with new ways of making art and new materials and tools for making art. They are always searching for fresh ways of expressing themselves visually.

Artists Can Work Alone or With People

If you want to be an artist, you should be able to work by yourself for long periods of time. This means having self-discipline. You must be able to set deadlines for yourself and to meet them. There won't always be someone there to remind you to get busy and finish your assignment. Self-discipline is a very difficult skill to master. When left alone with a task, all of us can be easily distracted, unless we are organized and disciplined to complete the job at hand.

Artists must also be able to work with people. There will be clients and customers who will have their own ideas about the job they are hiring an artist for. The artist must be able to adjust creative ideas to meet their needs. Artists in some careers must be willing to compromise.

If you recognize any of these qualities or traits in yourself and you enjoy making art, you might want to consider a career in which designing and art production are important parts.

The art world, however, is highly competitive. For young people just beginning, it can be very tough and filled with disappointment. But, you can succeed if you have the talent and desire. And regardless of what you might have heard, people can make decent livings creating art. You probably won't get rich, but you will be able to live a good life. Most of the careers listed pay reasonably well. You will also have the added benefit of having a job that you enjoy and that can be enjoyed by others.

HOW DO I KNOW I'M GOOD AT ART?

Believe it or not, there are some aptitude tests for art ability, just like there are tests for math and reading skills. Most of these tests, however, won't tell you how good you are in art or whether you will be happy in an art-related career. They are designed to help you judge whether your personality and temperament are suited to the kinds of tasks that artists must do.

A far better way to judge your ability is to ask other art professionals, starting with your art teacher. He or she knows your art and work habits better than anyone else at the present. You can also show your work to other art professionals. As you enter high school, you will have more opportunities to meet people who are professional artists.

Save examples of your work to show. Try to save works from a variety of projects and in a variety of media. You might want to keep your samples in a **portfolio.** A **portfolio** is a large folder, made of either cardboard or vinyl. Some professional portfolios can be very expensive, but you can make your own by taping two pieces of posterboard together along one edge. Ribbon or string ties can be added to hold your work inside.

Most important of all is to show pride in your artwork by seeing that it is properly stored and protected from accidents like being chewed by the dog or torn by your baby sister!

Most high schools have an art teacher who offers art classes at a variety of levels. You will probably find the high-school art program demanding of your skills and time. But, if you are serious about an art career, you should try to take art in high school.

If you intend to go to college, you will need to talk with your parents, art teacher, and guidance counselor about the best school for you. There are colleges and universities that have excellent art departments, where

EDUCATION
  Art Teacher
  Art Consultant
  Art Therapist
  Crafts Counselor
  Art Historian
  Art Lecturer
  Artist-in-Residence
  Art Reference Librarian
FASHION
  Hair Stylist
  Fashion Illustrator
  Fashion Editor
  Fabric Designer
  Makeup Artist
  Fashion Photographer
  Accessories Designer
  Color Consultant
FINE ARTS
  Painter
  Sculptor
  Printmaker
  Photographer
  Filmmaker
  Portraitist
  Muralist
GALLERIES
  Gallery Director
  Curator
  Lecturer
  Gallery Owner
  Artists' Agent
  Display Artist
INTERIOR DESIGN
  Interior Designer
  Decorating Studio Assistant
  Illustrator
  Color Consultant
  Lighting Consultant
  Fabric Consultant
  Draftsman
  Model Maker
JOURNALISM AND PUBLISHING
  Art Editor
  Art Critic
  Art Publisher
  Illustrator
  Layout Artist
  Cartoonist
  Comicstrip Creator
  Photography Editor
  Political Cartoonist
  Lithographer
  Photographer
  Graphic Designer
  Calligrapher
  Greeting Card Designer
  Type Designer

you can major in a variety of art-related subjects, while still receiving a general education in a variety of other subjects. There are also art schools in which the curriculum is primarily made up of art courses.

Many of these schools send representatives to high schools throughout the United States to talk about their programs. You and your parents can also send for brochures and course catalogs from these schools. Your school counselor will probably have a number of brochures for you to look at from different colleges and universities in the country.

Regardless of the kind of school you choose, it is important that you get advanced training in art, if art is going to be your career. The competition in art fields can be fierce, and you will want to prepare yourself in the best, most complete way possible.

Fine Art and Applied Art

"I just want to draw and paint. I don't want to work for other people."

If this sounds like something you have said or heard, you were talking about **fine art**. Fine art doesn't really have anything to do with the quality of the work. Fine art is simply a term that refers to artworks created for no other purpose than to be seen and appreciated for their own sake. Fine art isn't made to sell a product or to serve as decoration. Of course, it isn't at all unusual to find fine art used for just these purposes. The difference is in the artist's original intent.

Leonardo didn't paint the *Mona Lisa* to sell greeting cards or T-shirts, although her face has turned up on both! He painted her portrait because of what he could express about himself and the human condition through those memorable features.

If you choose a career in the fine arts, you will paint, draw, sculpt, or make prints all for the purpose of expressing yourself visually. If this is the way you want to spend your life, you are joining the ranks of a very distinguished group of people, including most of those you have read about in this text. Some, like Rubens, achieved wealth and fame during their lifetimes. Others were not so fortunate.

To draw, paint, or sculpt for a living is very difficult. You will more than likely need to consider other job alternatives to pay the house rent and the electric bill. It takes great courage to make the decision to be a creator of fine art. Those who make the commitment feel that no other career is as satisfying, although the financial rewards are small.

Applied art is art that serves purposes beyond that of just visual expression. Most of the products we use daily were designed by applied artists. Architects, graphic designers, and illustrators all work in applied art.

UNDERSTANDING ART CAREERS

Let's take a quick survey of some of the more popular art-related careers. Although each requires different skills and training, all use art to express ideas or to meet the aesthetic needs of modern society. Who knows, one of them may be just what you want to do!

Illustrator

An illustration, as you already know, is a drawing or painting that enhances or visually describes written material. Magazines, newspapers, book publishers, and advertisers all hire illustrators. Although each illustrator will have a personal style of working, those who can meet the needs of a wide variety of clients will fare well in the job market. Illustrators frequently work freelance, seeking work from many different sources.

Graphic Designer

Like an architect, a **graphic designer** organizes and arranges the structure of a printed page. Using drawings, paintings, or photographs supplied by an illustrator or photographer, the graphic designer creates a **layout** or composition for printed material. The layout may be for a page for a textbook, a poster, or a billboard. Some graphic designers also find work in television and the motion-picture industry. With the modern world's reliance on printed material, there are many different tasks for graphic designers (Figure 17.1)

Interior Designer

Interior designers choose and arrange the furnishings for homes, office buildings, banks, theaters, hotels, and numerous other interior spaces. Like architects, they must prepare plans and diagrams of room arrangements and color schemes. In today's complex world of innovative building materials and environmental and health concerns, interior designers must have extensive training in many areas of architectural and industrial construction. (Figure 17.2)

Figure 17.1. Ikko Tanaka. *Nihon Buyo.* 1981. Offset lithograph, 40½″ x 28¾″. Collection, The Museum of Modern Art, New York. Gift of the College of Fine Arts, UCLA.

Figure 17.2. *Modern Interior Design.* Walt Disney World, Swan Hotel, Lake Buena Vista, Florida. Architect: Alan Lapidus. Michael Graves Architectural Association. Photo: William Taylor. Interior designers frequently design as well as arrange the furnishings in a building.

Architect

Architects design homes and buildings. But, like the interior designer, the modern world has changed the job description of the architect. While still designing buildings, many architects have become **urban designers.** They are interested in the design of entire cities—from the layout of roads to the preservation of the natural environment. (Figure 17.3)

Industrial Designer

The design of the fork you eat with, the chair you sit on, and the bicycle you ride are all the results of an **industrial designer.** With so many different products, machines, and equipment used by modern society, industrial designers have a hand in almost everything we see or use. Door knobs, toys, computers, office furniture, lamps, toothbrushes—all were, at some point, drawings on the boards of industrial designers. This is one art career that seems to have endless possibilities for the future. In the following chapter, you will learn more about design in the modern world and some of the artist/designers who have achieved success in this fascinating field. (Figure 17.4).

Photographer

You have already seen the work of some well-known photographers. Although a relatively new art form, compared to painting, photography as a career in the modern world has almost as many possibilities as industrial design.

Some photographers specialize in portraits, while others work to capture events for newspapers and magazines. Some photograph food; others concentrate on sports. Photographic assignments can be as varied as the customers they serve—television, magazines, advertising, or law-enforcement. (Figure 17.5)

Teaching Art

Perhaps the most important art career of all is that of teaching art. Art teachers direct and encourage the talents and abilities of their students. Even if the majority of those students do not become professional

Figure 17.3. Michael Graves. *Public Service Building,* Portland Oregon. View from Fifth Avenue. Photo credit: Paschall/Taylor. Courtesy of Michael Graves.

Figure 17.4. American. *Silver Tableware with Salt and Pepper Shakers.* Designed c. 1930. The Metropolitan Museum of Art. Gift of Russell Wright, 1976.

Figure 17.5. Photographers can work in many different areas including television, motion pictures, newspapers, and magazines.

artists, art teachers still play a major role in educating the general public about the vital part art plays in the world.

There are many different art topics to teach at many different levels. Some teachers select to teach only art history or studio subjects at the university level. Others prefer to work with young people like yourself, or even younger, such as first- or second-graders. (Figure 17.6).

Teaching in schools, whether it be math or art, takes special training and education. A qualified art teacher must have a college degree, in addition to special courses in the behavior of children and teaching strategies.

Although you won't get rich teaching, it can be a very rewarding art career. Many of the great artists of history were also teachers. However, being a great artist does not necessarily make you a great teacher. Teaching requires special ability and commitment. For art teachers, the progress and accomplishments of their students are their creative expression, their "works of art."

Figure 17.6. Possibly the most important art job is that of teaching. Dedication and commitment are needed to open the wonderful world of art to the young.

Jobs in Art Museums

Art museums employ many people in a wide variety of jobs, from curator to docent. Like schools, museums educate the public about art. Many of the same instructional skills needed by teachers are important for museum educators. Some positions in art museums, such as that of docent, are voluntary, and provide experience and practice in public speaking. (Figure 17.7).

Figure 17.7. Museums offer many job opportunities for those interest in art.

Courtesy of Michael Graves.

BORN: 1934
BIRTHPLACE:
Indianapolis, Indiana

Figure 17.8. Michael Graves. *Singing Kettle.* Designed for Alesssi. Photo credit: William Taylor. Courtesy of Michael Graves.

Of Buildings and Tea Kettles

Michael Graves was originally trained as an architect, but has found a wider audience for his work as a designer of furniture and household items. He combines both humor and an unusual sense of visual balance in the objects he designs.

Michael Graves, as architect and designer, belongs to a movement or style called **Post-Modern.** There is some disagreement about the exact definition of this style, since it takes many forms. You can usually recognize it in architecture by the way certain elements of ancient architecture are combined with more modern developments. For example, parts of Greek columns will be placed near the top of a modern building, or an entrance will appear as if an ancient Egyptian temple has been blended with a modern office building (Figure 17.3) decked out in bright colors. In Post-Modern design, anything goes!

Yet for all its outrageous combinations, Post-Modern design can also be fascinating, fun, and quite beautiful. It is as if the architects and designers have tired of taking their work so seriously, and have decided instead to add wit, humor, and fun to the mixture.

By far, Michael Grave's most well-known design is that of a "singing" kettle (Figure 17.8). Made of stainless steel, this delightful object uses space as expressively as a piece of sculpture. With beautiful precision, Graves contrasts one material and texture against another. His final note is a funny, little bird perched on the end of the spout. After all, this is a "singing" kettle.

This design made such an impression on people that over 40,000 were sold in a single year! The designer became such a celebrity, that people asked him to autograph their kettles. So much for poor, struggling designers!

Did you learn

- The definitions of these words and phrases: freelance; portfolio; fine art; applied art; graphic designer; layout; interior designer; architect; urban designer; industrial designer; Post-Modern?
- At least three traits that artists have in common?
- The differences between fine art and applied art?
- What graphic designers do?
- What urban designers do?
- Some businesses and professions that hire photographers?
- At least two reasons teaching art may be the most important art career of all?
- A characteristic of Post-Modern architecture?

Student work.

Understanding and Evaluating

- Interview someone who has an art-related career that you think would be interesting. Find out why he or she chose the career and what they like best about it. Ask what skills or training are necessary to do the job. See if they share any of the artistic traits mentioned in this chapter.
- Select one of the careers from the list at the beginning of the chapter. Write a job description based on what you know or imagine the job to be. Include in your description any special qualities, education, or training you think essential for the job.

Student work.

Seeing and Creating

- Design a poster or advertisement for a space station or city. Use water-based felt markers or India ink and pen.
- Using two or three contrasting colors and at least three objects, create a design out of cut paper.
- Make some drawings of students in your art class. Try to capture them as they work on their own art.
- Illustrate a poem or story using a woodcut or
ⓒ linoleum block-print design. [CAUTION: Wood and linoleum block cutting tools should be used carefully and under the supervision of a teacher. Never cut toward your hands or body. Hold the block in the proper manner while cutting (see Figure 12.10)].

Chapter 18

DESIGNING THE MODERN WORLD

As you learned in the last chapter, there are many art-related careers that involve designing products and environments for modern life. The most difficult task of a designer is not developing the idea, but coming up with it in the first place. Sometimes, no matter how hard you try you just can't think of a new, fresh idea. When your next paycheck depends on new ideas, you better have some way to restart the creative machinery! There are ways to move around creative blocks, and you can practice them to improve your own visual and creative thinking.

VISUAL THINKING

Visual problem solving or **visual thinking** is simply a means to find creative solutions to problems. It is especially helpful in producing new solutions to art and design problems.

The first important skill needed for visual problem solving is to be able to create an image in your mind of what you see, hear, feel, taste, smell, and think. You may believe you always do this when you experience things, but you don't. Not as clearly as you can with practice. The more skillful you become at mental imaging, the better you will be able to create with art what you experience. Let's experiment!

Making Mental Pictures

As you read each of the following images, try to picture it in your mind as clearly as possible. Take your time. Try to hold the image, and see if more details appear.

- your house
- what you ate for dinner last night
- your favorite dessert
- a sneeze
- ice on your tongue
- smell of rain
- sound of a siren
- smell of a rose
- blowing a bubblegum bubble
- your hand in water

Which images were the easiest to visualize? Which were the hardest?

Remembering What You See

Figure 18.1. Study these shapes for one minute. Cover and see if you can draw them in the right order.

Students always complain that they can't draw what they see. Even though they may have seen a dog thousands of times, the shapes, textures, and details of a dog are forgotten when they begin to draw.

One way to overcome this is to learn to really look when you see something. Pay attention to the basic shapes first and then how the parts fit together. Then look closely at textures and other details. The more you practice being observant, the better you will be.

Another way to sharpen your visual memory is to practice recalling what you see and to create an image in your mind. For example:

Look at the row of shapes in Figure 18.1. Study them for one minute. Cover them, and on another sheet of paper, draw them in the correct order.

Place yourself in front of a light switch or door knob. Study it for one minute. Look away, and draw it, including as many details as you can remember. When you are finished, check your drawing against the object. How well did you do?

Look at the image in Figure 18.2 for two minutes. Cover the image, and make a list of as many of the objects as you remember.

See how many of these events you can picture in your mind. Imagine a piece of white paper. Now, imagine folding it in half. Fold it again. Unfold it. Cut a circle in one of the sections. Cut a square in another. Draw a circle in another. Write your initials in the last section. Do you still have a clear image?

Exercises like these sharpen your visual memory. You might want to create some other exercises for yourself and your friends. How many times can you imagine a piece of paper being folded?

Seeing objects in your mind and remembering them are important skills for artists and designers. But, what about getting those creative ideas? Where do they come from?

If you practice the exercises, they will help you prepare for the next step in creative problem solving—developing new ideas.

Brainstorming is a term you are already familiar with. It describes a way of considering or thinking about many possible solutions to a problem before selecting the best or most creative solution. Creative brainstorming is one method artists and designers use to overcome creative

Figure 18.2. Study the above image for two minutes. Cover and list as many objects as you remember.

blocks. It can sometimes be the answer to the statement, "I don't know what to draw/paint/sculpt/do."

Coming Up With Bright Ideas

⟦?⟧ Creative brainstorming can sometimes take the form of a "what if" game. Let's see how this method works.

By asking a series of "what if" questions, you can come up with some unusual and creative images that might be great ideas for an artwork or design project you are planning. Here's an example of some interesting "what if" questions. Can you add to the list?

What if. . .

> . . . everyone had three eyes
> . . . it rained all the time
> . . . plants could move around
> . . . right angles were forbidden
> . . . everyone had the same face
> . . . you had to buy air
> . . . everything was transparent

The best way to use a "what if" idea is to expand it by thinking about how the "what if" would change the environment or the way people would live their lives. For example, select one of the "what if's" and make a pencil drawing of how it would change details and how they would be changed. Would people dress differently? Would they need special equipment? Would buildings be the same? Often, it is the details of a "what if" that turn into the best, most creative ideas.

Another technique for coming up with new ideas is to doodle. That's right. Take a pencil and start to draw—anything. Most people don't take their doodles seriously. Artists do. From the curling lines of a doodle design, a jewelry designer may create a new shape for a bracelet. The repeated lines of a doodle might suggest a new pattern to a fabric designer. Some designers never work without a pencil or pen in their hand. As they think, they draw. Try it yourself. See how many interesting images you come up with.

Another creative brainstorming technique is to make mental connections between unrelated objects or ideas. Picture these two objects in your mind—a roller skate and a sofa. Now imagine them connected or combined in different ways. Their sizes can be changed as needed. After all, in your mind, you are not restricted to reality!

Once you have imagined a few interesting combinations, sketch them in pencil. As you draw, add details. Ask yourself if the new object has a use or function.

For more practice, imagine, connect, and draw the following:

- a fork and a wheel
- a pencil and a cloud
- a balloon and a loaf of bread
- a zipper and a kite
- a faucet and a typewriter

You can use this and the other techniques anytime you are looking for an idea. It may take some thought and several practice sketches, but you will be amazed at how many new ideas turn up.

DESIGN FOR A MODERN WORLD

Are artists and designers the same? Throughout this text, both artists and designers have been mentioned together and apart. So which is correct? In reality, it can be both!

Those individuals who work only in fine art media, such as painting, sculpture, and printmaking, are usually referred to as artists. However, throughout the centuries, artists have also designed furniture, jewelry, dishes, and fabrics. Some have even designed weapons. Even the great Leonardo designed Renaissance versions of super-weapons for combative patrons.

In the last chapter you learned that when art is put to work, or serves a purpose or **function,** it becomes applied art. Today, more than in the past, we refer to those who create functional objects as designers. So, an artist can be both fine artist and applied artist or designer.

In the following sections, the word *designer* will be used to refer to individuals who design functional objects. Like all art forms, the designs of everyday objects have undergone many changes through the years. In the 20th century, there have been a number of design styles that have influenced and altered everything from dinner plates to wallpaper patterns.

A Love of Decoration

Clothes, household objects, and even machinery designed in the 19th century can be identified by its **decorative** appearance. **Decorative design** uses patterns, textures, and curving shapes, plus swirling lines and ornaments to create visual interest. Of course, you have already seen other examples of ornamental design. Can

A.

B.

C.

Figure 18.3. A. American Rosewood Slipper Chair. Middle 19th century attributed to John Belter. 44¼" x 17½" x 16½". The Metropolitan Museum of Art. Gift of Mr. and Mrs. Lowell Russ Burch and Miss Jean McLean Morron, 1951. **B.** Bronze Candelabra. French 1st quarter of the 19th century. The Metropolitan Museum of Art. Gift of Mrs. Percy Rivington Pyne, 1947, in memory of James A. Scrymser. **C.** Silver teapot, American, 1840-50. Maker: Ball, Tompkins and Black, New York. The Metropolitan Museum of Art. Gift of Mr. and Mrs. Henry Mali, 1944.

Figure 18.4. *Gothic Revival Style Chair.* ca. 1860. Walnut and leather, 64½″ x 25⅜″ with 22½″ depth. The Metropolitan Museum of Art. Friends of the American Wing Fund, 1986.

Figure 18.5. William Morris. *Wallpaper.* Design, 1896. 22″ wide. The Metropolitan Museum of Art, Purchase. Edward C. Moore, Jr. Gift, 1923.

Figure 18.6. American. *Art Nouveau Vase.* 1890-1910. Blown glass and silver. The Metropolitan Museum of Art, Purchase, 1968. Edgar J. Kaufmann Charitable Foundation.

you remember the name of the style? Here's a hint. It was popular in the 18th century.

Figure 18.3 shows a selection of 19th-century objects. You can see how their design depends on decorative elements more than the function they were designed for.

In search of more decorative ideas, late 19th-century designers turned to the past. One very popular style was called **Gothic Revival.**

This style of design, as you can see by the name, revived the decorative elements of medieval or Gothic art and architecture. Pointed arches, elaborate plant and animal patterns borrowed from Gothic tapestries, painted scenes from medieval legends—all became part of the design of things from furniture to wallpaper.

Figure 18.4 is an example of the Gothic Revival style in furniture. Look back to Chapter 6 to the Gothic cathedrals and sculptures. What Gothic design elements can you identify in Figure 18.4?

Figure 18.5 shows a sample of a wallpaper design in Gothic Revival style. It was designed by William Morris, an English designer who helped popularize the Gothic Revival style. In building his own house, Morris tried to have everything crafted by hand and designed to his specifications. He hated the industrial, mass-produced objects of his day. He wanted to return to the medieval way of designing and handcrafting objects with care and beauty.

When the 20th century began, the decorative style was still very popular. Then it began to undergo some interesting changes. One of the most noticeable was in the style of decoration. Objects were still very decorative, but the edges of objects and the lines of the ornaments had started to swirl as never before. This was the birth of the design style known as **art nouveau** [new • VOH].

Art Nouveau

Figure 18.6 is an example of the art-nouveau style. The designer has used long flowing lines that coil and curl like a vine. While the Gothic Revival style borrowed design ideas from the past, many design elements of the nouveau style were borrowed from nature, especially the shapes and lines of plants.

For example, the water lily was a favorite design **motif.** A **motif** is a feature that recurs in a design. The use of plant forms in design was made famous by the Tiffany Studios of New York. The most famous product of the studio, was the Tiffany lamp (Figure 18.7).

Combining the curving line of the nouveau style with the stained glass craft of the great cathedrals, these beautiful lamps have become as treasured by collectors as masterpieces of painting or sculpture. Many museums have examples of these wonderful objects.

In Figure 18.7 you can see how both the base and shade of the lamp have been designed with plants in mind. Notice the graceful lines of the design. Each part seems to flow into the others. Can you imagine how beautiful this lamp would be if it were lighted in a dark room?

THE IMPORTANCE OF FUNCTION

The graceful line of the nouveau style was replaced by what was to be the most important design movement of the 20th century. This new style was known as **Bauhaus** [BOW • house].

The Bauhaus style developed in 1919 at a German school for architects and designers. The main purpose of the school was to train designers to improve the look and function of the machine-made, mass-produced products that were becoming part of every household. Bauhaus designers believed that design should be based on function, not decoration. They also believed that the materials of industry and mass-production—steel, concrete, and plastic—were proper materials for art, architecture, and product design.

You only have to compare the chair in Figure 18.3 with the Bauhaus chair in Figure 18.8 to see the difference this new style made. Gone are the decorative ornaments. In their place are smooth form and clean lines.

The chair in Figure 18.8 was designed by one of the greatest members of the Bauhaus School. Ludwig Mies van der Rohe [mees VAN • dur • Row]. Although this chair was made in the 1920s, its style is copied even today. You have probably seen chairs very much like it in restaurants, furniture stores, or perhaps in your own house.

The Bauhaus style had a great influence on design everywhere. The United States, with its interest in industry and technology, was especially receptive. As you will see in the next chapter, Bauhaus design became the model for architecture, as well.

Post-Modern Design

In the last chapter you met architect/designer Michael Graves. He designs in a style called **Post-Modern.** Post-Modern means "after modern."

The easiest way to understand Post-Modern design is to see it as a kind of rebellion against the Bauhaus or the International style it became. Post-Modern designers, like Michael Graves, grew tired of the rigid and, to them,

Figure 18.7. *Tiffany Lamp.* Bronze base, leaded glass shade, 26½" x 18½". The Metropolitan Museum of Art. Gift of Hugh J. Grant, 1974.

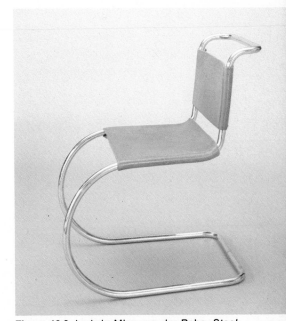

Figure 18.8. Ludwig Mies van der Rohe. *Steel Tubed Chair.* 1927. Chrome-plated tubular steel and leather, 31" x 18½" x 28 5/16". Collection the Museum of Modern Art, New York. Gift of Edgar Kaufmann, Jr.

Figure 18.9. *Post-modern furniture.*

boring sameness of the Bauhaus style. They began to look around for fresh ideas—maybe even to borrow a few from the grab bag of the past. What they came up with is amazing.

Critics of the style say Post-Modern design is like Bauhaus meets Disneyland! Others find the style witty and refreshing. The examples of furniture shown in Figure 18.9 give you an idea of the style's variety. You must admit, Post-Modern furniture is hard to ignore! Like a painting or sculpture, it captures your attention, making you consider its design and function. This is a new role for furniture. We are so used to taking our chairs, tables, and sofas for granted. Having seen Post-Modern furniture, would you like to have a piece for your room?

Design With Wheels

The design of the mass-produced automobile, since the first one rolled off Henry Ford's assembly line in 1913, has been of continual interest to the American public. Every year new designs are eagerly awaited. Automobile shows draw thousands of visitors, anxious to wonder at the designs of the future. Will the year 2,000 see cars that drive themselves? Will they be lower, higher, wider, faster? When will they fly?

Automobile companies hire hundreds of designers to meet the yearly public demand for something new, something different. Through the years, the designs have changed to make cars faster, more comfortable, and safer. Like all designers, those who design automobiles reflect the tastes and values of their day.

We look at cars manufactured during the early part of the 20th century and smile knowingly. How foolish those big, boxy shapes seem to us. However, we should remember, the latest car designs we now admire will seem hopelessly dated in the 21st century.

As you look at the automobiles in Figure 18.10, try to see them not as cars, but as design objects. See if you can describe how the designers of each one have used line and form. Do some look like they are moving even when they are standing still? How is that effect achieved? Are there any that remind you of Bauhaus design? Art nouveau?

Figure 18.10. Drawings of different car designs.

Mies van der Rohe. c. 1956. Photograph courtesy, Mies van der Rohe Archive. The Museum of Modern Art, New York.

BORN: 1886
DIED: 1969
BIRTHPLACE:
Berlin, Germany

Figure 18.12. Mies van der Rohe. *Barcelona Chair.* 1929. Chrome-plated flat steel bars with pigskin cushions, 29⅞" x 29½" x 29⅝". Collection, The Museum of Modern Art. Gift of Knoll International.

"Less is More"

Young Ludwig Mies van der Rohe learned the business of architecture from the ground up. He began his training as a stonemason for his father in 1890. In 1905 he became an apprentice to an architect, Bruno Paul. By 1911 he had established his own architectural firm and was doing business.

As an architect, Mies van der Rohe's most influential design was that of the German Pavilion at the Barcelona International Exposition of 1929 (Figure 18.11). This building, even today, seems modern and beautifully designed. Interior and exterior spaces appear unified, as the eye moves over smooth planes of marble and walls of glass. The design has been reduced to its purest form. All decoration has been eliminated. Mies van der Rohe's famous saying, "less is more" seems a perfect description for this beautiful structure.

Like Michael Graves, Mies van der Rohe's fame rests more with his furniture designs than with his architecture.

Figure 18.12 is a famous chair designed by Mies van der Rohe. It is known as a "Barcelona" chair. This chair design is still reproduced and sold in fine furniture stores everywhere. Like his architecture, Mies van der Rohe's designs are reduced to pure line and form. Notice the relationship between the chair and the footstool. The line of the steel legs of one leads the eyes toward the continuing line of the other. This chair is a sculpture, as well as a functional piece of furniture. Unlike some modern furniture designs, the "Barcelona" chair is a comfortable as it is beautiful.

Figure 18.11. Ludwig Mies van der Rohe. *German Pavilion.* International Exposition, Barcelona, Spain, 1929. Has been demolished. Photograph courtesy, Mies van der Rohe Archive, The Museum of Modern Art, New York.

Did you learn

- The definitions of these words and phrases: visual thinking; function; decorative design; Gothic Revival; art nouveau; motif; Bauhaus; Post-Modern?
- The difference between decorative and functional design?
- The name of the design style William Morris made famous?
- What inspired art nouveau design?
- The most famous household item designed by the Tiffany Studios?
- Two characteristics of the Bauhaus style?
- The design style that "rebelled" against Bauhaus?

Understanding and Evaluating

- Design a visual-memory exercise.
- Find an object you consider an example of decorative design. Select another that you think was designed mainly for function. In a short paragraph, compare the two. Include how shape is altered by decoration or function. Also include whether a design idea from the past or from nature is used? Decide which design you think is better and defend your choice.
- In a paragraph or two, explain what you think "less is more" means and why it is a motto for the design style of the Bauhaus?

Seeing and Creating

- Under the direction of your teacher, design and weave a small wall hanging. Base your design on modern architecture. Use geometric shapes and a limited color scheme. Try to create a design in which the negative space is as important as the positive shapes.
- Select functional objects that can be used for an object print. Old tools and kitchen utensils work well. Apply tempera or acrylic paint to each and print them on newsprint. Experiment with various ways to combine the impressions into a new design. Print your created design on fabric, as a sample motif.

Student work.

Student work.

Chapter 19

ART AND THE ENVIRONMENT

In the world of the late 20th century, most people live in **urban** areas or towns and cities. The physical and aesthetic environment of these areas has become of increasing importance to the people who live there. They want their cities to be beautiful, functional, and healthy places in which to live and work. Unfortunately, in many rapid growth, industrialization, and increasing population have outrun the abilities of city planners to keep up. Whether for lack of money, will, or resources, many cities are neither attractive nor safe places to live. But things are changing.

Within the last few years, there has been a growing interest in revitalizing and beautifying urban areas. Many cities and towns are restoring historic buildings to their former glory, making them both visual showpieces and comfortable dwellings.

In other cities, where funds are available for building and expansion, new emphasis is being placed on creating architecture that is functional, comfortable, beautiful, and compatible with the natural surroundings and the needs of people.

As you read in Chapter 17, many architects consider their professional roles expanded to include urban planning. Both modern architectural design and urban planning promise an exciting and more beautiful future for city dwellers.

WHERE PAST AND PRESENT MEET

No city or town is made up completely of one style of architecture (Figure 19.1). Buildings, abandoned over the years, are either torn down or restored. Many cities in the United States, especially those on the East coast, have buildings that were designed and built in the 17th century!

Have you ever looked for old buildings in your town? Do any look like the one pictured in Figure 19.1? Like other art forms, 20th-century or modern architecture has a history all its own. Also like other art forms, its style was influenced by designs from the past.

The Birth of the Skyscraper

There weren't any so-called skyscrapers in the 19th century. There were some buildings with three, four, or even six floors, but height for commercial structures just wasn't an important consideration. But things were soon to change.

Figure 19.1

Figure 19.2. Henry Hobson Richardson. *Marshall Field Wholesale Store.* 1885-87.

Figure 19.3. Van Allen. *Chrysler Building.* ©C. O. Slavens. Courtesy Peter Arnold, Inc.

First, there was the invention of a process for manufacturing steel called the **Bessemer process** after its inventor Sir Henry Bessemer. This process allowed the making of structural steel. Structural steel would soon replace the weaker cast iron as the building material of the modern age. Together with concrete reinforced by steel rods, the materials for the birth of the modern skyscraper had arrived.

Strangely enough, another important event in the development of the skyscraper was the great Chicago fire of 1871. Most of the wooden structures at the city's center were destroyed. There was now a place for the great building experiment to begin.

Of course, the first structures built couldn't be called skyscrapers. Barely ten to twelve stories high, these buildings are best called multistoried, or many-storied. Some of the first are now seen only in photographs, having long since been demolished.

An early example is the Marshall Field Wholesale Store designed by architect Henry Hobson Richardson (Figure 19.2).

One of the first and most successful skyscraper designs was the Chrysler Building in New York. It was designed by William Van Allen for the Chrysler Automobile Company (Figure 19.3).

Although it looks somewhat old-fashioned to our late 20th-century eyes, it was, in its time, the wonder of New York. Even today its unusual blend of past styles and automobile motifs attracts the interest of contemporary product designers and Post-modern architects.

The layered design of the building emphasizes the upward push of the structure. Crowned with an explosion of sunburst arches (the sunburst design was the Chrysler Company logo or signature), a needle for a top, and winged radiator caps at the four corners, in 1930 this building was the last word in modern style and technology. It was also the tallest building ever built. At least, until the following year when the Empire State Building was completed.

There had been an earlier challenger for the title of tallest building. The neighboring Chanin Building was declared the tallest, until the builders of the Chrysler Building, in the dark of night, put up the crowning needle from the inside!

A European Style

While American architects were busily putting up higher and more simple, box-like structures, some European designers were taking a different path.

Figure 19.4 is the Casa Mila Building in Barcelona, Spain. It was designed by Antoni Gaudi [AN•toe•knee GOW•dee]. Influenced by the curving lines of the art-nouveau style, this building doesn't seem to have a straight line in it!

The edges of the roof wave as if seen under water. The balconies ripple and curve. The wrought-iron decoration is fashioned like vines and moss cascading over the sides of the building. The chimneys are all different and look like soft ice-cream mounds. Perhaps Gaudi's design owes more to Surrealism than Art Nouveau!

The International Style

The glass, box-like office buildings you see everywhere today are newer versions of a style of architectural design that began after World War I. This style of architecture has come to be known as the **International Style**. It is a style that is easy to identify.

The building is designed as a block, with as little use of heavy materials as possible. Walls of glass are held together by reinforced steel girders. Most of the building materials are human-made rather than natural. Decoration and ornament of any kind are rejected. Those solid wall spaces that exist are usually white or some very neutral color.

From this description you should be able to identify the creative parents of this style—Cubism and the Bauhaus.

The Cubist love of planes and form, rather than texture; and the Bauhaus principle of function before decoration, can be found in this popular architectural design.

The Lake Shore Drive Apartments (Figure 19.5) were designed by Mies van der Rohe and completed in 1951. These apartments in Chicago were one of the first and purest examples of the International Style.

The word "international" is an appropriate one for this style of architecture. It has become the favorite style for the entire world. Glass boxes are everywhere—from New York to Hong Kong; from Nairobi to Paris.

The great number of buildings constructed to this design have, in some people's eyes, created boring and monotonous cityscapes. One of the rebellions against this sameness is the movement known as Post-Modern.

AN AMERICAN LEGEND—FRANK LLOYD WRIGHT

Easily the most famous American architect was Frank Lloyd Wright. He made his greatest contributions to

Figure 19.4. Antoni Gaudi. *Casa Mila.* 1905-1907. Barcelona, Spain.

Figure 19.5. Mies van der Rohe. *Lake Shore Drive Apartments.* Chicago, Illinois. Photo credit: Hedrich-Blessing, Chicago, Illinois.

Figure 19.6. Frank Lloyd Wright. *Robie House.* 1909. Chicago, Illinois. Photo courtesy of the Frank Lloyd Wright Memorial Foundation.

architectural design through a number of private houses he built for clients.

One of the first and most successful is known as the Robie House (Figure 19.6) after the original owners. Built in Chicago in 1909, it was innovative and daring in several ways.

First, it didn't look at all like the other houses of the time. Wright believed that a building should look like a natural part of its surroundings, rather than like an alien thing dropped down on a piece of land.

The Robie House is designed on various levels, almost like the shelves and ledges of a cliff face. It stretches horizontally, rather than vertically, matching the flat plains of its Midwest environment.

The rooms are only partially enclosed with walls. The interior space is allowed to flow from one room to another. This idea of a large interior space where rooms connect is so common today that we forget what a new idea this was for early 20th-century architecture.

Another innovation was Wright's use of the **cantilevered roof.** A cantilevered roof is one that projects into space without support from posts or columns. Such a design only became possible with the invention of reinforced concrete. It is weighted or attached at an opposite point.

The style of the Robie House may seem familiar to you. There are probably a number of similar designs in your community, especially if you live in the Midwest or Southwest. Wright's famous design became known as the ranch-house style.

POST-MODERN ARCHITECTURE

In the last chapter you were introduced to Post-Modern design in functional objects and furniture. Post-Modern design has had an even greater influence on architecture.

In some cases, Post-Modern design is a rebellion against the sameness of the International or Modern Style. Many Post-Modern architects borrow design ideas from the ancient and near past to give a new look and life to the basic glass box building.

One of the more controversial designs has been that of an art museum in Paris called the Pompidou [POM•pee•du] Center (Figure 19.7). This extraordinary building has been compared to everything from a gumball machine to a ride at an amusement park! There is little doubt that it is an unusual design, even for Post-Modern.

Notice that the steel structure of the building is on the outside, rather than on the inside. It looks as if the building were still under construction. Bright colors are used to define different levels. The use of color is a characteristic of many Post-Modern buildings.

Figure 19.7. Renzo Piano and Richard Rogers. *Pompidou Center,* Paris.

The Design of the Modern City

As urban populations grow, so do the problems. Simple transportation from one place to another can be a difficult and frustrating task. Freeways, meant to make travel easier, are frequently jammed with traffic. The sealed, air-conditioned office buildings, where most city dwellers work, can be as visually barren and uninspiring as a desert. Architects and urban planners are beginning to make serious attempts at improving life in the city. More new buildings are planned with considerations for their surroundings, as well as the design of the building. Greenscapes are being added or restored wherever possible, so people can take refreshing walks or eat lunch outdoors.

Even the underground mass-transit systems, so long places of depressing drabness, are beginning to receive the attention of designers.

Figure 19.8 shows the O'Hare Station of the Chicago Transit System. Its designer, architect Helmut Jahn [YAHN], has used lighted glass-brick walls to reproduce, as nearly as possible, the appearance and benefits of sunlight.

In all these innovative approaches to improving the environment and people's lives, art is playing a larger role than ever before.

Many large corporations are investing in art for both the interior and exterior of their buildings. This gives workers and those living in the areas a chance to enjoy important works of art without effort or cost. There is

Figure 19.8. Helmut Jahn. *O'Hare Rapid Transit Station.* Chicago, Illinois. Courtesy, Helmut Jahn.

215

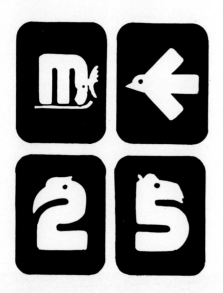

Figure 19.9

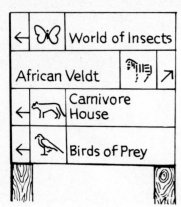

Figure 19.10. Directional signs and advertising can be informative and attractive.

little doubt that a comfortable and aesthetically pleasing workplace improves production and work quality, not to mention the personal well-being of the workers.

In Portland, Oregon three different public centers—The Western Forestry Center, The Oregon Museum of Science, and the Washington Park Zoo—commissioned artists to paint several buses with designs and images related to the center they serve (Figure 19.9). These buses are beautiful examples of how art can improve the looks of the most ordinary objects.

A shopping mall may seem a strange place to look for art, but many new malls are designed to meet the physical and artistic needs of people. They include works of fine art and interesting uses of applied design for advertising.

Zoos and other nature parks have been very imaginative in both their layout and designs and in signs that direct people to various exhibits.

Figure 19.10 shows signs from both the Minnesota and Cincinnati zoos. Notice the interesting graphic designs that have been created from animal shapes. Some of these graphic images are so clear that written directions are completely unnecessary. Can't you "read" each of this signs clearly?

In many cities, artists are commissioned to beautify the city environment with murals. Some of the artists commissioned, like those who paint the freeway murals in Los Angeles, are professionals. Others are part of youth and art organizations, who give their time and talent to adding interest and beauty to the urban landscape.

Large-scale murals like those seen in Figures 19.11 and 19.12 can transform unsightly buildings or freeways into works of art.

You might want to investigate art organizations in your community and participate in a project to beautify the community. Help is always needed. And think of your pride in seeing your work as a permanent part of your town or city.

Figure 19.12. Six photographs of the mural project *A United Community* sponsored by St. Joseph Multi-Ethnic Cultural Arts Committee, Inc. Location: St. Joseph School, Houston, Texas. Technique: Acrylic. Size: 34′ x 58′. Original painting: Sylvia Orozco and Pio Pulido. *A United Community*. 19″ x 30″. Acrylic on illustration board.

Figure 19.11. Highway Mural. Photograph by D. Watson.

Graphic Design and Advertising

A major part of urban life is advertising. Whether it is in the form of billboards, posters, record covers, magazines, or newspapers, graphic design is a vital part of advertisements.

Not all of it is good, by any means. Many examples are poorly designed in composition of art elements and unimaginative in ideas. Still others make us stop and take notice.

Figure 19.13 is a collage made up of advertisements. Many of you may recognize from newspapers, magazines, and television. Most modern advertisements combine both words and pictures into the graphic design. Notice, for example, the variety of lettering or type styles seen in the collage. Like any other visual design, you should look at and judge advertisements for the way the art elements and design principles are used. Try asking these questions: How is negative space used? Is the composition symmetrical or asymmetrical? How has color been used? Does it add to the meaning? Does the graphic design express the intended idea?

Figure 19.13. Collage of advertisements.

MEET FRANK LLOYD WRIGHT

Poetry in Concrete

Frank Lloyd Wright was born the son of a preacher and a music teacher. One of the first toys young Frank received was a set of building blocks from his mother. He was later to say that those blocks fired his interest in architecture.

When Wright was nineteen, he took off for Chicago to make his fortune. He was lucky. Chicago, still devastated after the great fire of 1871, offered young, ambitious architects golden opportunities to make names for themselves. This was what Wright intended to do. But even the most talented individuals have to start at the bottom.

Wright began work as a draftsman for the famous architect, Louis Henri Sullivan. Wright was influenced by Sullivan's feelings about using organic forms from nature in his houses and buildings.

In 1893 Wright decided the time had come for him to set up his own architectural firm. It was here that he was to begin his most famous designs for private houses.

BORN: 1869
DIED: 1959
BIRTHPLACE:
Spring Green, Wisconsin

Figure 19.14 shows another example of the Wright style of architecture. This house is known as "Falling Water." It was commissioned by the Kaufman family.

Like the Robie House (Figure 19.6), "Falling Water" uses cantilevered roofs to cut into the negative or surrounding space. It is easy to see where the house gets its name. Built over a natural spring and waterfall, the form of the house repeats the jutting rocks and falling water below. The design of the house is so beautifully matched to its surroundings that it seems a part of them, as natural as the rocks and water.

Wright was not only a gifted architect, but also a skilled engineer. In 1923 an interesting tribute was paid to his engineering abilities. A terrible earthquake hit Tokyo, Japan. More than 250,000 people were killed and 500,000 houses destroyed. One of the few large buildings left standing was the Imperial Hotel. It had been designed by Frank Lloyd Wright. A few days after the disaster, a telegram arrived for Wright from an official of the Japanese government. It read: "Hotel stands undamaged as monument to your genius. Congratulations."

Figure 19.14. Frank Lloyd Wright. *Falling Water, Bear Run, Pennsylvania.* Courtesy of the Frank Lloyd Wright Memorial Foundation.

Student work.

Student work.

Did you learn

- The definitions of these words and phrases: urban; International Style; cantilevered roof; Bessemer process?
- How the production of structural steel helped the development of the skyscraper?
- What part the great fire of Chicago had in the building of skyscrapers?
- The name of a European architect with a different view of design?
- At least two characteristics of the International Style?
- Two new building ideas introduced by Frank Lloyd Wright?
- Some areas of cities that are beginning to use art for beautification?

Understanding and Evaluating

- As you tour your town or city, see how many different architectural style you can identify. Make a list or sketches of the styles. Is the Post-Modern style represented? How do you recognize it?
- Visit several malls in your town. Take note of how they are designed. Is art used inside? Outside? Is it easy for people to move about? Is the interior attractively designed? Pick one mall and make a list the things you would change to improve it visually.

Seeing and Creating

- Locate some old houses or buildings. Study them and make several sketches of their shapes and details. Are they decorative? What do you think inspired the decoration—a past design or nature? Make a collograph or relief print from your drawings. Prepare your printing plate by gluing pieces of paper and cardboard into the shapes and textures of your building. Some simplification will be necessary. When dry, ink with water-based printing ink and print. Remember the raised parts will be dark; the recesses, light.
- Make drawings of buildings in a variety of media. Decide which works best for decorative structures, and which for simple. Use your sketches to design your own house from the details of others.

The most recent decades of the 20th century have been a time of great changes and advances in many areas of human life. Advances in science and technology have enabled humans to leave planet earth and walk on the surface of the moon.

Computers are so much a part of everyday life that it is difficult to imagine the modern world without them. Progress in communications now allows us to speak with just about anyone, anywhere, anytime. Through television, motion pictures, books, magazines, and newspapers we have the world at out fingertips.

TRENDS IN ART

In spite of these miracles of technology, it is still a world that is troubled in many ways. As struggles for personal freedom and equality continue around the globe, the future well-being of the earth itself is of growing concern. The future is filled with both promise and fear. The many possible directions for the future are reflected in the diversity of visual art styles and movements that have developed over the last thirty years. Let's take a look at some of them.

Pop and Op Art

Figure 20.1 by artist Andy Warhol [WAR•hall] is a famous example of the art style known as **Pop art. Pop art** is a shortened version of the term "Popular art." From its name, you can easily tell where Pop artists get many of the images and subjects they use. They come from the popular culture of the 20th century—advertising, movies, and comic books.

In Figure 20.1 American artist Andy Warhol has used as a subject something that most people recognize immediately—a can of soup. But it isn't just any soup. The brand name is displayed, and is, in fact, part of the image and symbol of the artwork. It is as if Warhol were saying to us, "Hey, look at this everyday object with its advertising. Why can't it be a subject for art?"

Not surprising, American culture, with its love of products and advertising, was both the primary target and generator of Pop art during the 1960s. Other artists who worked in the Pop art movement were Roy Lichtenstein (Chapter 16, Figure 16.7) and Claes Oldenburg (Book One, Chapter 10) with his "soft" erasers and potatoes.

Chapter 20

THE CUTTING EDGE—NEW DIRECTIONS IN 20TH-CENTURY ART

WORDWATCH
Pop art
Op art
Abstract Expressionism
color field
assemblage
printer
storyboard
installation
Earth art
serigraphy
silk screen
block-out
hard copy
pixels
electronic media
CAD program
hardware
monitor
disk drive
software

Figure 20.1. Andy Warhol. *Campbell's Soup Can.* 1962. Synthetic polymer paint on canvas, 20″ x 16″. Courtesy, Leo Castelli Gallery, New York.

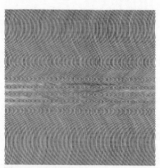

Figure 20.2. Brigit Riley. *Current.* 1964. Synthetic polymer paint on composition board, 58⅜″ x 58⅞″. Collection, The Museum of Modern Art. Philip Johnson Fund.

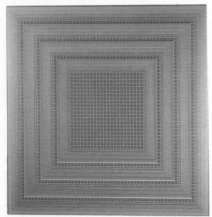

Figure 20.3. Richard Anuskiewicz. *Glory Red.* 1967. Acrylic on canvas, 60″ x 60″. Collection of the artist. © Richard Anuskiewicz/VAGA New York. 1991.

Another popular art movement during the 1960s was **Op art.** Once again, the name is a shortened version of the term "Optical art."

The name of this movement also tells you something about the subject and purpose of the work. Op art uses the human eye and the way it sees to create various illusions. Figure 20.2, *Current* by Bridget Riley is an excellent example.

Take a few moments to look at this work—if you can stand it! You will notice that there are two types of illusions taking place. One, is the illusion that as the lines curve near the center, actual ridges and folds appear in the paper. If you are still looking at the work, by now you see the second illusion—movement.

The black-and-white lines are placed so close together that your eyes are unable to hold them as separate images for very long. This creates a vibrating effect, or an illusion of movement.

Other Op artists, like Richard Anuszkiewicz [ah • NOOSE • key • wis] use optical sensations created by color. In Figure 20.3, titled *Glory Red*, the squares have variations in color value. Notice the colors used for the lines. Are they cool or warm colors? As you look at this work, do some panels appear closer, some further away? What other illusions do you notice?

Although most Op art is usually created in two-dimensions, like drawing or painting, at least one artist has tried to make it three-dimensional. For some who experience this amazing work, it seems as if the artist has taken them into the fourth dimension!

Mirrored Room, (Figure 20.4) by Lucas Samaras [sah • MARE • ahs] is an actual, three-dimensional room entirely covered in mirrors. Visitors to the work are allowed to step inside and experience the dizzying sensation of floating in space. When a mirror is placed facing another mirror, they reflect an infinite view. This idea is magnified in the mirrored room, because in every direction you look, there is infinity! The walls, objects, ceiling, and even the floor beneath your feet, seem to disappear. For some, the sensation is scary and unpleasant; for others it is thrilling.

Abstract Expressionism

As an art style, Abstract Expressionism dominated American art during the 1950s. Abstract Expressionist painters cared nothing about painting objects and scenes realistically. In fact, they rejected all recognizable images from their art.

Using only the art elements of line, color, shape, texture, and value, they tried to express and communicate

Figure 20.4. Lucas Samaras. *Mirrored Room.* 1966. Mirrors on wooden frame 8' x 8' x 10'. Albright-Knox Art Gallery, Buffalo, New York. Gift of Seymour H. Knox, 1966.

pure feeling and mood. You have already been introduced to one of the most famous Abstract Expressionist—Jackson Pollock (Chapter 10). Of equal fame and influence was Dutch-born painter, Willem De Kooning [WILL•um dee KOONING].

Figure 20.5, titled *Easter Monday,* is characteristic of De Kooning's work. The paint is applied thickly to the canvas with broad, slashing strokes, expressing the emotion and movement of the artist as he works. He even uses crumpled newspaper to blot the paint. Do you recall how Pollock applied paint to his canvases?

In Figure 20.5, colors and shapes are used to balance the composition; different line directions and widths add variety.

When you look at an abstract work of art, don't try to make out real images. Just let yourself react naturally to the colors, shapes, and lines you see. Try to feel the mood or emotion expressed by these elements.

Color-Field Painting

In reaction against the lashing brushstrokes and thick mounds of color found in many works of Abstract Expressionism, some artists during the 1960s went in the opposite direction. They developed a style of painting called **color-field** painting. This art style can be recognized by its use of large simple areas, or fields, of color.

Color-field artists filled their canvases with only one or two colors applied smoothly, with no brushstrokes showing. Shapes, when used at all, were made where two or more colors met. The edges of the colors are sharp and clean.

Figure 20.5. Willem de Kooning. *Easter Monday.* 1955-56. 96" x 74". The Metropolitan Museum of Art, Rogers Fund, 1956.

Figure 20.6. Ellsworth Kelly. *Red White.* 1961. Oil on canvas, 62¾" x 85¼". Hirshhorn Museum and Sculpture Garden, Smithsonian Institution. Gift of Joseph H. Hirshhorn, 1972.

Figure 20.6, titled *Red White,* is by artist Ellsworth Kelly. The red-and-white shapes are so smoothly painted and have such crisp, hard edges that this work could easily be made of cut paper. What kind of feeling do you get when you look at this work? Is there tension? Conflict? Harmony?

TRENDS IN SCULPTURE

In some ways, more interesting directions were taking place in sculpture than in painting during the 1960s and 1970s.

As the Pop artists were using commercial products and advertising as subjects, some sculptors began to look to the cast-off objects of modern life as materials for sculpture. Putting together "found" materials is called **assemblage** [ah•sohm•BLAHGE]. One of the most important artists to use this form was Louise Nevelson.

Artist Louise Nevelson created her large, impressive sculptures by putting together objects from many sources—old pieces of furniture, parts of demolished houses, boxes, wood fragments, and other bits of junk. Figure 20.7 is an example of her work. It is titled *Sky Cathedral.*

If you look closely at this work, you will see that it is made up of everything from chunks of driftwood to porch railings and posts. All these different objects, with their varying forms, give the sculpture variety and interest. We enjoy seeing how the shape of one object contrasts

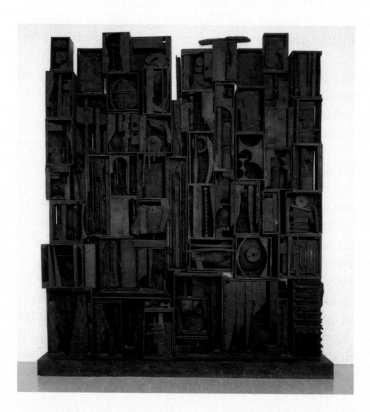

Figure 20.7. Louise Nevelson. *Sky Cathedral.* 1958. Assemblage: wood construction painted black, 11'3½" x 10'¼" x 18". Collection, The Museum of Modern Art, New York. Gift of Mr. and Mrs. Ben Mildwoff.

Figure 20.8. Judy Pfaff. *Supermercado.* 1986. Painted wood and metal, 25 units, overall: 8'4½" x 13'7¾" x 50". Collection of Whitney Museum of American Art, New York. Purchase with funds from the Louis and Bessie Adler Foundation, Inc., S.M. Klein, President and The Sondra and Charles Gilman, Jr. Foundation, Inc.

with another. Round against square; natural against human-made.

The entire work, as with other Nevelson works, is painted in one color. So no matter how diverse the objects, the composition is unified with a single color.

Louise Nevelson's sculptures are in some ways the ancestors of another kind of art known as **installation.** Sometimes a combination of both painting and sculpture, **installations** are constructed for an exhibition in the gallery or museum.

Unlike a single painting or sculpture which can be moved and placed in a particular setting, an installation work is composed of many different pieces which must be reassembled each time it is moved. Installations are assemblages with loose pieces!

Figure 20.8, titled *Supermercado,* will give you an idea of how complex installation art can be. This work by Judy Pfaff [faff] took hours of work to assemble and hang. This illustration is like an abstract painting you can walk through. A delightful circus of color, pattern, and moving shapes, it is filled with joy and fun. The shapes are made of everything from fiberglass and plastic to painted steel.

Obviously, the complexity of a work like Pfaff's requires careful preplanning and complete concentration in order to put everything in its proper place. How heart-breaking it must be for the artist to have to take it all down!

Figure 20.9. Robert Smithson. *Spiral Jetty.* 1970. Great Salt Lake, Utah.

Figure 20.10. Christo. *Valley Curtain, Rifle, Colorado.* 1970-72. 365' h. x 1250' span. ©Christo, 1972. Photo: H. Shunk.

Altering The Earth

Perhaps the ultimate in installation art is what is called **Earth art.**

How large can a work of art be? You have seen canvases and sculptures that cover many feet of space. But what about a work of art that covers miles of space? Many examples of **Earth art** do just that.

The term **Earth art** refers to those works that in some way alter the natural or human-made environment. Not content with mere canvases and marble blocks for materials, Earth artists use lakes, hills, valleys, harbours, and buildings for their media.

Figure 20.9, titled *Spiral Jetty,* was designed and created by Earth artist, Robert Smithson. The artist and his crew of engineers and construction workers created a coiling pathway out into a section of Utah's Great Salt Lake. Since much Earth art has a limited existence, because of its exposure to the natural elements, the construction of the works is recorded on film and videotape. This documentation is considered part of the total work of art. In fact, Smithson's *Spiral Jetty* can now only be seen in the film he made or the hundreds of still photographs taken of the work. The Great Salt Lake, like a greedy patron, has already submerged and claimed the work.

More famous than Smithson's works are those by Bulgarian-born artist, Christo. Christo doesn't alter the landscape by moving things around. Instead, he wraps and packages it with miles of fabric.

Figure 20.10 is a photograph made by the artist of the sculpture known as *Valley Curtain, 1970-72,* which was constructed across a Colorado valley. The wind, in this case, acted as an assistant to the artist.

As the wind whipped down the valley, it set the great curtain moving in beautiful and ever-changing drapes and folds, shapes and shadows. At a certain point, the curtain was released by the artist and his helpers due to strong winds. The wind then took over once more and carried the curtain down the valley.

Another Cristo work that thrills with its size and image is *Surrounded Islands, Biscayne Bay, Greater Miami, Florida, 1980-83,* (Figure 20.11.)

Seen from the air, the deep green of the small islands that dot Biscayne Bay leap into sight. They are surrounded by brilliant pink sheets of fabric. The contrast in colors and the scale of the work form an awesome spectacle.

Figure 20.11. Christo. *Surrounded Island, Biscayne Bay, Greater Miami, Florida.* 1980-83. 6½ million square feet of pink woven polypropylene fabric, 11 islands ©Christo, 1983. Photo: W. Volz.

Figure 20.12. Avebury Circle, Wiltshire, England. © Horst Schafer from Peter Arnold, Inc., New York.

Although Earth art seems completely a product of the technology and experimental spirit of the late 20th century, it has some very ancient connections. You have only to look at the great Earth mounds and circles built during the Neolithic (New Stone Age) period in Europe (Figure 20.12) or the endless miles of lines carved into the desert floor of the Nazca plain in Peru (Figure 20.13) to realize that earth art isn't such a new idea after all.

NEW MATERIALS—NEW TOOLS

Visual art continues to follow many different directions. What the future holds, no one can know for sure. What you can be sure of is that people will continue to express themselves with visual art.

Along with the traditional art forms—drawing, painting, sculpture, and printmaking—artists will discover and explore new materials and tools for communication that are the products of the technology for the future.

Some of these materials and tools will simply be newer, more flexible versions of traditional media. For example, take **serigraphy** [sur • RIG • raf • ee] or the **silk-screen** process of printing.

Long used in commercial and industrial applications, **serigraphy** is a stencil-printing technique. Silk or some other closely-woven fabric is stretched over a frame. A paper or plastic stencil is cut and attached to the fabric, or a **block-out** substance is used, such as glue. The stencil

Figure 20.13. Nazca desert plains, Peru. © Klaus D. Francke from Peter Arnold, Inc., New York.

Figure 20.14. Timothy High. *Rebel Earth-Maranatha.* 1980. Serigraph, 22″ x 36″. Collection of the artist.

or block-out prevents the printing ink from touching the printing paper placed beneath the frame. The open areas of fabric allow the ink to penetrate and print on the paper.

When many different colors are desired, a new stencil must be made for each color. A serigraph print like that shown in (Figure 20.14), titled *Rebel-Earth Marantha,* by Tim High, required dozens of screens to achieve the subtle color values you see. Some of the intricate screens are made by one of the newer versions of the traditional stencil process—photographic silk screen.

With special, and rather expensive equipment, the images to be printed can be transferred to the silk screen through photography. Not only does this simplify the work of preparing detailed screens, but it allows many new and exciting effects. *Rebel-Earth Marantha* is a combination of many different methods, including photographic silk screen. The Warhol work (Figure 20.1) is also a serigraph or silk screen. If you wear T-shirts with images and writing on them, they too were probably made by this versatile and creative process.

Neon, Casting Resin, and Fiberglass

Like the silk-screen process, neon, casting resin, and fiberglass are all products used originally in industrial and commercial settings. Little did anyone guess they could also be used to create exciting art!

Figure 20.15, titled *Chicago Cityscape II,* is by Vardea Chryssa [VAR•dee•ah KRIS•sah]. It uses lighted neon tubing in place of drawn or painted lines.

Many of the bright signs you see at night on the front of movie theatres and stores are made from neon. Las Vegas has miles of neon lights that blink, move, and dazzle with their images.

Neon gets its name from the gas that is contained within the glass tubing. When excited by a charge of electricity, the gas glows. The glass tubing can be bent and molded into many different shapes.

Casting resin is used commercially for everything from toys to coatings on restaurant tabletops. Made from a type of plastic, casting resin has the advantage of being both clear like glass, but tough and unbreakable. It is often used to protect surfaces from wear and the weather.

Artist Paul Hatgil has used casting resin to create a beautiful sculpture called *Diamond* (Figure 20.16). After a mold is constructed of plastic, the casting resin, in liquid form, is tinted with color and poured in layers. Each layer takes four hours to dry before the next can be poured. When the entire piece is dry, it is unmolded and polished to a high gloss. Suspended on a transparent stand of plexiglass, its shape catches the light, throwing off brilliant rainbows everywhere.

Fiberglass is a material that has been made by drawing glass into fine threads, which are then woven or molded together. Because of its strength and light weight, it has long been a favorite material for molding boats and car bodies.

It can also be used for monumental sculptures like *Progress I,* (Figure 20.17) by the Southwestern artist Luis Jimenez [Heh•MEN•es]. Like an enormous and outrageous plastic toy, the figures of buffalo, horse, and Indian are molded into a dynamic and slightly comic image. Even the eyes of the buffalo light up!

Jimenez takes three images from the historic American West and gives them a modern, humorous look. Can you imagine a more suitable medium to capture the look and mood of this sculpture!

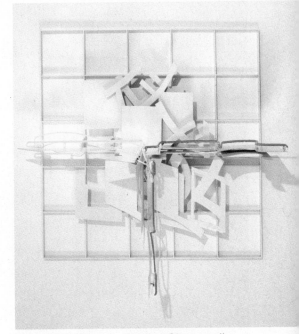

Figure 20.15. Chryssa. *Chicago Cityscape II.* 1988-90. Honeycomb, aluminum, paint and neon, 57″ x 52″ x 35½″. Courtesy, Leo Castelli Gallery, New York.

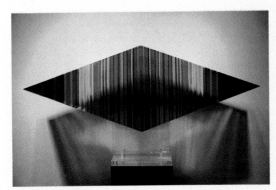

Figure 20.16. Paul P. Hatigil. *Diamond.* 1980. Resin sculpture, 40″ w. Collection of the artist.

229

Figure 20.17. Luis Jimenez. *Progress 1.* 1974.
Fiberglass, 7′7″ x 8′8″ x 9′9″. Private
collection.

USING ART MATERIALS SAFELY

Artists who use neon, resin, and fiberglass must use great care to avoid serious health problems that can occur while working with industrial materials. They must work in special areas where ventilation systems have been enhanced to eliminate toxic fumes. They also wear special masks and gloves when working with these materials.

Most materials produced today are safe, if used according to directions and health precautions. However, you should never assume that a product is safe. Read the labels and reject any that pose unneccessary hazards.

Some materials, while perfectly harmless to most, pose problems for others. Many people have allergies which can be aggravated by certain materials. These individuals should avoid using anything that causes discomfort. If you know you have such an allergy, or you begin to have a reaction to an art material, tell you teacher at once. Alternate materials for you to use can be found.

ELECTRONIC MEDIA—COMPUTERS, VIDEO, AND FILM

At least one future direction for art that seems to hold truly amazing possibilities is that of **electronic media**.

Electronic media use images created and projected by electronic technology—television and videotape; movies and film.

Computer Art

Today many people own computers. You may have one yourself. Your school may have several for teachers and students to use. In most instances, school computers are used in classes other than the art class. This is unfortunate, since using computers to make art, makes them interesting and exciting creative tools.

Computer-made images are so much a part of our visual experience that we sometimes fail to appreciate or even realize the source when we see them. Television commercials, special effects in movies, and computer games—all make extensive use of computer art. (Figure 20.18)

Computers have also become an important drafting tool for designers and architects. **CAD,** Computer Assisted Drawing programs, allows designers to complete drawings and plans in a fraction of the time it used to take. More important, the computer allows for almost instantaneous changes in viewpoint, perspective, and scale. An endless number of changes can be tried before the drawn image is printed. For these tasks to be done by hand, takes hours of very tedious work.

The computer, and the pieces of equipment that accompany it, are called **hardware.** Most computers have a keyboard for typing information, a screen or **monitor** to see what you type and what the computer says, a **disk drive** for storing and retrieving information, and a **printer** for printing out on paper the information or images made through the computer. These printed images of text are called **hard copies.**

To make art on a computer of any kind, you need a graphics program. These programs, stored on 3½″ or 5¼″ disks, tell the computer what to do, and how you can interact or draw with the computer. Computer programs are known as **software.**

All personal computers on the market today have some kind of graphics programs for creating art. Some computers have many, each able to perform a wide range of drawing and painting tasks.

Some programs allow you to add hundreds of colors, design the size and shape of the brushes you draw with, rotate images, enlarge them, make them small, duplicate them, and zoom in on a single point. You can even change the size of the computer's **pixels.** These are the small squares with which the computer creates the images.

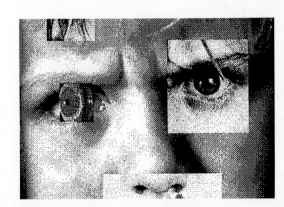

Figure 20.18. The computer will continue to be an important electronic graphic medium for the future as more artists learn to take advantage of its versatility and speed.

231

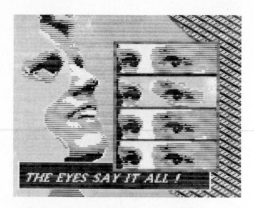

Figure 20.19. *Computer graphic.*

Figure 20.19 shows several examples of the images possible with a computer drawing or paint program. Once you become accustomed to the computer and the program, there is virtually no limit to the images and art you can create.

Video and Film

When we sit in the dark of a movie theatre, anxiously waiting for the feature to start, we rarely think about the creativity, art, and plain hard work that goes into the movie we are about to see. Once the movie starts, especially if it is a good one, we are lost in the action, characters, plot, and images of the film. We rarely think about the "art" of what we are seeing. We usually don't evaluate the visual qualities of a film the way we do a painting or sculpture. The power of motion pictures is such that we have a hard time seeing anything but the drama of the moment. They engage our attention as few other visual experiences do.

Films are also difficult to evaluate as art because they involve so many different people. You have but to look back at our art career list in Chapter 17 to see how many individuals are involved in just the artistic part of making a motion picture.

To get a small taste of this complexity, you might want to try your hand at making a small film or video.

If your teacher has a film or video camera available for class use, or you are allowed to use your family's, you can create simple "mini-movies," featuring your family, friends, or classmates.

For your movie to be a success, you need to follow the same process used by any video or film producer. The following steps will help you get started. But, first you need to be sure you know how to use the camera properly. Cameras, both film and video, are expensive. Always follow the directions of your teacher, or read the operating directions carefully.

Next, you need to decide the subject of your movie. Prepare a script. Outline the overall action and write any dialogue that your "actors" will speak. Before you begin shooting your movie, you might find it helpful to prepare a **storyboard,** a series of drawings that outline the main action and key scenes of the movie.

Next, shoot several sample scenes to check out your equipment. This is really only possible with videotape, which is less expensive than film and can be reused.

Finally, be sure you have all necessary props, costumes, and lighting. And now. . .

Lights! Camera! Action!

Sculptured Walls

Louise Nelson was brought to the United States when she was six. Her family settled in Rockland, Maine. In 1920 Nevelson moved to New York and began her study of art. She worked with several well-known artists, including Hans Hoffman, Ben Shahn, and Diego Rivera.

It was not until 1955 that she achieved real recognition. Three important museums purchased pieces of her work for their permanent collections. These were the "sculptured walls" that brought her international fame.

Figure 20.20, *Homage to the World,* is another example of her work. Painted a uniform black to give unity to the found objects, the sculpture is constructed in box-like sections. Within the sections are a combination of found objects, made mostly of wood. Nevelson likes to play straight-edged shapes against rounded profiles. Using what looks like wooden decorations from furniture or architecture, Nevelson creates an overall texture that changes as a viewer sees it from different angles.

Value plays an important part in these sculptures. The broken surfaces catch and reflect light from a hundred different points. Shadows, because of their overall flat color, vary in degree of darkness.

Some Nevelson sculptures fill entire rooms, creating a complete environment where a viewer can almost be enveloped in sculpture. Some have compared her work to ancient monuments or shrines. Looming and mysterious, they invite viewers to imagine and dream about their purposes.

BORN: 1899
DIED: 1987
BIRTHPLACE: Kiev, Russia

Figure 20.20. Louise Nevelson. *Homage to the World.* 1966. Wood, paint, 8'6" x 28'8". © The Detroit Institute of Arts, Founders Society Purchase, Friends of Modern Art Fund and other Founders Society Funds.

Student work.

Did you learn

- The definitions of these words and phrases: Pop art; Op art; Abstract Expressionism; color field; assemblage; printer; storyboard; Installation; Earth art; serigraphy; silk screen; block-out; hard copy; pixels; electronic media; CAD program; hardware; monitor; disk drive; software?
- Where Pop artists get their art subjects?
- How color-field painting is different from Abstract Expressionism?
- The kind of sculpture made by Louise Nevelson?
- The name for artworks that must be constructed in the museum or gallery?
- Why part of Earth art is the filming of the construction?
- Another name for the silk-screen process?
- The main parts of a computer system?

Understanding and Evaluating

- Rent or watch a movie on television. Watch it again and take notes. Notice whether color in sets, costumes, or lighting is used to create a certain mood. Watch camera angles, that is the viewpoint from which you see the action and characters. Is it always the same? Is there anything unusual about it? What about editing? Can you tell when the editor cuts from one scene to another? What kind of cuts are made? Quiet shots to violent action, or some other kind? After your analysis is complete, decide if you consider the film a work of art, or simply an entertainment, or both.
- Write a script for a video. Give brief descriptions of the characters and plot. Accompany your script with a storyboard or the key scenes to be shot. Your storyboard drawings can be small, fitting inside 5" x 7" rectangles.

Seeing and Creating

- Try your hand at creating an assemblage. Use found objects and different-sized boxes to hold your objects. When complete, paint with a single color of tempera or acrylic paint.

- **Abstract**—a style of creating art in which little attempt is made to reproduce visual reality; the art elements such as line; color; value; etc. are the subjects.
- **Abstract Expressionism**—20th-century art movement characterized by a rejection of realism in subject matter; artists were interested in expressing moods and emotions through the arrangement of art elements alone.
- **Analysis**—the second level of art criticism; offers information on how a work is put together or composed, using the art elements and design principles.
- **Analytical Cubism**—type of Cubism in which forms are broken down into basic, simpler shapes.
- **Applied Art**—created for a purpose in addition to visual enjoyment; advertising; architecture; industrial design; etc.
- **Archaeology**—science of uncovering and documenting artifacts from the past.
- **Architect**—individual who designs buildings.
- **Architrave**—part of the entablature above the columns, but below the frieze.
- **Art critic**—individual who evaluates the works of art.
- **Art historian**—individual who researches the historical and cultural background of artworks and artists.
- **Art Nouveau**—design movement popular during the early part of the 20th century; characterized by the use of curving plant forms as a design motif.
- **Assemblage**—artwork assembled from found materials.
- **Asymmetrical composition**—arrangement that is not symmetrical; no central axis to divide the composition equally.
- **Attribute**—a characteristic.
- **Avante-garde**—something new or the latest development.
- **Aztecs**—civilization that flourished in Mexico during the 15th and 16th centuries.
- **Baroque**—period of art (16th and 17th centuries) characterized by the use of dramatic elements of strong value contrasts and visual movement.
- **Bauhaus**—famous German school of design, established in 1919 to use the products and materials of industry as design elements; style characterized by simple lines and functional forms.
- **Bessemer process**—process of steel manufacturing developed by Sir Henry Bessemer, which allowed the building of tall buildings.
- **Black-figured**—a style of Greek vase painting in which black figures were painted on a light-colored background.
- **Block-out**—term used to describe the use of a material to block the passage of printing ink in serigraphy; in essence it is a resist.
- **Board or Trustees**—individuals responsible for policy and the budget of a museum.
- **Brainstorming**—creative thinking; technique for coming up with new ideas; all suggestions are considered and reviewed.
- **Brayer**—small roller used to spread ink onto a printing plate.
- **Bronze**—alloy consisting of copper and tin; favorite material of sculptors because of its strength.
- **Byzantine**—period and art style developed during the Holy Roman Empire, primarily in Constantinpole; style is characterized by rich color and the use of gold and silver; mosaics were the preferred two-dimensional form of art; subject matter was religious in nature.
- **CAD program**—Computer Assisted Drawing; programs are used by architects and designers to create perspective drawings of structures.
- **Calligraphy**—art of hand lettering.
- **Cantilevered roof**—concept developed by Frank Lloyd Wright; the roof is attached to the supporting structure at a single area and allowed to project outward without the need of supporting columns; reinforced concrete is essential.
- **Capitol**—decorative top of a column.
- **Cartoon**—in art a cartoon can be either a humorous drawing or a full-sized design for a mural.
- **Mural**—wall painting or fresco.
- **Celtic**—describing the culture and art of individuals living in ancient Britain.
- **Cenote**—well or natural sinkhole.
- **Centaur**—mythological creature; half man and half horse.
- **Chiaroscuro**—meaning light and dark; used to describe drawing or painting with dramatic contrasts in value.
- **Classical**—refers to an art style prevalent during the 4th and 5th centuries B.C. in Greece; refers to artworks which follow a certain artistic standard.
- **Color Field**—art movement in which large areas of color were smoothly applied to canvas; shapes were created where the color fields met.
- **Conservator**—individual responsible for the conservation of artifacts, art and documents.
- **Consumers**—individuals who consume or use information, goods, or services.
- **Content**—refers to the meaning of an artwork.
- **Corithian**—a style of capitol characterized by a decoration resembling the leaves of the acanthus plant.

GLOSSARY

- **Credit line**—written information that accompanies a work of art; lists information, such as artist's name, title of work, size, media; in a museum or gallery the credit is usually present on a card next to the work; in a book, it is listed beneath or near the reproduction.
- **Cubism**—art movement in which objects are simplified into basic, geometric elements.
- **Cuniform**—type of writing invented by the Sumerians; the triangular-shaped point of a stick was pressed into damp clay to make a mark representing a letter or word.
- **Curator**—individual responsible for the documentation, preservation, and display of collections; some museums have several curators, each responsible for a particular area of study or group of artifacts.
- **Decorative**—design or composition which uses decorative or ornamental objects or is arranged in an ornamental style.
- **Decorative design**—uses ornamental elements with no purpose other than visual enjoyment.
- **Description**—first level of art criticism; includes information, such as who painted the work, what is in it, etc.
- **Diptych**—a two-paneled painting or drawing.
- **Disk drive**—computer hardware which reads the software and stores new material.
- **Docents**—museum guides; individuals who enhance the public's enjoyment and appreciation of museums collections through guided tours and lectures.
- **Doric**—style of capitol characterized by a simple pillow-like shape.
- **Earth Art**—art movement which uses the environment as subject matter for giant sculptures; valleys are curtained, islands wrapped, bridges covered.
- **Electronic media**—materials and tools run by electricity or batteries; computers, cameras, projectors, etc.
- **Entablature**—flat surface area directly above the column capitols in a building; usually divided into two parts; the architrave and the frieze.
- **Etching**—printing method in which lines are cut into a metal plate directly or through the use of acid.
- **Evaluation**—level four of art criticism; asks for an opinion or judgment of the quality of the work.
- **Eye level**—horizon line in a perspective drawing; indicates the viewpoint of the observer.
- **Facade**—front of a building; in Gothic cathedrals, the facade was usually decorated with sculptures.
- **Fauve or Fauvism**—Early 20th-century art movement; characterized by violent use of brilliant color; the word "fauve" means "wild beast."
- **Federal style**—architectural style popular in the United States during the 18th century; based on architectural styles of ancient Greece and Rome.
- **Fine Art**—answers may vary; works of art created only for visual enjoyment.
- **Flying buttress**—an exterior architectural support used in Gothic cathedrals to support the weight of soaring interior vaults.
- **Folk art**—sometimes called primitive art; art created by individuals with little or no formal art training; subject matter is usually closely tied to traditional country or domestic activities.
- **Foreshortening**—method of creating the illusion of forms in space by drawing them shortened in relation to the angle from which they are viewed; type of perspective.
- **Form**—part of a work of art that refers to the method or process used to express the idea; for example, painting, drawing, or sculpture.
- **Freelance**—to work for oneself in a career; to seek out jobs and work from your own home, office, or studio.
- **Fresco**—a process of painting on walls; wet plaster is applied to a wall and painted on while still damp; as the plaster dries, the colors become part of the wall.
- **Frieze**—a surface area of the entablature on which reliefs may be carved.
- **Function**—use or purpose.
- **Gates of Paradise**—name given to the bronze door panels designed by Ghiberti for the Baptistry of Florence Cathedral.
- **Glazier**—a designer and maker of stained-glass windows.
- **Gothic**—style of art representative of the Middle Ages in Europe; characterized by soaring arches, stained glass windows, and flying buttresses of the great cathedrals of Europe.
- **Gothic Revival**—design movement during the late 19th and early 20th-centuries; used Gothic or medieval motifs, such as arches and carvings for decoration.
- **Graphic designer**—individual who works with images and print to create a pleasing and informative design.
- **Graphic device**—way of making lines, shapes, etc. in a drawing or painting that carries a message to the viewer; for example, repeated lines following a figure signifies movement.
- **Hagia Sophia**—crowning glory of Byzantine architecture; located in the present city of Istanbul, Turkey; now a museum attracting thousands of visitors each year.
- **Hard copy**—computer term referring to the actual printing on paper of written and graphic materials.

- **Hardware**—equipment part of the computer, including the monitor; keyboard; disk drives; etc.
- **Monitor**—television screen of the computer.
- **Hieroglyphics**—writing represented by images of pictures in place of letters; both the Egyptians and the Mayas of Central America used hieroglyphs for writing.
- **Horizon line**—in linear perspective, this is the same as the eye-level line.
- **Illustration**—two-dimensional image used to visualize an event or character in a narrative.
- **Industrial designer**—individual who designs the products, machines and equipment of modern life.
- **Industrial revolution**—period of social and economic change resulting from the invention and use of machines.
- **Interior designer**—designer who works with structural and decorative elements of interior space.
- **Interlace**—decorative design in which the elements appear to be woven or intertwined together; style popular in Celtic art.
- **International style**—architectural style popular during the last quarter of the 20th century; standard design used by architects around the world.
- **Interpretation**—level three of art criticism; gives an opinion of what the meaning of the work may be; what the artist is trying to say.
- **Installation**—sculptures which must be installed in an area of a museum or gallery each time it is exhibited.
- **Ionic**—style of capitol characterized by curling horn-like projections.
- **Layout**—to arrange the images and print needed for a graphic design; the arrangement.
- **Linear perspective**—method of drawing to create an illusion of three-dimensional space.
- **Manuscript illumination**—collection of writings, usually in calligraphy or hand-writing, decorated or illustrated with pictures; this art form reached its height during the Middle Ages; *The Book of Kells* and *The Lindisfarne Gospel* are examples of illuminated manuscripts.
- **Maya**—a culture and civilization of Central America and the Yucatan peninsula of Mexico during the 14th and 15th centuries.
- **Media**—art materials such as pencils, crayons, and pastels.
- **Medici**—famous and powerful Italian Renaissance family, whose members were patrons to many well-known artists.
- **Middle Ages**—period of history from about the 5th century A.D. to the 15th century.
- **Minotaur**—mythological creature; half-man and half-bull.

- **Mixed media**—use of more than one media in a work of art.
- **Mosaics**—technique in which small tiles, broken stone, or glass are assembled into a two-dimensional image; used in ancient Greece and Rome, as well as in Byzantine architecture.
- **Motif**—reoccurring design feature.
- **Mummification**—process developed by the ancient Egyptians to preserve the body after death; mummies of many Egyptian nobles have been found well-preserved in tombs thousands of years old.
- **Museum director**—individual in charge of a museum; administrator of collections and staff.
- **Mythology**—a collection of legends or stories about the origins of a civilization and its gods.
- **Narrative art**—art which tells a story.
- **Natural environment**—includes everything that is not human-made.
- **Neoclassic**—art period in which artists were inspired by the classical traditions of Greece and Rome.
- **Neolithic**—time period which means "new stone" age; time when the first great free-standing stone structures in the world such as Stonehenge in England, were built.
- **Non-objective**—in art, works which have no recognizable or realistically presented subjects.
- **Obsidian**—volcanic glass; dark brown or black in color, this semi-transparent material was used by the Aztecs and other Pre-Columbian artisans to create beautiful sculptures.
- **Op Art**—art movement which used visual tricks and illusions to fool the eye.
- **Paleolithic**—time period which means "old stone" age.
- **Panorama**—view which takes in a large area or space.
- **Parthenon**—famous ancient Greek temple; built in the 5th century on the Acropolis overlooking the city of Athens; dedicated to the cities' patron the goddess Athena.
- **Patron**—individual who supports; patrons support art by purchasing artworks for collections and by commissioning artists to create them.
- **Pediment**—the triangular section below the roof.
- **Pharoah**—king of ancient Egypt; the Pharoah was considered a god, as well as king.
- **Photorealism**—painting style which attempts to mimic visual reality as seen in photographs.
- **Picture plane**—surface area of canvas, paper, board, etc. upon which a two-dimensional work of art is composed.
- **Pieta**—representation in art of Mary and Jesus.
- **Pixels**—small squares which make up computer-generated images.

GLOSSARY

- **Pointillism**—technique of creating images by applying dots of color; in its purist form, the primary and secondary colors are not mixed prior to application, the idea being for the human eye from a distance to mix the dots of colors.
- **Pop Art**—art movement based on the use of objects of popular culture as subjects for art.
- **Portfolio**—collection of artwork, usually contained in a large envelope or folder.
- **Post-Impressionism**—art movement which followed Impressionism; a reaction against the transparent, melting shapes and colors of Impressionism. Post Impressionists like Cezanne and Seurat were more interested in color and form, than the effects of light on objects.
- **Post-Modern**—design movement in the last decades of the 20th century, characterized by the borrowing of design elements and symbols from previous ages and pop culture.
- **Potshard**—piece of a broken pot; from such items, archaeologists can date the site or the level at which they found the potshard.
- **Pre-Columbian**—referring to the art and civilizations of the Americas before the arrival of Christopher Columbus in 1492.
- **Prehistoric**—time period before written records were kept; the art of this period was primarily found in caves, where walls were covered with huge drawings and paintings of animals.
- **Printer**—computer hardware used to print out the hard copies of information processed by the computer.
- **Red-figured**—style of Greek vase painting in which red figures are painted on a dark background.
- **Relief**—shallow carving in which figures or areas stand out from the surface.
- **Renaissance**—important period in the world of art and learning, extending from about 1400 A.D. to 1600 A.D.
- **Rococo**—period of art (18th century) characterized by delicate and curving lines and gilded onament; more delicate and light in feeling than Baroque.
- **Romantic style**—19th-century art style characterized by subjects taken from dramatic events or exotic locations. The Romantic landscapes of Constable (Figure 9.6) and Turner (9.7) were considered romantic in their idealism of nature.
- **Roof comb**—architectural decoration found on many Mayan temples, such as those at Palenque.
- **Serigraphy**—sometimes called silk screen; printing process in which an ink is forced through a fine-weave material (silk) around stencil shapes to create a print.
- **Silk-screen**—see above.
- **Slip**—kind of clay glue made by mixing dried clay with a small amount of water.

- **Software**—computer programs.
- **Still life**—an arrangement of objects.
- **Stone Age**—time period identified by the production of stone tools.
- **Storyboard**—a series of images used to indicate key scenes in a play or movie.
- **Stucco**—type of plaster used in building and also by some cultures for sculpting.
- **Subject**—the part of a work of art that refers to the objects or elements portrayed or seen in the work.
- **Surrealism**—art movement which used dreams, fantasies, and imagination for subject matter.
- **Symmetrical composition**—arrangement that is more or less equal on both sides of a central axis.
- **Synthetic Cubism**—type of Cubism in which forms are combined in new ways to produce new forms.
- **Tapestry**—woven or embroidered wallhanging.
- **Thumbnail sketch**—small drawing, usually quickly done to indicate basic shapes or points of view.
- **Toned paper**—paper with a tint or value, other than white.
- **Trompe l'oeil**—technique of painting to create an illusion of space or three-dimensional objects.
- **Unicorn**—mythological creature popular in medieval literature and art; frequently pictured as a white horse with a long horn growing from the center of its head and a beard like a goat.
- **Universal**—having a common meaning for many different elements.
- **Urban**—referring to the city as opposed to suburban which refers to the outlying areas of a community.
- **Urban designer**—individual who designs whole communities, including which areas will be living spaces and which will be open landscape areas.
- **Vanishing point**—in linear perspective, the point on the horizon or eye-level line where horizontal lines converge.
- **Viewpoint**—view or angle from which a scene or object is seen.
- **Visual composition**—arrangement of art elements or objects.
- **Visual thinking**—ability to create images in a mind or visualization.
- **Western civilization**—cultures and countries influenced by ancient Greece and Rome, including Western Europe, England, and the United States.
- **Woodcut**—type of print in which an image is cut into a wood block; remaining raised portion will be inked and printed; while cutlines remain white.
- **Ziggurats**—pyramid-tiered temples of the Sumerians; constructed of clay bricks.